Promoting the
Social Development of
Young Children

Gabriel

Promoting the Social Development of Young Children: Strategies and Activities

Charles A. Smith
Kansas State University

 Mayfield Publishing Company

Library of Congress Catalog Card Number: 81-83085
International Standard Book Number: 0-87484-528-9

Manufactured in the United States of America
Mayfield Publishing Company
285 Hamilton Avenue
Palo Alto, California 94301

Cover photo: Elizabeth Crews
Compositor: Type By Design
Printer and binder: George Banta Company
Sponsoring editor: Judith Ziajka
Managing editors: Judith Ziajka and Pat Herbst
Manuscript editor: Mary Forkner
Designer: Nancy Sears
Illustrator: Elizabeth Boling
Layout: Mary Wiley
Production: Michelle Hogan and Cathy Willkie

Contents

Index to child and self studies and activities

Child studies

Activities to promote body awareness

Preface

This book responds to two basic questions teachers and students—and parents—may have about the personal/social goals for early childhood education: *What* kinds of skills do we want to nurture in children, and *how* do we proceed to accomplish these objectives? Goals such as "improving self-concept" or "promoting social relationships" do not serve as clear guides for involvement with children, and they are too vague to allow us to effectively evaluate our teaching. However, personal/social abilities can be more clearly defined, and teachers can use this book to identify a broad range of skills relevant to children from three to eight years of age. These skills are organized into five clusters or themes, which are explained in sufficient detail to make sense and be useful to teachers. Furthermore, theory and research describing the foundation and developmental changes in personal/social behavior are integrated to provide an in-depth understanding of the issues related to the skills.

Useful strategies for nurturing personal/social development are an important part of this book. Specific suggestions for utilizing informal relationships with children as an educational method are identified, and more than one hundred group activities are presented at the ends of chapters. Research findings and theoretical perspectives are included to help teachers form a clearer picture of what they might try to accomplish with children and how they might implement their ideas.

One reason that personal/social skills may not have been given the serious attention they deserve is their widespread association with an affective curriculum. Unfortunately, cognitive development is usually identified with abstract experiences like counting, spelling, or reading; but cognition is also involved when children think about their feelings or try to form friendships. In this book the integration of cognition and social behavior, especially among peers, is an important priority. Teachers no longer will need to consider such goals inferior to the "real" task of education.

This book was written for students of early childhood education and child development as well as for practicing teachers who would like to be better informed and to expand their list of what works with children. Parents may also benefit from reading the material and may wish to adapt activities for use in the home.

Promoting the Social Development of Young Children begins with an explanation of a social/cognitive model with an emphasis on forming ideas, using intuition, and solving problems. This approach is then applied to five general personal/social issues: body and sensory awareness, emotions, friendship and affiliation, conflict and cooperation, and kindness. Suggested classroom activities, ideas for improving relationships, and useful references are identified for each of these five skill clusters. "Self Studies" and "Child Studies" are distributed throughout the text to encourage readers to relate the material to themselves as well as to the children they work with or observe.

Students and teachers may use this material in a variety of ways. Some may wish to emphasize understanding the skills and how they change over time; others may refer primarily to the activities; some may integrate those features. Readers are encouraged to focus on both skills and activities. Familiarity with the skills will help teachers clarify their teaching goals and be more aware of the problems and constraints they may encounter in the classroom. The activities and suggestions for improving relationships will provide opportunities to translate theory into practice.

No book can *make* anyone a better teacher. This material will provide useful and interesting ideas, but you must supply the courage, sensitivity, and patience needed to make them work. Success in teaching depends on the resources you can find within yourself. After reading this text, use what seems useful and appropriate for the children in your classroom.

Completion of *Promoting the Social Development of Children* has been a long task. Over the past several years I have had the good fortune to be near people who believed in me and provided support when I needed a kind word. My greatest debt is to my delightful family—Betsy, Sarah, and Bill—for enduring my absences, accepting my frustrations, and extending helping hands during difficult times. Without their patience I could never have finished this book.

When this project began with my dissertation in 1972, the support from my Purdue "family," including Dave Englund, Mary Endres, Chuck Riker and Ruth Bogdonoff, was especially significant. They encouraged me to begin and showed confidence in my ability. Along the way, Ron Russell and Chuck Figley provided much-appreciated support, friendship, and encouragement. Teachers like Carolyn Foat, Sue Morrow, Bill Carver, Anne Ahlenius, Kitty Beverly, and Lois Bates expressed a need for this material and gave valuable feedback for improving the text.

Reviewers Diane Bridgeman of the University of California at Santa Cruz, Janet Gonzalez-Mena of the Family Service Agency in Redwood City, California, Willard Hartup of the University of Minnesota, Judith Long of California State University at Los Angeles, Evelyn Neufeld of San Jose State University, and Ned Schultz of Texas

Tech University offered many perceptive comments. I would also like to express my appreciation to the staff of Mayfield, and especially to Judy Ziajka, for their patience and support. Finally, I would like to thank my most important teachers—the children who attended my classes, those who were gentle and rough, kind and mean, happy and sad. Each of them helped make this book possible.

Charles A. Smith

To Betsy, Sarah, and Bill

Chapter one
Becoming a person:
The purpose of education

Do you remember the first time a child called you "teacher"? How did you feel? What did you think you should have been able to do? Perhaps you remember feeling self-conscious but proud at that moment and eager but afraid you might not be able to live up to this child's expectations. You were no longer just an ordinary person for this child. You were a "teacher," and you suddenly felt the full responsibility of that title. Teachers want to be worthy of having children view them as someone who can help them. They want to have the kind of *relationship* with children that will motivate them to learn and nurture them in their own personal *growth*.

Relationship means making contact with children, feeling their joy, and sharing their pain. Relationship means reaching out to children and showing them we want to share something of ourselves with them. Authentic teaching is a passionate profession which can challenge both our hearts and minds. True "teaching" can make a difference in the lives of others.

If we believe in this relationship we are likely to detest conditions which prevent us from making contact with children. Large classes bother us because children can remain anonymous in a crowd. Rigid schedules and uniform classroom behavior disturb us because children may fail to discover their own unique talents under these circumstances. We want to know and be known by our children and to be able to respond to their needs as we encourage their abilities. We want to celebrate with them their enthusiasm for learning.

Growth means using our relationships to nurture development in both children and ourselves. We want to reach out to children, to help them, and to answer *their* questions about *their* concerns. Children begin their school years with excitement and arrive with important questions about life: "What is happening to me? Why do things grow? What are things made of?" Children may initially think of school as a magical, powerful place and their teacher as its guiding force—a special person who can help them discover the answers to their questions.

As teachers we also want to learn and grow. We want to learn from children, to nurture our own childlike wonder of the world, and to continue to appreciate the usefulness of our own imaginations. By living and working with children our lives are profoundly affected for the better.

Those of us who believe in this personal growth of teacher and learner are troubled when we are asked to teach from a "canned curriculum." We grow weary of political pressure to establish such curricula, and we are disturbed by parents who take no interest in their children's education. We want respect and involvement—a dialogue with parents, administrators, legislators, and others about the needs and education of children. The welfare of children in our care is foremost in our minds.

Children's experiences of the world

Children want to deal effectively with three different experiences of the world.[1] The first experience is the world of *impersonal things*. Children want to learn about such things as bugs, animals, and machines. They want to understand where rain comes from, how ice melts, and why it gets dark at night. The second experience is that of *relationships with others*. Children want to learn about other people—how to make friends, resolve conflicts, and help others. And third is the world of *personal experience*. Children want to discover themselves and to know more about how they grow and develop and how to deal with their emotions. School can offer children an opportunity to master all three types of experiences.

Traditional academic skills like reading and writing receive a great deal of formal attention by parents and schools. As children master these skills they also discover that they are useful tools for better understanding their experiences. Reading, for example, increases a child's ability to gather information and discover how others live, work, and play. Writing enables children to communicate better their ideas and feelings to others. Even arithmetic is an opportunity to master the world of things and thus engage in more effective relationships. Traditional academic skills are useful because they enable children to master the three worlds of experience.

Of the three worlds, personal and social experiences may be the most meaningful. If we ask someone to think back to his or her childhood and recall a significant learning experience (see Self Study 1), the result is likely to emphasize personal or social issues. Teachers in workshops on social skills have recalled how significant teachers influenced them by identifying such consequences as: "She helped me learn to be myself"; "He gave me confidence"; "She helped me overcome a conflict and make a decision"; "I felt recognized and accepted as a person." For many of us the most important events in life are more personal and social than impersonal. Knowledge of impersonal issues such as size, shapes, and colors is important but only has real significance to children when it relates in some way to their personal/social concerns.

Take a few moments to think about when you were a child and try to recall someone who had an important positive impact on your life. It could have been a classroom teacher, a relative, a friend, or even someone you did not know very well. Try to remember how this person looked and how he or she reacted to you. Now identify some important effect this person had on you. Complete the statement, "Because of this person I learned...."

When you think about what you learned from this special person, how important has it been to your life? Could this special skill or insight be important to the children with whom you work? Can it be appropriately nurtured in them? How? Do you think they would be interested in learning it? Is what you learned something you really can believe in? Is it something you would like your children to remember about you?

Personal/social skills and meaningful success

Even though mastery of the impersonal world may be necessary, personal social skills provide the foundation for real success in life. The lawyer who is a technical master of the impersonal worlds of judicial procedure and precedent may lose cases because she lacks self-confidence. Also, the highly-skilled factory worker who is repeatedly fired because she argues with her supervisors and the brilliant doctor who cannot maintain a practice because he lacks a gentle bedside manner are examples of failure to deal effectively with the world of relationships and personal experience. In each of these cases impersonal, technical skills are neutralized by personal social incompetence.

Mastery of personal experiences and social relationships must be learned. As children grow they begin to acquire a broad range of knowledge about themselves and others in a predictable, age-related manner.[2] Temperamental attributes like mood and adaptability which begin at birth affect the quality of children's relationships with others.[3] But children do not arrive in this world with ideas about themselves and others. Personhood is something they must learn.

Through experience, observation, and the comments of other people, children gradually acquire concepts of how their world does and should operate. They also begin to form ideas about how they should behave in relationship to that world. For example, through the experience of physical contact with their mothers and fathers infants begin to differentiate between themselves and the rest of the world. Through observation they learn to recognize themselves and because of adult comments like, "Oh, I think you are beautiful!" or "Yuk, you sure are stinky!" young children begin to form certain attitudes toward themselves. Children's ideas about their physical characteristics have a strong influence on the way they involve their bodies in dance, play, or other forms of movement.

What can personal/social development include?

If we want to promote children's personal/social development where do we begin? This book emphasizes five key themes: body and sensory awareness, empathy and emotional development, affiliation and friendship, conflict and cooperation, and kindness and affection (see Figure 1.1). All personal/social issues are included within one or more of these five areas and the skills relating to these themes are examined thoroughly.

**Figure 1.1
Five personal/
social themes**

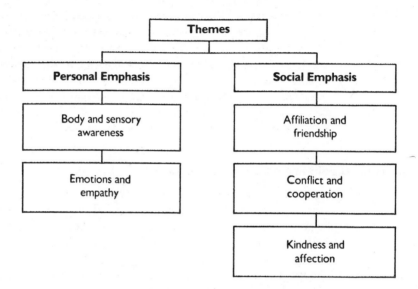

The theme of *body and sensory awareness* is considered first because all experiences of the world begin with the human body. For young children this involves, for example, learning the names and functions of various body parts, accepting the physical traits of themselves and others, understanding the changes associated with growth, expressing themselves through movement, and using their senses to make contact with the environment. *Emotional development* follows because emotions are interpretations of body experiences. For young children we emphasize acquisition of an emotional vocabulary, recognition of emotions in others, and verbal expression of feelings. Body awareness and emotional skills tend to emphasize the more personal aspects of development and are likely to contribute significantly to successful interpersonal relationships.

The interpersonal themes of affiliation, conflict, and kindness are based on William Schutz's theory of group development.[4] Schutz suggests that the first social task for any person is *affiliation*, the ability to approach others and initiate relationships. Children are concerned about affiliation when they seek recognition from parents and try to establish friendships with other children. Once affiliation is resolved in a relationship, *conflict* and the acquisition of influence and respect emerge as key issues. This concern for developing a sense of personal power is manifest when children refuse to obey their teachers, fight with their peers, or cooperatively resolve conflict. When children in a social group deal with conflict problems, *affection and kindness* can emerge in relationships. According to Schutz's theory, when recognition and respect are present children are more likely to express their affection, show compassion, offer help, and decide to share with others.

In addition to identifying relevant personal/social topics, we examine the kinds of behaviors or processes we might encourage in children as they begin to deal with these issues.[5] For example, we might emphasize the topic *cooperation* in our classroom, but a goal of cooperation alone is not sufficient. We must decide what specific behavior or cognitive process we want children to learn. We might, for example, ask children to point out or define cooperative behavior. We might also ask them to describe the social or emotional consequences of cooperation and encourage them to practice cooperation with others. Each of these suggestions involves different behaviors or processes directed toward the same topic. In the next chapter we examine the cognitive processes which serve as the foundation for personal/social skills.

Chapter two
Personal/social development:
A mind-growing experience

During outdoor play in kindergarten, a five-year-old boy saw one of his playmates fall off a tricycle and begin to cry. Jamy ran to his friend and gently patted him on the back. "You be better," he said. When the teacher arrived Jamy picked up the trike, looked around, and walked quickly to a small storage shelter. After a few moments he emerged with a fireman's hat which he offered to his friend. "Let's play fireman," he suggested. Jamy and his friend then returned to their tricycles and cheerfully began to pedal around the schoolyard.

Seven-year-old Doris was playing quietly with her tool set when her three-year-old brother arrived and grabbed for her hammer. "That's my hammer!" she insisted. "No, *me* play with it!" was her brother's reply. After a brief struggle Doris regained the toy. But then her brother began to cry. "Just a minute, Zack," she said. "Let me find one for you." After rummaging through the toy chest she discovered a toy saw. "Here, Zack, you play with this," she suggested. By the time their mother arrived to referee the conflict the children were playing together quietly.

In each of these situations children tried to deal effectively in a social situation by reflecting on how they might respond to the problem. In the first instance Jamy may have attempted to show kindness by helping his friend, and in the second Doris tried to resolve a conflict with her brother so she could proceed with her own activity. Their efforts to respond to a social problem were thoughtful and intuitive rather than mindless.

Children's minds are actively involved in giving meaning to their personal/social experiences. This application of thinking to personal/social behavior is called "social cognition."[1] A suggested sequence of events and related examples illustrating social cognition are presented in Figure 2.1.

Figure 2.1
Social cognition:
A sequence of
events

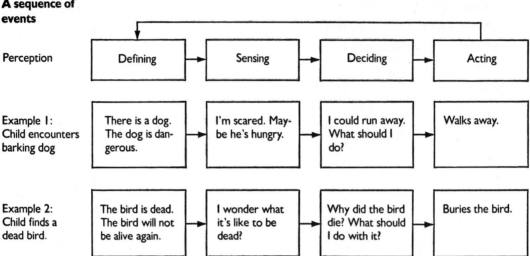

Perception

| Defining | Sensing | Deciding | Acting |

Example 1:
Child encounters
barking dog

| There is a dog. The dog is dangerous. | I'm scared. Maybe he's hungry. | I could run away. What should I do? | Walks away. |

Example 2:
Child finds a
dead bird.

| The bird is dead. The bird will not be alive again. | I wonder what it's like to be dead? | Why did the bird die? What should I do with it? | Buries the bird. |

Defining a situation or observation involves assigning meaning to what we perceive. For example, we might notice someone smiling and then define his experience as being "happy." In the previous examples Jamy may have decided that his friend was hurt and needed help, and Doris may have believed the toy hammer to be her sole property. Their definitions of what they saw influenced their actions. Some children may look in the mirror and define themselves as being "ugly," and this negative self-evaluation may cause them to withdraw from social contact. Other children may believe they are "bad" and then act accordingly. Their definitions can become prophesies which are later confirmed by their own actions.

Sensing our feelings or drawing on our creative intuition comes after defining a situation. Because Jamy may have felt alarmed, he looked around for some way to alleviate his friend's sadness. Doris may have experienced frustration with her brother's behavior, but she also was aware of another child's need for something to play with. When they defined the situations it triggered their feelings and creative sensitivity to what may have been happening to the other children.

Making a decision follows defining and sensing. At this point we might consider causes, alternative solutions, and the consequences of our actions. Jamy first decided to respond to his friend's distress by offering a hug. Later, he reflected on other alternatives and decided to offer him a fireman's hat. Doris also hoped to solve her problem by finding something interesting for her brother. Thus, both children combined their definitions with their own intuitive sensing to make decisions about how to solve a problem. It is important to note that if the original reasoning is faulty, the problem may not be completely resolved. For example, children who believe they are "stupid" may give up trying to deal with problems or may avoid situations in which they might feel foolish. For such children, lack of self-confidence distorts their decision making.

**Personal/social
development**

By encouraging children to reflect on how they define their experiences, to get in touch with their intuition and feelings, to think out their problems and take action, we can improve their chances for personal growth and successful interpersonal relationships.

Taking action is the final event which completes the sequence of social cognition. Jamy implemented his ideas by actually trying to help his playmate, and Doris looked for a toy her brother might like. These actions may have an effect on the situation which is then redefined as the sequence begins again. When his friend responded positively to his offer of the fireman's hat, Jamy suggested they return to their tricycles. When Doris's brother stopped crying, she returned to playing with her tool set. The actions of both children depended a great deal on their interpretations of events.

Defining personal/social experiences

Children define their experiences because they want to be able to predict what might happen and decide how they should respond to various situations. A toddler, for example, sees a match and defines it as "something to put in my mouth." As he puts it in his mouth, his mother intervenes because her definition of the match differs dramatically from his. In order to convey her point of view, his mother may take it from his mouth and say, "No! No, mouth! Matches are dangerous!" Now his view of the match has changed, and in addition to being interesting it is now a vaguely risky object. When he finds matches from now on, he may bring them to his mother. He has modified his definition and thus conformed to an adult view of the world.

Children begin to assign meaning to their internal and social experiences in a similar way. The work of sociologists Erving Goffman[2] and Peter Berger[3] has demonstrated the relationship between the way we define our personal/social experiences and our actual behavior. Although their work has been done primarily with adults, the underlying principles apply to children as well.

Children gradually become more conscious of how social settings can vary relative to their obligations as well as to their expectations of others. *Places* begin to acquire meaning. For example, to a very young child, a church, grocery store, and living room all may be defined as places for free exploration and play. However, as their definitions begin to conflict with those of others, children begin to discriminate between situations and make corresponding adjustments in their behavior. A church becomes a serious place, a grocery store becomes a place where they must be careful, and a living room is a place where they can act sillier and be less inhibited. Every society expects children to learn how places are defined within that culture.

Children make adjustments in behavior by becoming more aware of what they consider to be their *obligations* in various situations. They become more conscious of how others expect them to act. In some schools, for example, children learn that a classroom is a serious place where they are expected to remain quiet and orderly. On the playground, though, these same children may be much more active and informal in their contact with each other. Grade-school children who make no situational adjustments to their behavior are likely to receive disapproval from both adults and peers.

**Defining
situations**

There are developmental changes in the way children view social situations. For example, children of different ages are all likely to behave differently during church. The youngest may talk and wiggle at the "wrong" times, and the oldest child may do his best to act "appropriately." Select one of the following settings and observe three children of different ages. Record their behavior:

Supermarket
Church
Shopping Mall
Restaurant

How are the three children different? How much of their response is due to personality, and how much of their behavior seems due to age differences? How are these children defining the situation? Did any of the children come into conflict with adults? What happened? How do you think parents should respond when their views clash with those of their children? Can you recall instances from your own childhood when you misunderstood a situation or differed with adult views. What happened?

In addition to trying to ascertain their obligations in a situation, children gradually begin to form *expectations* of how others are supposed to act. Kindergarten children, for example, would probably be quite startled if their teacher suddenly threw herself on the floor with a temper tantrum or if one of their friends came to school wearing pajamas. Similarly, if one of their playmates were to become very bossy someone might insist, "Stop doing that! You're not my mommy or daddy!" In each of these instances children have formed expectations about how others are supposed to behave in certain situations. Their experiences with people have enabled them to anticipate other people's behavior in different settings.

Research by Malcolm W. Watson and Kurt Fischer demonstrated that young children's awareness of social roles follows a developmental sequence.[4] By eighteen months of age children are able to differentiate between reality and fantasy by engaging in pretend play. By two years of age they can make a doll do something as if it were acting on its own and most three-year-olds can make a doll carry out several activities related to role, for example a doctor or mommy. By four years of age children can act out a social role in dramatic play and integrate that role with another, for example, doctor and sick person or mommy and baby. When they are about six years old, children can coordinate one role with *two* other complementary roles, such as doctor, nurse, and sick person. As children grow older they are more aware that simultaneous roles can influence behavior. For example, they may now understand that a doctor may react differently to a patient who is also his daughter.

**Personal/social
development**

Concepts: Building blocks for thinking

Children begin to differentiate between situations and roles through a process of forming concepts, the building blocks for thinking. Concept formation is very significant for children's social development.

When children first begin to talk, they use words to refer to *specific* objects or activities. For example, a two-year-old might use the word *mama* to refer to one specific person, her own mother rather than all mothers. Similarly, a word like *gentle* might refer only to a very specific action like patting another person's face. Words used only with such narrow meaning are called *symbols*.[5]

Children gradually begin to transform their symbolic use of words into *concepts*.[6] Concepts have a general rather than specific meaning. Instead of referring to a specific person, *mother* can represent the entire category of mothers. Preschool children can use the word *mother* to refer to their own and others' mothers and what some of them might become someday. When used as a concept, the word *gentle* may also refer to a variety of compassionate behaviors, such as hugging, touching, and holding. Concepts help children order and simplify the experiences they have with their impersonal, personal, and social worlds.

Concepts are powerful tools for communication because they help children and adults respond more effectively to each other. Concepts reduce the complexity of experiences by making shared meaning possible. For example, one child may ask another, "You be the daddy and I be the mommy, OK?" Both children have an idea of what a daddy and a mommy are and use the words to refer to the general roles. Similarly, children who are asked to be gentle can more correctly interpret the request if they have several interpretations of the word from which to choose.

Differences between concepts

Concepts can differ greatly from one another in their level of difficulty for children. There are important differences among concepts in terms of the degree of abstraction, complexity, differentiation, and centrality of dimensions.[7]

One basic difference is that concepts vary along a concrete-abstract dimension. *Concrete* concepts are those with characteristic dimensions that can be observed directly. *Gentleness, hitting, crying, soft,* and *face* are concrete concepts. *Abstract* concepts refer to more intangible events and cannot be directly observed. *Sadness, honesty,* and *courage* are abstract concepts. In general, children learn concrete concepts before learning more abstract ones.

Concepts also differ in complexity based on the amount of information needed to define them. The concept of hitting has a *low complexity* because the behavior is relatively easy to define. Hitting involves some type of striking in which the hand is used. In contrast, a concept like violence has a *high complexity* because more detailed information is needed to define the concept. A complete definition of violence would include many different kinds of destructive behavior. Children typically acquire concepts of low complexity more quickly than those of high complexity.

Concepts may differ also in the number of words that can be used to represent them. For example, the concept mother is *not highly differentiated* in the English language because there are very few words that describe varieties of mother (momma, mommy, ma, etc.). The concept nose is even less differentiated because there are fewer recognizable words to refer to this easily defined part of the body. In contrast, the concept home is *highly differentiated* because a large variety of different terms can represent it. For example, hut, cabin, igloo, and palace are all homes. Young children are more likely to learn concepts that have a low differentiation before learning concepts that have high differentiation.

Concepts also vary in terms of their number of critical dimensions. Some concepts derive their essential meaning from only one or two central dimensions. For example, the concept cooperation refers to two or more people working on a task of mutual benefit. Other concepts, though, may have a *large number of equally important dimensions.* The concept kindness has several equally significant dimensions including offering help, sharing, giving, and showing affection. Children tend to form a greater number of misunderstandings when referring to sickness because of the number of characteristics needed for its correct definition.

The easiest concepts to learn are those with characteristic dimensions which are

Personal/social development

concrete, only slightly complex and differentiated, and have few central dimensions. Thus, children might learn concepts for gentle, family, body, and fighting earlier than for affection, group, learning, and violence. We might be more effective teachers if we introduced concepts easier to understand and more relevant to young children.

Developmental changes in concepts

Three attributes of a concept are validity, status, and accessibility.[8] All of these attributes help describe how concepts change as a child's intellectual development progresses.

The *validity* of a concept refers to the degree to which the child's understanding of the concept agrees with that of the larger social community. Piaget's studies[9,10] have demonstrated that young children's conceptual behavior is dominated and limited by their perceptions. For example, a young child's understanding of the concept of life may be based on movement. The child may believe that a tree and balloon on a windy day are alive because they are moving and seem to be alive. Thus, the child might insist that they are not alive when they stop moving. As they gain more experience children gradually broaden the meaning of their words to reflect more valid concepts.

A second attribute of concepts which changes over time is the status of a concept, or its degree of clarity and exactness for use in thinking. As children have experiences and begin to grasp more complex meanings, their concepts become clearer and more useful to them. For example, the concept parent undergoes dramatic transformations in meaning as young children become adolescents, young adults, and finally parents. A change in age and its corresponding change in perspective broadens the status of the concept.

The third attribute of concepts which changes over time is *accessibility,* or the availability of a concept for use in thinking and the degree to which the concept can be communicated. Young children sometimes find it difficult to express what they want to say. For example, a five-year-old boy might struggle with his feelings of wanting to have his friend's toy but not know the word *jealous* to communicate how he feels. Instead, he might say he is angry. Children gradually learn to use more specific concept labels as they interact with and listen to other people.

Organizing concepts into convictions

Concepts can be combined in a number of ways to form ideas or convictions. If concepts are the basic building blocks of thinking, convictions are the structures which result. Children interpret their experiences with ideas that are constructed from their concepts.

A *conviction* is a belief, generalization, or rule which brings together two or more concepts to form a unique relationship.[11] For example, a child may combine the two concepts people and feelings in the conviction, "all people have feelings." Similarly, a child might think, "I'm a bad boy," combining his concept of himself, badness, and his gender. Children begin to form convictions as a way of logically organizing their experiences.

Complete the statement, "I believe that . . . ," and identify and list evidence to support your conviction. Now write a statement which is the direct opposite of your conviction. For example, if you wrote "people are good" you would now write "people are bad." Identify and list whatever evidence you might think of to support this point of view. Now compare the two lists and make a decision about the acceptability of your conviction. Does it seem better to change your conviction to increase its validity? For example, "people are good" might be changed to:

People are bad.

People are sometimes bad or good.

People are neither bad nor good, only their behavior can be judged.

Some people are bad, some are good.

In a similar fashion adults can encourage children to evaluate their beliefs in light of evidence they have experienced.

Convictions can be rational, blind, or irrational.[12] *Rational* beliefs are those which can be supported by evidence. "People bleed" and "friends sometimes disagree" are convictions that are realistic and accurate. Rational beliefs enable people to relate effectively to others.[13] For example, children who believe "hitting hurts people" have an idea that could help them respond more sensitively to others. Similarly, children who have acquired the idea "getting into a stranger's car is dangerous" have a guideline which will enhance their own safety.

Blind beliefs are those which cannot be supported or denied by available evidence. "Third grade will be easy next year," or "when I am a mommy my children will love me," are examples of blind beliefs. Blind beliefs can cause problems because later experience may not confirm the idea being advocated.

Irrational beliefs are illusions or distortions which can be disproven by evidence. The person who says, "fear is always a sign of weakness" or "I must be perfect to be liked," has adopted an irrational belief which interferes with his or her own personal development and relationship with others.

From a child's point of view these irrational beliefs may be quite logical. Children often place a great deal of confidence in what adults tell them, and some comments contribute to their irrational beliefs.[14] For example, a parent might casually tell her child that he should not feel afraid. Despite the fact that fear can be a very useful emotion, the child may decide that fear is bad. Then if there are times when he really is afraid, he may conclude that something is wrong with *him* because he believes that these feelings are unacceptable.

Some irrational beliefs reflect a growth process in the child's logical thinking.[15] Children may say, for example, that the sun moves around the earth, that clouds are caused by their daddy's smoking, or that dead people can come back to life. In each case children are trying to make sense out of an experience by drawing conclusions which make sense to them.

Select three children of different ages (e.g., three, five, and seven years) and ask each separately to describe their views on the same issue. You might talk with them about what fathers do, what they can or cannot do when they grow up, or what happens when they are afraid. Do not contribute your own opinions until you are sure the children have said all they would like to about the matter.

What changes in ideas do you notice as you listen to children of different ages? Did any of the children have a definite misunderstanding about some aspect of the issue you discussed? If so, how did you respond? How should parents respond when this happens?

Even though they may have been logically acquired, some irrational beliefs may cause psychological pain and lead to ineffective or destructive behavior. For example, one child may despise his natural feelings of fear, another may fight constantly because she perceives all other children as threats, and a third may believe himself responsible for his sister's death because of a wish he once made in a moment of anger. In each situation the child's conclusion is logical but irrational.

A direct approach to introducing ideas

Teachers take a direct role in helping children acquire concepts and convictions which relate to personal and interpersonal issues by using a procedure which allows children to gradually increase their understanding.

The first step is to *name or identify the concept or conviction* during an activity with children. Teachers can also point out what the concept is not. While gently stroking a two-year-old child's face, we could say, "*Gentle* touches are nice to give." Or if a two-year-old child hits us we might say, "Ouch, hitting is *not gentle!* Hitting *hurts!*" If a young child brings a dead bird to us we could say, "You found a *dead* bird. It's *not* alive." Or when we feel sad we might say, "I feel *sad.*" This type of response is most effective to introduce a concept or to provide evidence which disputes a misconception or irrational belief.

The second basic step is to *question children about the truth of a concept or conviction.* We might gently touch a three-year-old child's face and ask, "Is this being gentle?" We could point to the picture of a child who is crying over a broken truck and ask, "Is this child happy?" Or we could touch her nose and ask, "Is this your ear?" This is a fairly simple strategy because all the child needs to do is give a yes or no. These types of exchanges let us know how well children understand an idea and draw their attention toward the concepts or convictions we want to emphasize.

The next step is to *request that children perform some action related to the concept or idea.* We could say to a four-year-old, "Please give me a *gentle* hug." If we needed assistance we could say, "Will you *help* me?" We might also give a child a picture and crayons and request, "Can you draw a *sad* picture for me?" Or we might say to a child, "Point to your nose." This strategy draws attention to the concept and provides us with an opportunity to check a child's understanding of our request.

The fourth step in this sequence is to *encourage children to describe the concept or* **17** *behavior.* If two six-year-old children are working together to clean up a mess we might ask, "What are you doing?" If the children say, "We're *helping* each other," we know that they have a working understanding of the concept help. If they cannot label their social behavior then we can name the concept for them or answer the question ourselves. In the same way we can ask children how they or someone else feels. This approach challenges children to verbalize concepts.

Finally, we can check the success of our efforts by *observing and listening to children as they play and relate to others.* Do children demonstrate an understanding of the ideas we have been emphasizing? Do they talk about gentleness or emotions? When they see someone hurt do they attempt to help them? The success of our teaching ultimately depends on children actually using the ideas in their everyday lives.

An indirect approach to introducing ideas

We convey ideas to children by what we say, but there are also more subtle or indirect ways of introducing personal/social concepts and convictions to children. How we behave and how we organize our classrooms influences children. Therefore, we should *examine the ideas children might acquire from being a part of our classrooms.* If we acknowledge how we feel during class, for example, we lend support to the belief that emotions can be useful. If we give children opportunities to make decisions, we affirm their self-confidence—a conviction that they are able to make some choices for themselves. In contrast, by frequently comparing the work of one child to another we might be contributing to the idea that competitive success is the only way to gain approval.

How do we deal with blind beliefs which can neither be supported nor disputed by evidence? How should we respond when children say such things as "The devil is going to put me in hell," "My daddy says there is no God," or "I'm going to be a doctor when I grow up."? If we teach in a church school we might feel obligated to nurture children's faith in certain blind beliefs appropriate for our religious community. Because blind beliefs are more open to debate, however, teachers in non-denominational and public schools may prefer to take a neutral position.

Instead of remaining silent, though, there are two simple ways of responding when children express blind beliefs: *we can restate what children say or we can ask for additional clarification of their idea.* We can do this without passing judgment on what the child says. The following conversation between a five-year-old and her teacher illustrates a neutral response to blind beliefs.

CHILD: When I die my mommy says I will go to heaven.

TEACHER: That's what your mommy says?

CHILD: Yes, and my Sunday school teacher.

TEACHER: Amy, what do you mean by heaven?

CHILD: Oh, it's a place where good people go to be with God when they are dead.

TEACHER: What do you think they do there?

CHILD: I don't know; I've never been there.

Personal/social development

16

The emphasis in this approach is to encourage children to examine their blind beliefs. But, most importantly, the teacher respects the child's and parents' position without advocating a different point of view. With this type of response we tell children that we are willing to talk with them about anything which concerns them. We do not, however, express our own blind beliefs or points of view as facts.

Sensing: The intuitive mind

A child's belief system is not entirely intellectual. A second important aspect of children's orientation toward their personal/social world is their sensitivity and intuition.

The defining aspects of social cognition tend to favor logical, rational, and analytical mind activities. Children use analysis when they think about their experiences, such as taking apart a toy, counting blocks, or spelling a word. But this cool logic is usually balanced by the warmer, more emotional aspects of intuition.

Intuition involves learning from sensation, feeling, and imagination. Children use intuitive thinking when they imagine a world of fantasy, write poetry, sing, or playfully explore a new toy at Christmas. The two modes of thinking, analysis and intuition, can work together to provide a balanced perspective on children's experiences, as well as our own.

Intuition is responsible for sensing possibilities and implications which may not be readily apparent.[16] Why would a child, for example, shy away from one adult stranger but show interest in another even though both are attractive and friendly? An onlooker may be bewildered by the child's inconsistency. But the child may be reacting to more subtle differences between the two adults, sensing such cues as body movement, posture, odor, and appearance. Although the child may not be able to explain his reaction, one adult "feels" right to him while the other does not. The child's sensing faculty or intuition served as a guide for decision making.

CHILD STUDY 3

Intuitive learning

Observe at least two children of different ages finger painting, working with clay, building with tinker toys, or playing a game. Can you find evidence of intuitive learning such as just "fooling around" to see what happens, responding to emotions, or using imagination? Can you detect any flow between intuitive and analytical thinking as children proceed through their activity? Do children respond differently to the same activity because of age differences?

Examine the following observation and reflect on the questions that follow it.

> One afternoon at school, Jason (five years old) decided to work with play dough while wearing a blindfold. After a great deal of kneading, rolling, and poking, he molded a bowllike structure. When he took off his blindfold, he looked at his "dish" and added several clay marbles. "Look at this, teacher!" he called, "Grapes!"

How does this example reveal intuitive learning? What kinds of responses can teachers make to promote or inhibit this form of learning? Give examples of effective and ineffective teacher responses to Jason's reaction.

Because our educational system often has emphasized analytical skills, many of us have learned to disregard our intuitive capabilities.[17] When we meet someone, for example, our conviction that we are *supposed* to like this person may overshadow our real feeling of discomfort with him or her. As teachers we might depend exclusively on abstract theories and analysis to guide our responses to children rather than acknowledge and trust our own hunches and feelings.

The integration of these two *complementary* modes of thinking, defining and sensing, provides a foundation for our personal/social effectiveness.[18] Verbal thinking (defining) helps us to analyze, clarify, and communicate our experiences while intuitive thinking (sensing) allows more subtle aspects of our experiences to be absorbed by our minds. By synthesizing intuition and logic we become "whole-mind" learners.[19]

Find a quiet place where you are not likely to be interrupted. Relax, get comfortable, close your eyes, and imagine yourself going into a toy store . . . How old are you?. . . What does the store look like?. . . Who else is in the toy store with you?. . . Picture yourself going up and down the aisles of the store looking for something you would like to have. (Someone has given you enough money to buy any three things you want.) Take your time, look at everything, and select your three toys. . . When you have selected your toys, pay for them with the money you were given, put them in a sack, and leave the store. . . Next, find a quiet spot and take out each of your choices, one at a time. Take a good look at each toy, turn it over, open it up, touch it, do something with it. . . If your toys could talk, what would they reveal to you? What needs do they help you meet? If you want, have a conversation with the toy. When you are through, put everything back in the sack and go on your way. How do you feel?

This self study may help you get in touch with your intuitive, sensing mind. Each toy may reveal something important to you that your more analytical, defining mind may have overlooked.

[a]Take your time with this activity. Read the entire description before beginning or have a friend read it to you. The dots (. . .) mean that you should stop reading and visualize the previous directions.

Education for the sensing mind

By developing a whole-mind teaching style we can nurture intuitive skills in children. Whole-mind teachers encourage children to develop their *creative* talents. For example, we can encourage children to participate in creative movement and dance activities, to play musical instruments, and to sing together. We can provide them with material so they can work with their hands to create sculptures, crafts, and other works of art. Creative activities challenge the receptive, experience-centered aspects of our minds.

Whole-mind teachers may also emphasize *imagination* in children. The ability to envision alternative worlds is an important characteristic of flexible thinking. Children who can visualize such things as yellow elephants, houses made of flowers, or a giraffe in a milk bottle are allowing their minds to be free from the rules we consider "reality."[20] Because of this mental flexibility, imaginative children can brainstorm consequences and solutions to problems. They can reflect on the past or what might happen in the future without committing themselves to action.[21]

Whole-mind teachers can nurture sensing skills in children by encouraging them to pay atttention to and learn from their *emotions*. The Ford-Esalen Project in Affective Education demonstrated that personal experiences of emotion could be integrated into the teaching of subject matter.[22] For example, while discussing the characteristics of helping, children could also identify how they felt when they offered or received help. Similarly, during an argument children could be asked to describe to each other how they feel. This exchange of information can help them better understand their emotions and those of others.[23]

Interpersonal problem solving: A whole-minded approach

The development of *effective* problem-solving strategies is a critical step in helping children organize their thoughts about personal/social experiences. The ability to enhance one's emotional well-being and relate successfully with other people depends on several cognitive skills. These skills include the ability to plan ahead, the ability to consider the consequences of one's actions, and the ability to consider alternative solutions to interpersonal problems.

Problem solving involves the *integration* and *application* of the defining and sensing modes of thinking and is the third aspect of children's orientation to their personal/social world. With encouragement from their teachers, young children can believe in their ability to produce worthwhile ideas and contribute to resolving problems. Spivak, Platt, and Shure have identified four interpersonal thinking skills for young children: (1) the ability to perceive a problem when it exists; (2) the ability to conceptualize solutions to typical age-relevant social problems; (3) the ability to describe potential consequences of social behavior; and (4) the ability to describe the anticipated causes of social behavior.[24] Each of these social problem-solving skills is very important to young children.

By employing techniques which Myrna Shure and Dave Spivak call "interpersonal problem-solving dialoguing," we can promote social reasoning in young children.[25] In this exchange of ideas teachers guide children to think about a past problem and describe the effects their responses may have had on themselves and others. Children may be guided to think further and explore what else they might have done, what the consequences of those actions might have been, and how other children might have reacted. As teachers, we must adjust our conversations with children so they can understand what is being discussed. Note that instead of solving problems for children, our effort should be directed toward helping them understand as best they can the dynamics of interpersonal behavior.[26]

Identify a problem you have had with another person, possibly a child. Visualize the situation or draw a picture which represents the problem. Try to identify all of the possible causes of the problem or factors that influenced it. What kinds of ideas or personality traits do you and the other person have which contributed to the difficulty?

Now try to brainstorm as many alternative solutions to the problem as you can. List whatever comes to your mind, and visualize each of the solutions as you think they might occur. Once this list of possibilities is completed, visualize and reflect on the possible consequences of each potential solution. Picture in your own mind what might happen.

With these solutions/consequences in mind, select what you think would be the best two. Devise a plan for actually implementing these solutions.

Sensitivity to problems and causal thinking

Perceiving problems or sensitivity to problems means that children become aware of a problem when it exists. *Causal thinking* is the ability to identify events that influence behavior. For example, two four-year-old children begin to fight over the use of a toy truck. The teacher intervenes, stops the fighting, and asks:

TEACHER: Hey… What's the problem here!

BILL: Tim is being mean.

TEACHER: What is he doing?

BILL: He's taking my truck.

TIM: It's my turn!

TEACHER: Bill, listen to Tim. Why is he grabbing your truck?

BILL: He says it's his turn, but I had it first.

TEACHER: Tim, why won't Bill give it to you?

TIM: He still wants to play with it.

In this interaction the teacher is attempting to direct the children's attention toward the real problem. The emphasis is on *behavior* and its causes rather than on labels. To emphasize this point the teacher asks Bill to describe Tim's behavior rather than simply allowing him to use the label *mean.*

Alternative-solution thinking

A child's ability to identify different ways a problem might be solved is called *alternative-solution thinking.* For example, how many solutions can a child think of if her toy is taken away by another? Grab it back? Threaten the other person? Ask for it? Tell the teacher? Cry? The emphasis in developing alternative-solution thinking is on encouraging children to think of various ways they might respond to a problem. Children who have only one solution will become powerless and frustrated if their first attempt fails.

In the previous example, alternative-solution thinking might result in the following exchange:

TEACHER: OK, the problem is that you both want the truck. Think of some ways you can solve this problem.

BILL: Tim could wait 'til I'm done.

TEACHER: What else?

TIM: We could play together.

BILL: Or we could take turns.

TEACHER: What else?

TIM: Bill could give it to me now.

If the children are not able to come up with any solutions we might mention some of the possibilities that come to mind. The strategy at this point is not to have the children guess the "right" solution but to encourage them to generate as many ideas as they can. Spivak, Platt, and Shure reported on a series of research studies which demonstrated that interpersonal alternative thinking has a significant influence on improving

the quality of children's social relationships and reducing adjustment problems.[27] Thus, socially competent children are more likely to be flexible and creative in their thinking about social relationships.

Consequential thinking

A third problem-solving skill involves *consequential thinking,* the ability to identify the effects of social acts. For example, the child whose toy was taken by another might think, "If I grab it back she'll hit. Teacher will tell me to solve the problem myself. So maybe if I ask her to play she'll give it to me." Proper evaluation of any course of action depends on being able to consider the consequences of various potential solutions.

In the example of two boys fighting over a truck, an emphasis on consequences might result in the following:

TEACHER: OK, what happens when you get into a fight?

BILL: We get hurt.

TIM: And cry.

TEACHER: What would happen, Tim, if Bill asked you to wait until he is finished?

TIM: I want to play now.

TEACHER: One of your ideas was to play together. How would you do that?

BILL: We could build a house and put the truck in it.

TEACHER: OK, that sounds interesting. What would happen if you took turns?

TIM: We could take turns after building the house. We wouldn't fight then.

TEACHER: Hey, you are really thinking now. Tim, one of your ideas was for Bill to give the truck to you now. How about that?

BILL: I want to play too!

TIM: Oh, Bill doesn't want to do that.

If children cannot identify consequences we might have to describe them ourselves. Of course, the heat of a fight might indicate that we should pick a better time for a dialogue.

Selecting and implementing a solution

The last step in the problem-solving process involves helping children select and implement solutions. The previous discussion continues:

TEACHER: Well, what do you want to do?

BILL: Let's take turns. You and me play together.

TIM: Yea, let's make a house too.

TEACHER: Sounds like a good idea.

Children use their concepts, convictions, and intuitions to influence their problem-solving responses even though they lack some of the logical abilities to understand and analyze social problems as adults might do. Yet patient discussion, consistent encouragement, and positive feedback to children during their efforts to talk with each other

Personal/social development

will help children *define themselves as problem solvers.* Although some of the intellectual aspects of the activity may not be fully understood, children will begin to learn to think about possible solutions, consider the possible consequences, and select and try out what seem to be the best solutions.

Social cognition and personal/social issues

Understanding the nature of social cognition and the three related processes of defining, sensing, and problem solving emphasizes the importance of thinking for personal/social development. Children are constantly trying to establish some type of logical order in their world, to make sense out of their experiences, and to deal as best they can with the problems that life presents.

However, this integrated approach to experience does not occur in a vacuum. Children do not just think—they think *about* something. This interaction between content (themes) and process (social cognition) is presented in Figure 2.2. The five themes and four steps in social cognition can be combined to form a matrix of twenty potential skill areas. In examining this matrix we can identify one aspect of social cognition and apply it across all five themes, or we can identify one theme and apply it to all four steps. This latter approach, focusing on each theme, is the primary emphasis for the rest of this book.

Figure 2.2 Matrix of potential personal/ social skills

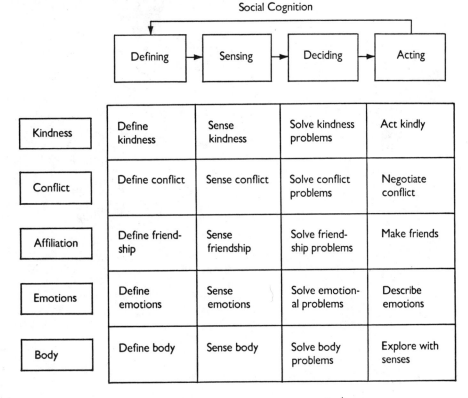

	Defining	Sensing	Deciding	Acting
Kindness	Define kindness	Sense kindness	Solve kindness problems	Act kindly
Conflict	Define conflict	Sense conflict	Solve conflict problems	Negotiate conflict
Affiliation	Define friendship	Sense friendship	Solve friendship problems	Make friends
Emotions	Define emotions	Sense emotions	Solve emotional problems	Describe emotions
Body	Define body	Sense body	Solve body problems	Explore with senses

Social Cognition

Personal/Social Themes

25

Chapter three
Body and sensory awareness:
Becoming somebody

S elf-discovery begins with body awareness. How do newborns experience life? Body sensations are likely to dominate their awareness.[1] Infants feel pain when hungry or uncomfortable and experience pleasure when fed, held, and rocked. These sensations add to their emerging sense of self.

Physical experiences bring children into contact with the world. Infants have a nearly insatiable desire to make sensory contact with their surroundings. By tasting, hearing, seeing, and touching they begin to differentiate themselves from other objects. Touching and being touched by others helps them map out their own body contours. The reactions of others also begin to contribute to children's attitudes toward their bodies. A child, for example, may notice a parent's disapproval and disgust during a diaper change and then begin to form a negative or mixed attitude toward elimination.

Children also learn that many of their physical characteristics are singled out by others for special recognition. For example, children become aware that they are boys or girls and that they are expected to behave accordingly. They also gradually learn that their appearance is evaluated by others in terms of its attractiveness. This type of recognition influences children's attitudes toward their bodies and can have positive or negative effects on their social development.

Children also discover that their bodies change over time. They begin to outgrow clothes and discover that they can do things that were previously too difficult. They also discover that growth and development are part of the cycle of life that eventually leads to death. Both the beginning and the end of life are baffling events of great significance, and the resolution of these and other body-related issues has a profound influence on the way children respond to life and relate to others.

Body awareness and education

Body awareness is a relevant and important issue for our educational program for many reasons. First, children do not leave concerns about their bodies at home, but they bring pressing questions about birth, death, disease, and health to school with them. Our educational programs can be designed to help them better understand these issues. If their need for information and support is not met, children may acquire misconceptions about their bodies.

An undergraduate student, for example, once revealed that during his early grade-school years he believed that he was filled with tar instead of blood. This was because his parents frequently corrected him with the warning, "If you don't stop that I'm going to beat the tar out of you!" He interpreted the threat literally and believed he had tar instead of blood. His worst fears were confirmed soon after his initial suspicion when he scraped the back of his arm and later examined dry but darkened blood in the mirror. He was convinced that he was an oddity, a shameful freak of nature. Even though he learned the facts when he became older, he acknowledged a lingering uneasiness about his body. If a teacher or parent could have penetrated that fear and confronted his misconception that confused child could have been saved a great deal of anxiety. A simple and accurate discussion with a trusted adult may have been all that was needed to resolve his anxiety.

Second, children come to school with a way of learning which includes *all* of their senses. By involving children in multisensory experiences we can keep alive their childlike appreciation of the world. If we isolate children at desks and emphasize only passive seeing and listening we may be depriving them of opportunities to utilize other senses in learning. We might instead look for opportunities to nurture children's senses of taste, smell, and touch. Children, for example, who have smelled, touched, seen, and heard a real pig will have learned much more about that animal than if they only saw its picture.

Third, children's attitudes toward themselves can be influenced by their teachers' responses. Sex-role stereotypes and feelings of attractiveness may be either reinforced or diminished. Some teachers, for example, may be especially critical of boys or give special attention to more attractive children. Other teachers may be fair in their relationships, but their choices will ultimately have some effect on children's attitudes toward themselves.

Finally, children's physical well-being is affected by how the classroom is organized. What kind of desks are most suitable for children? How long can they be seated before their need for energetic activity becomes frustrating? How does stress in school affect a child's body? The appearance and movement of our bodies reveal much about ourselves. Similarly, a child in an uncomfortable desk and with little opportunity for creative movement will look and move differently from a child whose desk is supportive and comfortable and who has a classroom schedule which allows for creative movement. Every classroom experience will have some impact on the structure and capabilities of a child's body.

Defining body features

As teachers we can help children understand their physical structure and development and become more sensitive to their actual body experiences. Children can gain a perspective on the structure and function of their bodies as they begin to understand themselves better by labeling and assigning meaning to their physical characteristics. Children ask many questions about their bodies. What is a heart, stomach, or a brain? Where are these body parts located? What is their function? Are boys and girls supposed to act differently? What kinds of standards are used to judge attractiveness? Each of these questions reveals a concern about physical self-definition.

The knee bone is connected to the leg bone: Understanding body parts

Understanding body parts begins during infancy. Infants begin to discover their physical dimensions in their sensory exploration of their world. They stick their toes and fingers in their mouths and discover their extremities. Pleasurable contact with their parents and their own self-exploration help them differentiate between what is and what is not a part of themselves. At about six months of age they reach out to touch their image in a mirror, a significant step in the development of self-recognition. By two years children typically can state their own name when parents point to the mirror and ask them to identify who they see.[1] Although they may not be able to say so, young children have a fairly well-advanced concept of their bodies by the end of infancy.

Physical awareness progresses rapidly in the years immediately following infancy. Toddlers name their major features and body parts and can respond to simple requests for specific types of movements such as "Point to your eyes," or "Can you point to your mouth?"[2] When children acquire control over their bladder and sphincter muscles, they take a significant step in body awareness. For some children this advance is accompanied by a sense of shame of their bodies as they experience disapproval and pressure from parents to master these body functions.

Preschoolers' growing awareness of their bodies involves the coordination of two perspectives. First, children get to know themselves as others see them. They begin to form a concept of how they look, feel, sound, and smell. Second, they begin to form a concept of their inner physical space. This perspective is difficult to develop and is easily distorted because children are not able to directly observe what goes on inside them. A growing awareness of inner physical space was sensitively portrayed by one four-year-old boy:

> Sometimes I wonder about the blood in me. Inside me is all wet and blood is moving and lots of insides, but outside is all dry and careful and you would never know about the inside part by looking at the outside part. Not unless you get a hole in you and some blood came out. All the people are like that. Their skins keep them in. But underneath their skins is such a lot . . . Your insides never stop . . . It is so funny to think of you being all wet inside and all dry out-

side. Everybody is like that. I am. Why, Miss Willimas, *you* are [laughs]. Did you ever think about it? [Teacher offers to show him an anatomical picture.] A picture that would be for you would be for me, too? Then we are alike. You me are alike.[3]

When one young girl was first learning to use the bathroom by herself, she experienced an unsettling incident which caused her some insecurity with her concept of her body's interior. She got up during the night to use the bathroom, but before she flushed the toilet she noticed a bug floating around in the water. Not realizing that the bug had been placed there by another family member, she concluded that the bug actually had been inside her. She awoke her father immediately saying, "Daddy, daddy, there are bugs inside me! There are *bugs inside me!*" When her father saw what had happened, he explained that he had placed the bug in the toilet. After being reassured she returned to bed and slept soundly the rest of the night. She never mentioned the incident again.

SELF STUDY 5

How children view themselves and you

Select one or two children who are at least four years old. Seat them individually at a table with paper and crayons (or colored pens) and ask them to draw a picture of you. Encourage them to take their time and include as much as they want. When they are finished give them another sheet of paper and ask them to draw a self-portrait.

When both pictures are completed cut them out and paste them side by side. First look at each child's drawing of you. What features appear to be most important to the children? Did they overlook any important characteristics, such as a beard, long hair, or glasses? Compare the drawing of you with the self-portrait. How are they similar? How are they different? Is there more detail in your picture or in the self-portrait? Is one bigger than the other? Is there a difference in emotional expression? Do these drawings reveal anything about how these children viewed themselves and you? Treat these ideas as speculation rather than fact since we cannot be absolutely sure of what these drawings mean.

What physical parts of you are most interesting to children in general? Why? Are you satisfied with the way children contact you physically? Do you like to touch and be touched, to sit close with children, to hold hands or roughhouse?

Sugar and spice or puppy dog tails:
Gender identity and sex roles

One aspect of defining body appearance for children involves their knowledge of and attitudes toward sexual differences. To put this issue into a better perspective, it is important to discriminate between gender identity and sex roles.[4] *Gender identity* refers to children's ideas and feelings about their biological sex, being a boy or a girl.

For example, a child might say to himself, "I am a boy. It's OK to be a boy." On the other hand, a *sex role* is the collection of qualities children believe are culturally appropriate for each of the sexes. Sex roles involve definitions of masculinity and femininity. Thus, a boy might shy away from dolls because he defines them as "girl stuff." His preference, in this instance, reveals his ideas about both the male and the female sex role.

Gender identity begins at birth with selection of the child's name and other sex-related labels adults use to identify the child, for example, "You're such a cute *boy*. You're *daddy's boy*!" By twenty-four months children can discriminate between the two sexes but not correctly apply the boy-girl label to themselves. By thirty months their self-labeling gradually becomes more accurate, and by three years of age children do acquire a firm gender label.[5] Because young children distinguish between sexes entirely on the basis of outward appearance rather than less noticeable biological differences, e.g. size of breasts, genitals, they do not have gender constancy, the realization that one's gender remains constant over time.[6] Length of hair and body build have been found to be the most important physical cues for four- to six-year-old children in establishing sex.[7] Six-year-olds view deviation from existing observable differences as a violation of the laws of physical reality as well as a threat to their gender identity.[8]

Once children make the decision about their maleness or femaleness they quickly begin to make decisions about how they are expected to behave and the kind of sex role they need to assume to maintain that self and social definition. On one hand, children are influenced by their social group and the kind of expectations others have of them. But they are also involved in a process of self-socialization, their interpretation of what they see, and the kinds of expectations they make of themselves to conform to social rules they consider appropriate for their own sex.[9]

Well-defined sex roles have been clearly established in our society. Traditionally, masculinity has been associated with an *instrumental* orientation toward life involving an emphasis on achievement, autonomy, and personal control. Femininity has been associated with an *expressive* orientation which emphasizes communion, commonality, desire to relate effectively, and expression of feelings.[10] Beliefs about masculinity and femininity, however, have not always been supported by research. For example, girls are not necessarily more sociable or suggestable than boys, nor do they have to have a lower self-esteem. Yet adolescent girls do have a greater verbal ability than boys and adolescent boys excel in visual-spatial and math skills. Also, boys generally are more aggressive than girls.[11]

Adults tend to respond to children in a manner which reinforces traditional sex stereotypes and strangers may exert more pressure on children than parents.[12] Several research studies have demonstrated that adults treat the same infant or toddler differently depending on the gender label provided.[13] For example, if adults were told that a crying infant was a boy they said "he" was angry. If they were told the same crying child was a girl they said "she" was frightened.[14] If they were told the infant was a girl they chose a doll for her to play with, and if they were given no gender information they spontaneously labeled the child's sex. If respondents said the infant was a boy they claimed they did so because of male-type characteristics like strength. If they said the child was a girl they cited traits of softness or fragility. These observations were made of the *same* child by different adults.[15]

Stereotyping responses also occur if the child is older. When a toddler was introduced as a boy, adults tended to encourage active play with typical "boy's" toys. But if the same child were introduced as a girl more interpersonal, nurturant play occured between the adult and child.[16] Female teachers have been observed to encourage feminine-type behaviors in both boys and girls.[17] Gender is clearly an important characteristic that adults use to influence what they do with children.

Children do not react passively to adult encouragement of stereotyped sex roles. The work of Kohlberg, Lewis, and Maccoby supports the notion that children possess and use their observations to construct a set of rules which they then use to govern their own behavior.[18] Once children make the differentiation between males and females they begin to adopt behaviors which they define as appropriate for their sex. This process is promoted by the kinds of labels adults use to identify correct sex-typed behavior.[19]

Young children may be especially rigid in their sex-role behavior because observable, concrete characteristics are the only features they can use to define their masculinity or femininity. They may have some difficulty, for example, understanding that girls can grow up and do most of the things boys can do or that their mothers have a variety of traditionally male occupations available to them. They simply do not see sufficient evidence to support these points of view.

Children begin to differentiate and encourage "appropriate" sex-stereotyped play in their peers as early as three years of age.[20] By this time children have already established a firm notion of their sex role.[21] In one study two- and three-year-old girls tended to assign positive aspects to their own sex (e.g., "look nice," "give kisses,") and negative characteristics to boys (e.g., "are mean," "like to fight," "are weak") while boys of the same age did the reverse (e.g., boys "work hard" or "are loud," while girls "cry" or "are slow").[22] This study also revealed that some behaviors were not stereotyped. Neither boys nor girls believed, for example, that one sex more than the other "runs fast," "is strong," "is not scared," "is the leader," or "is smart." Evidently young children do not assign sex appropriateness to all of their actions.

Sex stereotyping continues during the grade-school years. At six and seven years of age children were found to conform their preferences to items allegedly preferred by peers of the same sex.[23] If a boy, for example, were told "this object is the one the boys like best," he also claimed to like it more.

Eight-year-olds have acquired *gender constancy* which enables them to recognize that masculinity and femininity are partly a function of experience and environment. Because of this they become more capable of accepting variations in sex-role behaviors than preschoolers.[24] However, some stereotyping may continue to occur, since second graders' views of competence were more rigidly defined according to sex appropriateness than kindergarteners'.[25] During the fifth grade children were found to remember more of the masculine-type traits and behaviors of male characters in stories as well as the feminine-type traits and behaviors of female characters even though each character depicted an equal number of male and female type characteristics.[26]

CHILD STUDY 4

Clothing and self-image

Developmental changes in body awareness may be revealed in children's attitude toward their clothing. Look through a department store catalogue and cut out pictures of male and female clothing for infants, older children, and adults. Select two or three children of different ages and show them the pictures. Ask them to pick out one or two items they would want their mothers to buy for them. Do their selections reveal a choice which considers age and sex? Are their choices different from how they typically dress? Ask them to describe the kind of clothes they like to wear. Do their choices show an understanding of body awareness?

Recall your own childhood attitudes toward clothing. What kind of clothes did you like to wear, and how did your preference change as you grew older? How did you feel when you dressed up on Halloween? Were you ever self-conscious about the changes these costumes made to your self-image?

The color of people:
Racial awareness in children

Mary Ellen Goodman, in her study of racial attitudes in young children, identified three essential but overlapping phases in the development of racial concepts.[27] Phase 1, *awareness,* is the realization that racial differences exist (racial identity); phase 2, *orientation,* is the acquisition of race-related preferences, values, and beliefs (racial roles); and phase 3, *true attitude,* involves the establishment of full-fledged racial attitudes.

Research has demonstrated clearly that racial *awareness* emerges sometime between three and five years of age.[28] When preschool children, for example, were asked to select a photo which looked like them they were able to select one of their own race.[29] Exceptions to this conclusion have been demonstrated with Native American and Canadian children who misidentify themselves with their own race and insist that they are white.[30] This observation may be due more to strong negative feelings Indian children have of themselves than a lack of racial awareness.

In terms of *orientation*, research has shown that young children of all races generally show a preference for white over nonwhite dolls, animals, or pictures as playmates. This tendency may decrease with age in some children.[31] Thus, young black children may be more oriented toward outsiders as they more positively value whites than blacks. White children, with their attraction to their own racial group, are more oriented to insiders.[32] The result may be strong feelings of racial self-doubt and inferiority by black children though research has revealed that this trend may be changing.[33]

Children as young as three years old have demonstrated negative racial *attitudes* or stereotypes. Black and white American children have labeled black dolls as looking "bad," and Native-American and white children have done the same for Native-American dolls.[34] When black children drew themselves they were observed to produce small and incomplete people in comparison to the more powerful and strong appearances of their drawing of whites.[35] One group of researchers asked black, white, and Latino elementary school children to rank and evaluate photographs of children from each of the three ethnic groups. All three groups ranked the photos of white children highest on kindness, happiness, and school grades.[36]

The process of moving through the three phases of awareness, orientation, and attitudes toward race is influenced by children's cognitive development. If parents, schools, and the media make racial differences an important issue (as they do with gender), young children will apply the labels to their own behavior and will look for and exaggerate the distinctions between themselves and people of other races. Young children are likely to identify race with appearance rather than genetics and may believe that people can change their race with a change in their appearance. They may also associate race with very concrete, observable experiences. For example, a preschool child might believe black children are dark because of exposure to the sun.

Mirror, mirror on the wall:
Attractiveness and behavior

In addition to race and gender children consider attractiveness an important physical characteristic and are aware of their culture's definitions of beauty. During the early preschool years children begin to differentiate between attractive and unattractive appearances.[37] Attractiveness may even serve as a more powerful cue to influence behavior than race.[38] Even though they may be told otherwise, both children and adults use attractiveness as a guide to influence their thinking about themselves and others.

Three outcomes of defining attractiveness are the acquisition of stereotypes labeling people as attractive or unattractive, differences in peer relationships, and effect of adult appraisals. Children's concepts and definitions of beauty can have powerful impact on their own self-respect and their relationships with others.

Stereotypes of attractiveness begin during the preschool years. Attractive children are thought of in more positive ways than unattractive children. Children as young as four years of age have labeled unattractive children as antisocial and attractive children as more self-sufficient and independent.[39] And children who actually know attractive children tend to describe them as behaving both prosocially *and* antisocially.[40] In other words, stereotypes occur when attractive children are not known, while more attention and significance is given to the actions of attractive children who are known.

Children in kindergarten and fourth grade have labeled pictures of attractive children as smarter, more likely to share and be friendly, and less likely to be mean and hit than pictures of unattractive children.[41] Unfortunately, studies are not available which reveal how children evaluate their own attractiveness. Nevertheless, research clearly indicates that children use attractiveness to predict another child's personality and behavior.

These stereotypes influence children's peer relationships. In one study, children between three and six years of age more frequently chose attractive over unattractive pictures to view.[42] Children as young as three years were more likely to select pictures of attractive children as friends.[43] Kindergarten and fourth grade children liked pictures of attractive children more than those that were unattractive.[44] Although no differences were observed in three-year-olds, unattractive five-year-olds were found to be more aggressive than their attractive peers.[45] Attractive fourth and sixth graders were also likely to have more positive peer relationships than their unattractive counterparts. Apparently, standards of beauty emerge during preschool and are influential through grade school.

Attractiveness also influences adult-child relationships. Teachers were more likely to give a better appraisal of attractive children's academic ability, intelligence, success in school, and peer popularity.[46] They were also more likely to give them better grades.[47] When an attractive child misbehaved adults evaluated the behavior less negatively and were less likely to assign an antisocial label to that child. In this same study, however, there was no difference in the *intensity* of punishment advocated by the adult.[48] Research indicates that attractive children may at least begin their relationship with adults with a favorable bias while the reverse is true for their unattractive peers. The age at which attractiveness becomes important to parents and the extent these stereotypes may change during the course of an actual relationship is not known.

Defining growth

Children's attitudes toward themselves and their relationships with others are influenced by the manner in which they define their appearance (i.e., their body structure, gender, race, and attractiveness). Children may also be confused by the changes which occur in their bodies over time, but growth and development are difficult to define because they occur so slowly. Age is one attribute which is constantly but gradually transforming children's experiences of themselves and their social relationships.

In the beginning:
Children's ideas about conception and birth

Conception and birth, the origins of development, are difficult issues for children to understand. Conception is an abstract idea which cannot be directly experienced by children, and birth is an event which, in our culture, is typically a private, antiseptic **35** occasion which excludes them. Children do, however, pick up bits of information and misinformation regarding conception and birth.

Anne Bernstein and Philip Cowan interviewed sixty children from three to twelve years of age to elicit their ideas regarding how people get babies.[49] An analysis of the responses revealed six stages of understanding. At level 1, *geography*, younger children believe that babies always existed, and that they arrived in their mother's tummy from somewhere else like another woman or a "baby store." At level 2, *manufacturing*, children believe that instead of always existing, babies have to be built from various components. At level 3, *transitional*, children combine the importance of a social relationship, external mechanics of sexual intercourse, and fusion of biogenetic materials, but their explanations must be technically feasible and logical from their point of view. For example, one subject said that "the daddy plants the seed like a flower, I think, except you don't need dirt." These first three levels characterize children from three to seven or eight years of age.

At levels four through six, eight- to twelve-year-old children describe conception primarily in physiological terms. At level 4, *concrete physiology*, children may identify the physical facts of life but not understand the nature of genetic contributions of both sperm and egg. At level 5, *preformation*, children assert that the baby is a preformed miniature person in either sperm or egg and begins to grow when the two are combined. At level 6, *physical causality*, children can identify (at about age twelve) the physical explanations of conception and birth and the genetic contributions of both mother and father. This sequence demonstrates that children gradually progress from explanations based on their own direct experiences to more abstract notions not directly observable.

Other researchers have found that the vast majority of four- and five-year-old children knew that an enlarged abdomen in a woman was associated with the growth of a baby.[50] Some children asserted that the baby started because the mother became fat from eating, and others believed that the baby was always there and that the mother had to eat good food to make it grow. A small number of children thought that the mother had to swallow the baby in order to bear it later. Regarding birth, most children said that the baby would emerge from the mother's abdomen which would have to be cut open. On a somber note, 75 percent of the girls thought that the baby was miserable inside the mother—that it cried, and was lonely or afraid. Other explanations of what happens to the baby while it is inside the mother were that it eats the food mother eats, and that it grows, sleeps, and plays. At this age children try to take a very complex issue and reduce it to what they consider to be its simplest terms.

I'm not a baby any more:
Awareness of age differences

Awareness of age progresses in the same manner as awareness of gender, race, and attractiveness. Children first classify people into age groups and then develop expectations for themselves and others in terms of age. For example, a six-year-old boy may define himself as "big" and assume the characteristics he thinks a "big boy" should have. He may insist that he can now walk to a friend's house on another street, be left alone with a friend in a movie theatre, and stay up later in the evening. He is different now that he is "*big*." He may also believe, however, that he cannot babysit for himself or cook his own dinner. Children use age as a sign for acquiring skills and assuming responsibilities. For an excellent review of research on children's definitions of age, see Edwards and Lewis's article on young children's concepts of social relationships.[51]

SELF STUDY 6

Your approach to change

Life is a series of changes in which something old but predictable is left behind for something new and risky. As children we left the security of our immediate surroundings to explore our neighborhoods, and we gradually left our toys behind. Later, as our relationships with those of the opposite sex began to change, we went on our first date. And now many of us have left the security of our parents' home to risk a life on our own. Our future still holds inevitable changes, and to some extent we will lose our physical strength, experience diminished sensory abilities, and possibly gain a sense of wisdom toward life. Of course, we also face the biggest risk of all—death. Growth is change.

How do you feel about change? Do you look forward to the future with enthusiasm, or do you begrudgingly hold on to the past? Do you accept or fight change? Does your view of the life cycle include both a longing for what has been and an excitement for what might be?

How does your approach to change affect your relationships with children? Do you shy away from their concerns about growth and development or their questions about death and aging? What kind of attitude toward change do you convey? Are you satisfied with your impression, or is it something you would like to change?

In their review of the literature, Edwards and Lewis found that awareness of age begins about two years of age when toddlers use age-relevant labels for themselves and others. They will label photographs of infants as "baby" and those of adults as "mommy" or "daddy." At this point they have no word for "child." When asked how old they are, they may label themselves ("Two!" shouts one child) without really understanding the chronological basis for the term. Children do not really understand the basis for age until grade school.

Older three-year-olds can sort out and classify photographs of people of all ages. Preschoolers can differentiate between "little" and "big" children (using five years as the average cutoff) and parents from grandparents (using forty years as the cutoff). The ability to discriminate between teenagers and adults and to rank-order people according to age generally does not emerge until the early grade-school years. By eight or nine years old, children are able to assign ages to photographs of others.

The emergence of age roles also begins during the preschool and kindergarten years when children begin to form expectations about behavior which is most appropriate for a particular age category. Between three and six years children generally view adults as fulfilling dependency roles and asserting power as they punish, make demands, provide information, and help. Same-age and older peers are considered more appropriate for play activities, and older peers are considered good resources for learning. Infants and toddlers are generally viewed as dependent persons who need both nurturance and dominance. Thus, when kindergarteners view toddlers they may provide help and comfort or become "bossy" with their commands or corrections.[52]

Sing no sad songs for me: Awareness of life and death

Children are also concerned about death. In one study, a group of five-year-olds clearly demonstrated a stronger emotional reaction to three death-related words, *burned, kill, dead,* than to other words.[53] Young children are aware that death is something mysterious and, like sex, is something they may be apprehensive about discussing. Three basic questions children have about death are: what happens when a person dies (*metamorphosis*), what causes death (*universality*), and how long does death last (*permanence*)?

Children's ideas about the nature of life and death undergo dramatic transformations. They may first attribute life to anything that moves (at this stage a five-year-old may insist that clouds and trees are alive when they move), but soon they revise their thinking and attribute life to anything that moves on its own accord. Thus, a child may consider a clock alive because it appears to move by itself. At about eight years of age children begin to restrict their definition of life to plants and animals.[54]

Similarly, preschool children may associate death with stillness. Some children are afraid of bedtime because they think sleep is death, and they may be confused when something that is dead refuses to wake up. Some young children may believe that dead people still have use of their senses but cannot move.[55] A five-year-old girl, for example, may ask her teacher how dead people get food when they are trapped inside a coffin. Between seven and nine years of age children gradually begin to realize that death is a drastic *metamorphosis* involving the disintegration of the body, but they may still not understand that death is a natural part of the life cycle. Instead, they may personify death as a ghost, skeleton, or boogeyman—someone who causes death to occur.

Young children also struggle with the *universality* of death. They may think that death is the result of accident or illness. Thus, they assume that if they can avoid these unfortunate conditions they will be able to escape death. Around nine years of age children generally become aware that death naturally occurs for all living things including themselves.[56]

The *permanency* of death is another difficult issue for children to grasp. Maria Nagy discovered that children between the ages of three and five may act as though death is only a temporary event. At this stage children may define death as something reversible, a departure, a state of sleep, separation, a change of environment, or a form of limited life. Children may expect the dead to return or may speak of the dead as though they were alive. Some children, for example, may dig up the grave of a pet to see if it is still there.[57]

By their tenth birthday children have progressed enough in their thinking to understand that death involves a dramatic transformation in existence, that it is universal, and that it is final and permanent. During the first nine years, however, children's ideas about aging and death profoundly influence their views on human development.

Sensing body experiences

Children's attitudes toward themselves and others is affected by how they define their appearance and development, but the human body is much more than some object to observe and categorize. We *experience* our bodies and know what it means to be hungry, to feel pain, to smell a flower, or to hear a symphony.

Body contact:
The importance of body experiences

The importance of body experiences in our contact and relationship with the world is revealed in the many metaphors and expressions in our everyday language. When we are in a hurry we are "pressed for time," when faced with something unsettling our experiences are "mind blowing" or "hair raising," when we have a hunch we "feel it in our bones," when we are anxious we have "butterflies in our stomach," and when we are upset with someone he or she is a "pain in the neck." The way we use language illustrates the significance we attribute to body experiences.

Our bodies bring us into contact with the world and in harmony with the spontaneous rhythms of nature. There is a natural rhythm to all life as night gives way to day, sleep to wakefulness, and calm to turbulence. Rhythmic activities of the body fall into three categories: internal, sensory, and movement.[58] *Internal body rhythms* are involuntary and cannot be consciously controlled. The sensations of hunger, bladder fullness, digestion, and heartbeat are examples of involuntary rhythms. *Sensory activities*

of the body are involuntary to some extent but can be controlled. These rhythms include eating, breathing, sneezing, coughing, sleeping, and sensory contact with the external world (such as seeing, touching, or tasting). These are partially controlled because we can stop ourselves from eating, change the rhythm of our breathing, inhibit our sneezing, etc. In the third category our conscious mind assumes dominant control over *movement experiences*. Dancing, drawing, and singing are fully creative because they can be self-directed. In everyday life these three types of rhythmic activities merge together to form a complex and fascinating system of human action.

That tickle in my tummy:
Awareness of inner space

When do children become consciously aware of internal experiences like fatigue, thirst, and sickness? What kinds of physical cues do they use to interpret these experiences? Since research on these and some other issues is not available, two children were interviewed separately for this book and asked to describe their experiences. Here these children discuss feeling sleepy, thirsty, hungry, sick, and healthy.

INTERVIEWS   *JASON (five years)*

How do you know when you are sleepy? *Means you're tired. When you yawn — that means you sleepy.* How do you know when you're thirsty? What does "thirsty" feel like? *Means you feel like drinking something.* How do you know when you feel like drinking something? *Cause I hadn't anything to drink.* How do you know when you're hungry? *Means you eat something like meat or roast beef.* How do you know when to eat? *That's a toughy . . . I don't know.*

How do you know when you're hurt? *Like when your knee is bleeding.* How do you know when you're sick? *When I'm coughing or sneezing.* How do you feel inside? *I feel low down.* How do you know when you are healthy, when you are well? *Not sneezing or coughing.*

JENNY (seven years)

How do you know when you are sleepy? How does it feel to be sleepy? *I feel kind of lousy — can't run as fast because you're getting tired — feel like I'm going to drop out so I just lay down.* How do you know when you're thirsty? What does "thirsty" feel like? *That's a health kind of thing — you need some amount of water and salt in your body . . . and your mouth sends a message to the brain.* How does your mouth feel? *My mouth feels like play dough, gooey like . . . it feels really dry.* How do you know when you're hungry? *My tummy aches and my stomach begins to growl. Sometimes my mouth begins to water.*

How do you know when you're hurt? *You begin to cry. You know, you bump into something like when I skin my finger and it gets sore.* How do you know when you're sick? *Sometimes I get a tummy ache, sometimes I get a sore throat. When I run my lungs push together real fast — I got air sick from all that air. Sometimes I get kind of grumpy.* How do you know when you are healthy, when you are well? *I feel terrific, I start running around, let my brother play with my things. It feels tickly-like . . . makes me feel like I'm some big clown.*

Although these interviews do not qualify as a scientific study, the children's responses suggest a few tentative conclusions. Jenny was much more verbal than Jason and was more comfortable and confident in her answers to the questions but if we examine the *quality* or content of their comments we find an interesting developmental trend.

Jenny's comments related more to internal than external body experiences while Jason's were the reverse. Jenny made such comments as "feel lousy . . . need water and salt in your body . . . stomach begins to growl . . . finger gets sore . . . it feels tickly-like. . ." Each of these responses describes an inner experience. On the other hand, Jason focused on "when you yawn . . . drinking something . . . eat something . . . knee is bleeding . . . coughing or sneezing. . ." These responses emphasize ob-emphasize observable or external experiences.

Cognitive developmental theory suggests that young children's thinking is influenced by their perceptions, by what is available to their senses. Older children, however, are more able to understand the less obvious and the more abstract. Jason (at five years) focuses on external signs of inner experiences because he is influenced by what he can directly sense. He cannot conceptualize something that is going on in a more subtle way inside his body. On the other hand, Jenny (at seven years) is very aware of her interior space and tries to find words to describe these more personal experiences. On one occasion, for example, when she was feeling distraught she said, "I feel like my stomach is gone, like there is nothing there." Once when she was angry she stated that her "blood was shaking." Additional research is needed to see if the differences between children like Jason and Jenny are due to age, personality, or psychological orientation.

Learning to become sense-able:
Sensory knowledge and sensory awareness

In addition to demonstrating an active interest in their physical selves, from infancy onward young children display an eagerness for engaging in a sensory investigation of their environment. Children are drawn into this exploration by the apparently inexhaustible novelty of everything around them. They want to discover that tempting world with all of their sensory capacities—touching, tasting, looking, listening, and smelling.

The ability to recall and to talk about sensory experiences is an important capacity for both personal and interpersonal development. *Sensory knowledge* enables a person to recreate from memory an earlier sensory experience and recall, for example, the taste of salt, the feel of satin, the smell of roses, and the sight of a brilliant sunset. These images can be either pleasant or unpleasant. For example most older children eagerly look forward to Christmas morning because the excitement and ritual elicit pleasant sensory images of past Christmases. However, other sensory images, like recalling the sights, sounds, and odors from a hospital stay, can be equally unpleasant. As a child experiences the world in a variety of circumstances he or she begins to form a vivid "mental map" which enhances confidence in being able to cope with the environment and relate to others.

Sensory knowledge is also important in interpersonal communication. Art, literature, and drama, for example, involve an attempt to elicit sensory experiences by verbally or visually recreating for another the feel of grass, the smell of springtime, or the touch of a loved one. Sensory experiences can provide the foundation for a vocabulary and imagination which gives depth and clarity to communicating experiences.

This special sensitivity is beautifully portrayed in the poem one child wrote while in a concentration camp.

Birdsong[a]

He doesn't know the world at all
Who stays in his nest and doesn't go out.
He doesn't know what birds know best
Nor what I want to sing about,
That the world is full of loveliness.

When dewdrops sparkle in the grass
And earth's aflood with the morning light,
A blackbird sings upon a bush
To greet the dawning after night.
Then I know how fine it is to live.

Hey, try to open up your heart
To beauty; go to the woods someday
And weave a wreath of memory there.
Then if the tears obscure your way
. You'll know how wonderful it is

To be alive.

An anonymous child in Terezin concentration camp, 1941.

This child's sensory experience was translated into a form he or she could communicate to others. Yet the foundation of sensory awareness is not interpretation and communication but direct experiential contact with the environment.

[a]From *I Never Saw Another Butterfly*, Edited by H. Volavokova, McGraw-Hill, 1964. Used with permission.

CHILD STUDY 5

Sensory awareness

Observe two or three children of different ages in direct sensory play, for example, finger painting, kneading dough, smelling flowers, or playing at a watertable. How do the children differ in the way they approach and become involved in sensory activities? Does one become immediately involved while another hesitates and approaches the experience cautiously? Does one tend to rely only on one sensory modality (such as vision) while another tends to involve all possible senses? What do you think are the reasons for these differences? Do you think the differences in age have an effect?

Sensory awareness is a general attitude of openness to the world and a willingness to experience what it has to offer. It is the enjoyment of essentially non-social stimulation, an engagement in *sense-pleasure play*.[59] This form of play begins in infancy with the sensing of light, color, movement, sounds, tastes, odors, and textures. Later, an increase in physical-motor coordination enables the young children to seek, control, and modify their own sensory experiences. Children who have just learned to walk, for example, actively explore any new experiences available in their environment. They try to go anywhere their legs can take them. In adulthood, sense-pleasure play has its counterparts in the enjoyment of art, music, painting, dancing, or in the pleasurable contemplation of such beautiful events as the birth of one's child.

This playful exploration of the environment is not a mindless act. On the contrary, sensory awareness is a *cognitive* experience which involves our full, undivided attention. This consideration is similar to Maslow's concept of "being-cognition," a noncomparing, nonevaluating, nonjudging openness to experience.[60] For example, a toddler seeing a bug for the first time examines it with great interest, tries to touch it, and (if successful in catching it) may try to put it in her mouth. This sensory sensitivity enables her to make real contact with the bug. The child does not question the wisdom of her act or judge the value of the creature, she simply explores the novel phenomenon with full attention and fascination.

CHILD STUDY 6

Child movement

Observe two or three children of different ages as they move during a movement activity or nonstructured play. Are they graceful or clumsy? Do they "hold back" or "let go" when they move? What is their posture during movement? How cautious or reckless do they appear to be? How enjoyable does movement seem to be for them? To what extent are these differences due to age or individual personality?

Recall your childhood experiences with movement. Did you feel clumsy? What kinds of movement did you find most satisfying? Did your attitudes toward movement and yourself change as you grew older?

The dance of life:
Sensing movement

Children are concerned about making better sense of their external experiences and using their senses more fully to make contact with the external world. They are also interested in how their bodies move and how they can use motion to express themselves.

Life is energy which is transformed into movement, and movement provides the means for establishing contact with the world. Toddlers, for example, are excited with life and seem to be in constant motion. Once they learn to walk, they walk everywhere possible. Every step and incline invites them to climb. Despite bruised knees they playfully experiment with running, hopping, and twirling, and they vigorously resist any parental attempt to restrain their movements. Only sleep seems to slow them down. This insatiable desire for motion is a part of an ongoing self-discovery for children, the realization that their bodies are capable of doing much more than they once could do. It not only feels good, but this expression of self in movement is a confirmation of their sense of power and energy.

When children move they are also exploring their relationship with the earth and gravity. They learn to stand, for example, only after discovering how to balance themselves properly so they won't fall down. The same struggle with the force of gravity is necessary for walking, running, roller skating, and bike riding. Children perform these movements only after they achieve harmony with gravity. Their efforts to remain in proper balance and experience satisfying movement is called *centering*.[61]

Ida Rolf is a physical therapist who has devoted her life's work to understanding the structure of the human body.[62] She believes that there is a centered, inherent pattern of such body parts as head, neck, shoulders, trunk, and legs which can exist in strain-free arrangement relative to gravity. This "centered" balance involves a symmetrical relationship of all body parts to each other. According to Rolf, centered body alignment enables a person to experience movement in a satisfying and pleasurable manner.

Chronic tension affects the body and movement by forcing a rearrangement which is "off center."[63] Tension in one part of the body may disrupt natural balance and force other muscles and body parts to compensate. The result is unnecessary fatigue and stiff, awkward movement. Thus, a child who is constantly under pressure from adults and has no opportunity to openly express feelings may experience tension which changes the natural body symmetry. The head and shoulders may slump forward and muscles in the back of the legs and feet may tense to prevent falling. Whether or not Rolf's theory is correct, poor body symmetry and muscle tension may prevent children from developing in a healthy manner.

SELF STUDY 7

Sensing your center

Body and sensory awareness

Find a quiet place where you are unlikely to be disturbed. Stand with your knees slightly bent and your feet separated about shoulder width. Begin rocking very slowly from side to side and gradually increase your motion as much as you can without falling or stumbling. Feel yourself beginning to move off balance and then return to your center as you change direction. Then gradually and slowly reduce your motion until you return to your centered and balanced standing position.

Without moving your feet, slowly shift your weight to the left. Hold the position and become aware of the increased muscle tension throughout your body. Slowly return to your balanced center and note the difference in muscle strain. Repeat the same action to your right.

Now slowly begin rocking forward and backward. Gradually increase your motion as much as you can without falling or stumbling. Then gradually reduce your movement until you return to your centered position.

Begin to slowly walk around the room. As you walk, shift your center of gravity to the right, left, front, and back. When you walk "off center" in what parts of your body do you feel most tension? After a few moments of being off center return to your balanced position. How does this contrast feel? Move off center in a different direction and repeat the process.

When you are finished, stop walking and find your centered, balanced position as you stand. Your weight should be equally distributed to both feet while your toes and heels have good contact with the ground. Breathe smoothly and peacefully. How do you feel in a centered, balanced, relaxed position?

Body problem solving

Getting in touch with body experiences and defining appearance and growth are two general issues which underlie body awareness. The third and final component is *body problem solving*, the strategies or ideas children can use to resolve unpleasant changes in their bodies.

When children experience problems with body functioning, what kinds of interpretations, consequences, and solutions do they make in response to the discomfort? Physical troubles disrupt children's sense of body integrity—a feeling of being in control of themselves and of remaining intact. Two kinds of physical experiences trouble children: observable discomforts (e.g., cuts, bruises, and scrapes) and more hidden interior distresses (e.g., upset stomach, headache, and coughing).

Toddlers have a difficult time understanding the causes of discomfort.[64] Because of their difficulty in localizing pain, they may not know how to ease their discomfort. There may even be occasions when they are unaware that they are soiling themselves. Because of these limitations in awareness toddlers may become quite disturbed when a toy is broken because of their close identification with such objects. The thought processes of young children can make body problem solving quite difficult.

Due to their limited reasoning abilities, children's concepts of physical distress may be very frightening or confusing. Some children, for example, are terrified of cuts because they think all their blood will leak out. Some children think of germs as bugs that crawl around inside them. ("Sorry honey, you've come down with a 'bug' today and have to stay home.") Others may think illness or injury is a punishment for some misbehavior. Thus, children's fears and confusions may cause them to acquire distorted convictions.

Preschool children often believe that exterior agents like bandages or pills restore health and resolve distress. If a young child has a cut, no matter how small and insignificant, he or she may insist that a bandage be applied to "make it **45** better." One group of researchers reported about a boy who believed that soda pop would heal him by keeping cuts from traveling from his foot to the rest of his body.[65] During the early grade-school years, children are more likely to identify internal healing processes and mention specific diseases.[66] They basically understand that cuts will heal and that medicine works inside the body, but they are still likely to have some misconceptions of this complex issue.

Children also learn about expected sick-role behavior. A child who falls down may cry more strongly if an adult is nearby because he or she believes that adults expect crying under those circumstances. Similarly, adults who define children as being sick or hurt may expect them to act accordingly by staying in bed and remaining quiet even though initially the children may not want to conform to these expectations. Young children gradually learn that they are supposed to act a certain way when they are sick.[67] Play therapists in a children's hospital sometimes encourage children to get up and play as soon as they are able to do so. Many believe that children who are encouraged (within limits, of course) to act "well" will recover more quickly than those who remain bedridden. The problem is to help children learn to take care of themselves without fostering images of an irrational sick role they might expect themselves to play when they are not feeling well.

Body awareness education

The first step in forming an educational program is to decide on the types of skills that program will emphasize. Table 3.1 identifies body awareness skills, defines components of the skills, gives examples, and lists the basic concepts. No specific age guide-

Table 3.1
Summary of body awareness skills for children

Skill	Definition	Social/cognitive processes
1. Understanding of body structure and function.	1a. The ability to identify those characteristics that differentiate people from other living things and to recognize those features (e.g., food intake and elimination) which are common to all forms of life. *Example:* A four-year-old says, "People can drive cars but animals can't. People and animals both eat food."	Defining (Basic concepts) *People Trunk* *Boy Arms* *Girl Blood* *Skin Walking*
	1b. The ability to identify body parts and functions; to realize that individuals differ in terms of the appearance and use of these body structures; to accept one's own physical self and the physical characteristics of others. *Examples:* A two-year-old points to her mother's eyes and says, "Eyes!" A three-year-old says, "Your stomach is where your food goes when you eat."	*Head Running* *Eyes Vagina* *Mouth Penis* *Chin Legs* *Tongue Feet* *Nose Toes* *Teeth Hips* *Cheeks Elbows* *Ears Hands* *Hair Fingers* *Neck*

Body and sensory awareness Becoming somebody

Skill	Definition	Social/cognitive processes
	1c. The ability to describe the concept of *learning*; to realize that all people have performance limitations (i.e., some activities are more difficult than others and people sometimes *forget* how to do something); to accept one's learning limits. *Examples*: A four-year-old says, "I can't learn to fly, but I can run fast." A six-year-old says, "I can't run as fast as Michelle, but I tried."	(Advanced concepts) Brain Trachea Heart Esophagus Stomach Nerves Intestines Breathing Arteries Relaxing Veins Tensing Lungs Skipping Skeleton Remembering Muscles Forgetting Cartilage
2. Understanding of growth and development.	2. The ability to recognize the fact that one is always growing up (i.e., changing over time) and that this change is occurring for all living things; to recognize that an increase in growth also means a change in both abilities and responsibilities; to recognize that physical growth has a beginning (birth) and end (death), which is usually reached late in life, and that life moves through a continual cycle of sleep and wakefulness. *Examples*: A three-year-old sees a dead bird and says, "Oh look, teacher, the bird is dead." A four-year-old, after using the weight scale, says, "Look Mommy, I'm getting bigger. I weigh 35 lbs., now." A six-year-old describes the pain in her legs as ". . . growing pains of the muscles."	Defining Growing up Birth/death/life Baby/child/teenager/ adult
3. Getting in touch with body experiences.	3a. The ability to attend to such body processes as breathing, muscle tension, heartbeat, and other body rhythms. *Examples*: A five-year-old demonstrates a lack of muscle tension in her arm when the teacher checks it during rest time. A six-year-old compares heart rate before and after physical exercise.	Sensing
	3b. The childlike ability to experience what the environment offers at any single moment without categorizing or defining. By becoming totally absorbed in the experience, the child makes contact with his or her world and develops an auditory sensitivity for rhythm, timbre, and volume; a touch sensitivity for texture and temperature; a visual sensitivity to forms, colors, light, shade, and space; an olfactory sensitivity to a wide range of odors; and a taste sensitivity for sweet, salty, sour, and bitter foods of varying textures and temperatures. *Examples:* A three-year-old boy is totally involved in eating ice cream. All his attention is given to what he is tasting.	

Skill	Definition	Social/cognitive processes
	A seven-year-old girl is watching the rain trickle down her bedroom window. All her attention is given to the patterns and shapes the water makes.	
	3c. The acquisition of a sensory vocabulary which includes each of the sensory systems—visual, auditory, olfactory, tactile, and gustatory (taste). Rather than being absolutes (e.g., "This sponge is *soft*."), this vocabulary can be expressed in a *continuous* hierarchical manner (e.g., "This sponge is *softer* than this wood."). This vocabulary can be used to describe, identify, and compare different objects. *Example:* A five-year-old tastes a piece of chocolate and says, "Oh, that's sweeter than a cookie."	Defining Sensing
	3d. The ability to use a variety of media (e.g., paint, clay, and wood) to express ideas and feelings about sensory experiences. *Examples:* A three-year-old completes a series of finger paintings. A six-year-old makes a collage of materials taken from a nature walk.	Sensing Acting
	3e. The ability to engage in movement unrestricted by excess muscle tension; to demonstrate both comfort and self-confidence in movement. *Examples:* A two-year-old laughs as he begins to run. A four-year-old shows noticeable lack of skeletal-muscular inhibition as she moves and shows good range of motion of body parts.	Sensing Acting
	3f. The ability to express feelings and ideas through dance and other forms of creative movement; to demonstrate the ability to utilize the varying dimensions of space, force, movement tempo, and flow in expression through movement. *Examples:* A three-year-old dances in a relaxed and spontaneous way to a record the teacher plays. A six-year-old learns some basic mime movements. A seven-year-old acts out the life-span of a tree from germination to deterioration.	Sensing Acting
4. Exploring causes, consequences, and solutions to body distress.	4. The ability to identify the realtionship between body damage and physical pain; to describe the characteristics and consequences of being sick; to identify the ways other people can help a sick person become well; to understand that hospitals are special places where people who are hurt or sick can get special help to become well; to understand the consequences and causes of fatigue. *Examples:* A five-year-old shows a small cut to his teacher.	Defining *Pain/hurt* *Sick/well/health* *Hospitals/doctor/nurse* *Medicine* *Nausea* *Fever* *Rest*

48

Skill	Definition	Social/cognitive processes
	A four-year-old tells her teacher she feels sick. A five-year-old tells his parents that he is tired because he played so hard.	Deciding

lines are provided, but the skills are defined broadly enough so they can be adapted to the abilities of a particular child. Although written primarily for three- to eight-year-old children, these skills relate to learning at any age.

Our relationships with children

Our relationships with children can be significant factors in body awareness education. Planned activities and curriculum materials cannot substitute for the everyday, spontaneous encounters we have with children. The suggestions in this section are intended to strengthen the impact of that relationship.

First, we can talk with children to explore their perspectives toward body awareness. What ideas do children have about such body concepts as growing up, death, gender, sickness, and disability? By showing interest in what they have to say about these issues, we tell children that they can talk about their ideas without fear, and that nothing is too horrible to discuss. The following exchanges from a teacher's journal reveal children's eagerness to discuss something which is unsettling or confusing.

> The first two days of this week involved discussion of people in general. Today we talked about what happens when we feel sad. The response was great. We talked about sadness and about loved ones (especially grandparents) dying. Ben was especially eager to become involved. At one point he said, "Would you feel sad if I died when I got old?" Wow! What a question! I responded, "Yes, Ben, I would feel very sad. I would probably cry."[68]

> We found a dead bird outside today. Julie, Pam, and I buried it under the big pine tree. Dan was very thoughtful about the experience. He asked if the bird would be in the ground forever. I tried to find out if he could articulate any religious beliefs, and he could not. We talked briefly about the permanency of death. When we walked up the steps to our class he said, "I wonder if the bird knows it is dead?" A very thoughtful comment from a four-year-old. He asked me again and I responded, "I don't know, Dan. That's a very difficult thing to understand." The problem was primarily intellectual, and I did not detect any anxiety or fear regarding death.[69]

By assuming a receptive, listening role we can try to convey to children that we hear and are interested in what they say. If they know their ideas will be heard in a non-judgmental way, children are much more likely to talk about their concerns.

Second, we can take a more active role by introducing information which contributes to their self-understanding. We can, for example, help children gradually understand that death happens to all living things and is a natural part of the life cycle. **49**

We can help them learn that certain changes in the body are a natural part of growing up and that the human body is a sophisticated structure for self-healing and self-care. We can also help children realize and accept that people differ in their rates and directions of growth and that old age is not something to be feared.

Some of our suggestions may contradict misunderstandings children have acquired about their bodies. In our discussions we might discover, for example, that one child is afraid to eat watermelon because she thinks one will grow in her stomach if she swallows a seed; another might be afraid of sleeping because he thinks he will die; and a third may think lying causes warts. These ideas are not bizarre responses of seriously disturbed children. They are understandable conclusions reached by children who are naturally limited in the complexity of their thinking.

One goal we can have is to encourage children to revise their misunderstandings by providing them with contradictory evidence. Some rational contrasts to these mistaken beliefs are provided in Table 3.2. For example, if one or more boys think playing with babies is for girls only, we could invite a father to visit the class and bring his infant son. He could show his baby to the children and demonstrate some of the games they play together. We can then discuss what happened to reinforce the basic idea that daddies (males) can take care of and play with babies. If a five-year-old states that a

Table 3.2

Contrasting examples of irrational and rational beliefs about body awareness

	Irrational belief		*Rational belief*
Structure and function	• Boys are sissies if they play with dolls. That's only for girls.	vs.	• Boys can play with dolls because someday they might enjoy taking care of children.
	• Black people are unfriendly and dangerous.	vs.	• Some people are unfriendly and dangerous.
	• When you breathe all the air goes into your stomach.	vs.	• When you breathe most of the air goes into your lungs.
Growth and development	• My body will never die.	vs.	• All living things die.
	• People get sick because they are bad.	vs.	• People get sick because their body has a problem and needs rest and care.
	• There is something wrong with you when you begin to look old. I can avoid old age. Old people are ugly.	vs.	• Growing old is a part of growing up. Changes in my body due to change are natural and OK. Old is beautiful, too.

baby grows in its mother's stomach we can say something like, "No, a baby does not grow in its mother's stomach. It grows inside its mother's *uterus*, the part of her body which is inside here [point]. The stomach is up here and that's where your food goes right after you eat."

Children are more likely to accept our ideas if we respect their pace in internalizing new information. We can present an idea in a very simple form and restate it to be more helpful. But we should not attempt to force an idea on a child. The more emotional an issue, the more important this principle is. For example, some young children may need to believe that death is *not* permanent, because such a belief may be necessary to help them gradually face the permanency of death. Our gentle presentations will not "catch on" with a child if she or he is not ready. If stated simply enough these more rational ideas will be adopted when children are able to grasp their relevance.

Third, we can treat children as individuals rather than stereotypes. We can encourage them to participate in all that our classroom offers regardless of their sex, age, color, or attractiveness. We can encourage problem solving and assertiveness in all children rather than contributing to stereotypes through differential treatment of boys and girls.[70] Every child is a special person with unique talents waiting to be expressed, and this individuality deserves our attention.

Fourth, we can make awareness of experience an important part of our educational program. Awareness involves establishing sensory contact with ourselves or our environment. The emphasis is to *experience* something as it occurs rather than just to *think about it.*

Every experience offers an opportunity for a new discovery, but as children begin to form concepts of the world, this novelty and appreciation may fade. Familiarity can lead to a form of "mental contempt" in which the individual allows his or her ideas *about* something to replace their actual *experience.* Older children may see an orange, for example, and drink its juice without focusing their attention on the actual sensory experience they are having. Over time some children may gradually disinherit their senses until they finally look without seeing, eat without tasting, sniff without smelling, listen without hearing, and hold without touching. Their preoccupation with memories, fantasies, and anticipations of future possibilities cuts them off from enjoying what is available to them in the present.

We can, however, keep sensory awareness alive in children and help those who are beginning to show signs of sensory isolation rediscover an important aspect of themselves. It is a tragedy when young children distrust and avoid sensory involvement. For example, children who refuse to finger paint because "it's dirty," or insist on keeping their shoes on when everyone else in class is going for a special sensory walk are tragic figures. Many of us have known these children without joy who are no longer childlike. Children and adults who can keep their sensory channels open can continue to rediscover new experiences. Active contact with the environment when motivated by a sense of wonder comprises real sensory awareness.

Fifth, we can encourage children to monitor their own natural body rhythms. For example, children can listen to their heartbeats, observe themselves sweating, and discuss how they feel inside when they are hungry. If they have a cold we can ask them how their nose, throat, and chest feel. In a similar fashion we can help children experiment with their voluntary but partially controlled body rhythms. For example, children can practice different ways of breathing and relaxing. They can also discuss how they feel when they get sleepy and when they get up in the morning. Finally, teachers can help children creatively express themselves in movement. Creative movement is more than just dancing or singing. It means being "in touch" and finding enjoyment in one's own motion. Children who have been given opportunities to run, jump, and play in a joyful way discover that their bodies are magnificent tools for creative expression.

Six, we can make physical contact with children, we can hold, hug, and rock them, and we can gently reach out and touch them when we talk with them. This physical contact is important because it helps to build our relationship with children and actually has a positive, soothing effect on their physical well-being.[71] A style of offering contact rather than initiating it may be more acceptable to children who are cautious and may not know us very well. If a preschool child is in distress we might approach him or her and hold our arms out to indicate a willingness to hold and comfort. This type of gesture allows children to decide if they want that contact. If a child does not respond we might (depending on the situation) quietly sit near him or her, remaining available to provide comfort. It is generally much more comfortable to assume the receptive, inviting style instead of a more pushy, intrusive manner.

Finally, we can introduce a classroom schedule which accommodates children's natural body rhythms. Periods of quiet activity, for example, can be scheduled to follow more active play periods. Children can be given opportunities to move and explore without becoming overstimulated and exhausted. Also, opportunities for rest can be personalized as much as possible since endurance and fatigue vary a great deal among children. We can use our schedule and daily routine to help children better understand how their bodies function.

The suggestions above can be the most important part of our program to promote body awareness in children. We can also introduce planned activities which help us emphasize particular aspects of body awareness. When these activities are used in concert with a growth-producing relationship, our overall educational impact is likely to be strengthened.

Activities to promote body awareness

The following activities may be helpful to you as you design a program to nurture body awareness in children. A review of Tables 3.3 and 3.4 is suggested before beginning.

For an additional activity on sensory awareness see Activity 55, The Lonely Star.

Table 3.3
Suggestions for choosing and implementing activities

1. *Personal comfort:* Select activities with which you feel at least moderately comfortable. Do not try activities that seem inappropriate or too difficult for you to lead successfully.

2. *Group and individual match:* Activities should match the needs and interests of the group and of individual children. At the beginning of the year "name learning" games are useful since children may want to get to know each other better. Some games may be too threatening to children who are unfamiliar with each other.

3. *Concerting:* Group and individual activities should be used in concert with each other to increase the impact of teaching. For example, to emphasize the concept *cooperation* a leader can read a story illustrating it, organize cooperative painting, and lead the children in a cooperative finger play. Try to select activities that fit together in a logical manner.

4. *Sequencing:* Many activities are more likely to be effective if a different activity has already been successfully experienced by children. Ask yourself if there is another, more simple activity that should be introduced before you try something more complex. For example, children should have the opportunity to become familiar with blindfolds well before they are asked to put one on and perform any difficult task.

5. *Readiness:* No child should ever be physically or psychologically coerced into any activity. Some children are not ready for some activities and others may need to move more cautiously as an activity unfolds.

6. *Flexibility:* An activity is likely to be more effective if the leader can make changes while the activity is going on. This is especially important if we want to take advantage of unplanned incidents or resolve a problem. Feel free to change activities to suit the needs of your group.

Table 3.4
The structure of a group experience

Each activity in this book is organized into the sections described below. Additionally, each activity has a recommended *minimum* age for participants. In some cases younger children may benefit from the activity, so consider the age level a general guideline for selecting activities.

Purpose: This section identifies the target skills for the activity, drawn from the material presented earlier in the chapter. Keep in mind that although children have their own reasons for participating and may benefit in ways unintended by the teacher, this section can be used to select and coordinate activities. More specific objectives can be identified by translating these goals into outcomes for a specific group of children.

Setting: This section specifies the type of arrangement appropriate for the experience (e.g., community group, small group, partners, individuals, or learning center). Whenever possible arrange the groups in a circle to promote discussion. This arrangement is particularly important when the entire class (community group) or small group meets to talk with each other.

Materials: This section identifies the types of materials a teacher will need to successfully present the activity. In each case the materials are easily available to early childhood teachers and are uncomplicated to prepare.

Activity: The step-by-step explanation of how to introduce and complete the activity is presented in this section. Examples of what a teacher might say and do are suggested where needed. Rather than rigidly following this outline in minute detail, teachers are encouraged to use this section as a means to understand the intent and approach of the experience. The actual implementation of the experience should reflect the unique characteristics and style of the teacher.

Suggestion: When necessary, comments about the limitations or strengths of an activity and suggestions which might make an activity more successful are offered in this section.

Growing Flowers (three years +)

Purpose   To help children understand growth processes and express creative movement.

Setting/Level   Community group arrangement

Materials   Potted flower (optional)

Activity   **1.** Talk to the children about the growth of a flower from a tiny seed. Begin with the planting of the seed and then describe watering, sprouting, and stem and leaf growth. Finish with a description of the flower.
2. When finished show the children the plant you were talking about.
3. Act out the following finger play with children:

Say this	Do this
Tiny seed planted just right. Not a breath of air, nor a ray of light.	Make a fist with the right hand and place it underneath left arm which is parallel to the ground.
Rain falls slowly to and fro, And slowly the little seed begins to grow.	Slowly uncurl right hand while left hand makes motion of falling rain.

Slowly creeping up to the light	Right hand makes creeping motion
With all its energy and all its might.	upward with fingers together, left arm remains parallel.
Now the little seed's work is almost done,	Fingers on right hand begin to fan
To grow up tall and face the sun.	out. Palm of right hand turns to left hand as it forms a sun.

---

2 Plant Life (three years +)

Purpose To help children understand growth processes. Key concepts are *growing up* and *life.*

Setting Community group arrangement

Materials Enough seeds for all of the children (use dill, chive, or other seeds that germinate quickly)

A container filled with dirt or cotton for each child

Activity **1.** Take the seeds out of the package and show them to the children. Talk about seeds and discuss what happens when they are put into the dirt and watered. Introduce the concept *life* and discuss how things grow.

2. Pass out containers and have the children plant seeds. Put the children's names on the containers and place them in a sunny spot.

3. Refer the children back to the plants after germination. Emphasize the care needed to help them grow. Extend the discussion to how people grow and what their needs are.

---

3 Growing Up (three years +)

Purpose To help children understand growth processes and the differences in physical abilities between people, especially during the early years. Key concepts are *people, babies,* **and** *growing up.*

Setting Community group arrangement

Materials A four- to ten-month-old baby (If a real infant is not available a lifelike doll can be substituted.)

Activity **1.** Introduce the baby to the children. If possible, allow children to come up and touch him or her. Some children might even be allowed to hold the baby in their laps for a few moments.

2. After the greetings are over, ask the following questions: What are some of the things you can do that this baby cannot do? How are you different from this baby? Summarize and restate the children's comments as you go along.

3. Make further clarifying comments as needed, emphasizing the idea that the children are changing as they grow up. As they grow their abilities are also improving. You might also ask the children to identify some skills older people have that they have not yet attained.

4

Stick Together (four years +)

Purpose   To help children identify body parts and understand the physical similarities between people; to promote children's cooperation. Key concept is *cooperation*.

Setting   Children are arranged in pairs

Materials   **None**

Activity   **1.** Ask the children to find partners.
2. Tell them to pretend that their bodies are really sticky and that you would like to see how well they could stick together. Then give a series of commands such as, "Partners, your hands are stuck together . . . now your toes (knees, ankles, elbows, etc.) are stuck together." After a few such commands ask them to switch partners.
3. Discuss cooperation and the children's response to the activity.

Suggestion   The difficulty of this activity can be increased by asking the children to put two body parts together, for example, "Your knees and elbows are stuck together!" or two different parts could be put together, such as, "Your finger is stuck on your partner's knee!" Partners can also be asked to walk a short distance while remaining "stuck."

5

Space Person (four years +)

Purpose   To help children develop an awareness of their bodies, especially its spatial dimensions. Key concepts are *body* and *space*.

Setting   A large, open space to allow for movement activity

Materials   **None**

Activity   **1.** Have the children move away from each other so they have sufficient space between them. Ask them to get down on the floor and curl up into a tight ball.
2. Ask them to stick one arm out slowly and, without moving their bodies, to reach out as far as they can. Then ask them to move the other arm, then

a leg . . . and so on until they are completely spread out to take up the empty space. Reverse the process.

3. Ask the children to stand up and make themselves as small (taking up the least space) as possible. Then ask them to take up slowly as much space as possible, making themselves as big as they can get.

4. When finished, discuss how bodies can take up space in various places (e.g., theaters, cars, buses, etc.).

Suggestion Find different size large containers or closed-in areas (e.g., a refrigerator box, a closet, under a table, etc.) and have the children find out how many of them can fit in each area. Use different combinations of children to see if the final count is affected.

---

6 Frankenclass (four years +)

Purpose To help children acquire an understanding of the physical similarities and differences between people. Children also will practice cooperative behavior and become more aware of their school group.

Setting Community group and learning center arrangement

Materials Crayons
Paint
Construction paper
Butcher paper

Activity **I.** Tell the children that you would like to give them the opportunity to work together to make a very special "paper person." Tell them that this person will be composed of drawings of body parts of everyone in the class. Have the children decide on which body part they would like to be. One child could be the left hand, another the right foot, another the head, and so on.

2. Have each child lie on the construction paper so that you can draw an outline of the assigned body part. Then have the children cut out and put their name on the body part they are contributing. Each segment can also be decorated with paint or crayons. The body parts can then be taped or stapled together to be put up on the wall or used as a large mobile.

3. Use the occasion to discuss the physical differences of those in the class, for example, hair, eyes, and size.

Suggestion Make several different "people" if there are too many children to develop one. Also, be sure to note that the discussion of physical differences should be done lightheartedly. The purpose is to promote the idea that differences in appearance are normal and acceptable.

7 Me and My Shadow (three years +)

Purpose   To help children understand and accept their physical characteristics as well as their similarities to and differences from others. Key concepts involve various body parts such as *face, hair, neck,* **etc.**

Setting   A room that can be darkened

Materials

Large sheets of white paper	Paint
Table lamp with shade or film-strip projector or flashlight	Crayons
Table and chair	Collage materials

Activity   **1.** Tape a large piece of white paper to the wall, and place a chair in front of it very close to the wall. Turn the chair sideways and have a child sit on it. Darken the room and shine a light from a filmstrip projector or a bright flashlight on the side of the child's face. Next, trace the silhouette or shadow that appears on the paper.
2. Take the paper down and have paint, crayons, and collage materials set out so the children can decorate their "self-portraits." Discuss the various parts of the face that might be included or added to the shadow.
3. Tape all the portraits around the room at a later time and ask the children to identify who matches each portrait.

Suggestion   Because the teacher is working with one child at a time, this activity may not be suitable for large groups (more than six children).

8 Body Drawing (three years +)

Purpose   To help children understand the physical similarities and differences between people and to help them identify and accept their own physical characteristics. Key concepts are various body parts.

Setting   Individual activity either inside or outdoors

Materials

Large sheets of paper	Collage materials
Crayons	Chalk (if outside)
Paint	

Activity   **1.** Ask each child to lie down on a large sheet of paper so that you can draw around the contour of his or her body.
2. Set out crayons and paint for decoration.
3. Discuss and relate various body components to the picture.

1. The same activity can be done outside with outlines being drawn on cement (weather and authority permitting). Colored chalk can be used for decoration.

2. Older children can be involved in drawing the initial outlines around each other.

3. Also, don't forget to have one of the children draw around you.

---

9   I Like Me (three years +)

Purpose   To help children understand physical similarities and differences among people and the feelings associated with satisfaction and acceptance of one's physical self; to encourage children to praise themselves. Key concepts are *me* and *liking*.

Setting   Community group arrangement

Materials   None

Activity   1. Begin the activity by saying something like, "You know, I really like my body. I like me. I've got a head, a face, arms, fingers, and toes. All sorts of wonderful parts." Then continue with statements like, "You know what? I really like my _____. I like my _____ because _____." For example, "I like my *hands* because *they are often gentle*, because *they can pick things up*," etc.

2. Ask the children to describe something about themselves they like or something they feel happy about. Try to include everybody if you can. If needed, encourage responses by saying, "What is good about our _____?" eyes, ears, head, etc.

3. Be sincere in your comments regarding yourself. Prompt, but don't push, those children who fail to respond. Even young children feel self-conscious about their bodies at times.

---

10   Go So (three years +)

Purpose   To help children express themselves in creative movement. Key concept is *movement*.

Setting   A large open space to allow for movement

Materials   None

Activity   1. Tell the children you would like to see how well they can move in different ways. First tell them to pretend they are babies and to begin moving around the way babies would. After a few moments tell them to "freeze," and while they are motionless ask them to pretend that they are growing bigger and older. Now ask them to walk and move as though they are older children. After a few moments have them freeze again and continue your description of the aging process. "You are getting older and older. Now you are grown up. Begin to walk around like you are an adult, a grown up." Again have the children freeze, imagine growing even older, and then move as very, very old people.

2. Repeat this cycle several times. First help children to get into the mood or fantasy of what they are trying to portray and then ask them to move like they think the character would move.

Suggestion In addition to the aging changes identified above, you can have the children move like birds, fish, monkeys, clowns, etc. They can be asked to portray actions like climbing a mountain, driving a car, swimming, digging a hole, sleeping, etc. They might pretend to walk on ice, in mud, sand, on a sticky floor.

┃┃ Stories with Hands (four years +)

Purpose To help children learn that they can express themselves and their feelings in creative movement. Key concepts are *hands* and *movement*.

Setting Community group arrangement

Materials None

Activity **1.** Tell the children that their arms, hands, and fingers, can "tell stories" or convey ideas without the use of words. Ask them, for example, to portray the following images using finger and hand movements:

> There are waves along a river.
> A fish is swimming fast (or slow).
> You are climbing a tall tree.
> A snake is moving through the grass.
> You are dancing happily.
> A bird is flying.
> The rain is falling softly (or quickly).
> The snow is falling softly (or quickly).
> Someone is arguing, then fighting.
> Two children have decided to become friends.
> One feels sad, the other wants to be kind.
> One is scary, the other is afraid.
> One knocks on a door, the other answers and says hello.

2. Ask the children to make their own suggestions. Tell them that you and the others will discuss what they are doing. Have the children who are interested take turns.

---

12 Playful Scarves (three years +)

Purpose   To help children express themselves in creative movement. Key concept is *dancing.*

Setting   A large open space to allow for movement

Materials   Scarves made from discarded curtains or other inexpensive materials. Suitable "movement" records with varying tempos and styles

Activity   **1.** Hand out the scarves and play a record. Then encourage the children to make personal interpretations of the rhythms as they wave their scarves and move about. Vary the rhythm and tempo of the music. Let children join hands with a partner if they want.
2. As in other creative movement activities, avoid, if possible, performing the actions yourself, particularly if the children repeatedly copy what you do.

---

13 Shake and Wake (three years +)

Purpose   To help children learn to be aware of their bodies and understand how move-ment can be used for relaxation. Key concept is *relax.*

Setting   Community group arrangement

Materials   None

Activity   **1.** Tell the children that you would like to help them wake up their bodies and to help them relax. Ask them to do what you do. One by one begin to shake various body parts, verbally identifying each part as you shake it. For example, "Now I am shaking my hand. Now I'm shaking my whole arm." etc. Begin by thoroughly shaking one hand, and then stop and shake the other hand. Stop again and shake one entire arm. Each time you stop show how your body part becomes relaxed. Repeat this process moving to the following body parts: other full arm, one foot, other foot, one leg, other leg, head, hips. As you direct them to vigorously shake their bodies, put on some fast music with a good beat. Begin to move around shaking as much as you can. After a short while turn off the music and sit down.
2. Ask the children to sit quietly and think about how their body feels. After a moment of quiet discuss the experience.

3. Try to convey to children that "relaxed" does not mean limp—being relaxed means to be calmly ready for action; it is a productive way to use our energy and should not be associated with weakness.

Suggestion   This activity is excellent when children seem particularly tense or overactive. It is also appropriate as a relaxer for many other activities.

14

Wow! This Is Me! Part 1 (four years +)

Purpose   To help children understand and accept their physical characteristics. Key concepts involve various body parts such as *face, head, hair, and neck.*

Setting   Community group arrangement

Materials   **None**

Activity   **1.** While children are seated in the circle repeat the following chant while performing the appropriate actions.

> I am rubbing my head.
> I am tapping my head.
> I am feeling my hair.
> I am touching my ears.
> I am tapping my ears.
> I am rubbing my neck.
> I am tapping my neck.

2. After this warm-up give the following directions (pausing and rephrasing to make yourself clear). "Now touch your head all over. Try to find out if you have any bumps on your head. Now run your fingers around the outside of your ears. Feel for soft parts, hard parts, and bumpy parts. Can you bend your ears? Close your eyes. Very gently and softly touch your eyelids and feel your eyeball underneath. Be gentle with yourself. Touch your eyebrows. Rub them one way. Now the other. What happened? Now rub them both ways again. Rub them back to where they were. Move your fingertips down to your nose. Feel the hard bone up by your eyes. Feel where the bone stops at the tip of your nose. Feel your breath go in and out over your fingers. Is it warm or cold? Do you like the way it feels? That's all for now. We'll do more another time."

15

Wow! This Is Me! Part 2 (four years +)

Purpose   To promote children's understanding and acceptance of their physical characteristics. Key concepts involve various body parts such as *face, head, neck, hair,* etc.

Setting   Community group arrangement

Materials   None

Activity   **1.** While children are seated in the circle repeat the following chant while performing the appropriate actions.

2. Now say something like, "Remember when we were exploring our heads? Now we are going to explore a different part." Ask the children to lie down in comfortable positions.

3. Say, "Now, put your hands on your lips. Put your fingertips over your lips. How many lips do you have? Do they feel alike? Are they soft? Are they rough? Put your fingers just at the bottom of your neck. Now make a noise. Listen with your ears and feel with your fingertips. Where does the noise come from? Can you feel your voice with your fingertips? Put your fingertips on your chest and make a quiet noise. What do you feel there? Now put your fingers on the side of your nose and make a sound. What do you feel there? OK, that's all for now. We'll do some more another time."

Suggestion   The same type of activity can be directed toward encouraging children to explore bones, ligaments, and muscles in their hands and feet, arms, and legs.

16

Finger-licking-good Finger Paint (three years +)

Purpose   To promote children's sensitivity to touch and taste. Key concepts are *smooth, sweet,* and *awareness.*

Setting   Learning center arrangement in kitchen area

Materials   Vanilla pudding   Finger-painting (slick) paper
            Food coloring   Aprons

Activity   **1.** Make several different colors of pudding in separate bowls and encourage the children to finger paint with the pudding and to lick their fingers. (Make certain they have washed their hands.)

2. As they are engaged in this experience, call their attention to how the pudding feels and tastes. When everyone is finished, discuss the experience and make certain to point out the special circumstances of the activity, such as the fact that food usually is not used this way.

Suggestion   Some children may refuse to lick their fingers. They may be mistrustful of the teacher or concerned about cleanliness. Encourage them to taste the pudding and observe others who are doing so. If they refuse, though, allow them to continue to finger paint or to clean their hands with a wash cloth. Or you might allow children to taste the pudding before the finger painting.

17 The Nose Knows (three to four years +)

Purpose   To promote children's sensitivity to odors. Key concepts are *spicy, woodsy, pungent fruit and flower odors,* **and** *awareness.*

Setting   Community group or learning center arrangement

Materials Blindfold for each child (optional)
Containers or jars with the following types of substances:
Floral odors (perfumes with flower fragrances)
Fruit odors (lemon and lime)
Spicy odors (clove, cinnamon, and nutmeg)
Woodsy odors (lavender, thyme, and pine)
Pungent odors (vinegar, onion, and butter)

Activity   **1.** Talk briefly with the children about the idea that people sometimes do not think about what they smell. Mention that you have some things for them to smell, but first you want to "wake up" their noses. Ask them to watch and do what you do. With just your fingertips gently tap all around your nose for 15–30 seconds. Take your hands away and ask the children to be quiet and feel the tingling in their noses.
2. Tell the children that you are going to pass around some jars that have special things to smell in them. Explain the blindfold and blindfold those present who seem willing (to reduce distractions). Others might just close their eyes. Pass the jars around. Do not demand that children identify or describe what they smell. Simply encourage them to smell each odor.
3. After the jars have been passed around discuss preferences, dislikes, or observations. Line up the jars and group them into the five categories listed above. Identify these for the children and help them learn the terms, but don't overstress this part of the activity. Allow the children to smell the jars in each category.

Suggestion Purchase scented candles which fit into each of the odor categories. For example:

Rose or jasmine (floral)
Lemon or green apple (fruit)
Sandlewood or spice (spice)
Pine or evergreen (woodsy)
Musk (pungent)

Light a separate candle each day and identify the odor category.

18 Tangerine-a-peeling (four years +)

Purpose To promote children's sensitivity to taste and touch. Key concepts are *sweet, sour,* and other sensory concepts.

Setting Community group arrangement

Materials For each child:
One tangerine
One paper plate
One napkin

Activity **1.** Tell the children that you have something to show them. Pass out the tangerines and ask them to watch and do what you do. You can make verbal comments as you perform the actions. Hold the tangerine in the palm of your hand. Lightly tap it and listen to the sound it makes. Gently squeeze it and feel how firm it is. With your eyes closed, roll it around on your cheek to feel its texture. Smell the tangerine.
2. Gently break the skin to peel the tangerine. Watch the juice come out and smell it again. Continue peeling and watch how the skin separates from the rest of the tangerine. Look at the inside of the peels. Feel and compare the different texture of the inside and outside.
3. Next slowly separate the tangerine sections and place them on your paper plate. Watch closely how they come apart. When you are finished, slowly and quietly eat the sections one at a time. When you and the children are completely finished discuss what happened.

19 I Cannot See (three years +)

Purpose To promote children's sensitivity to touch and to help explore feelings associ-ated with uncertainty. Key concepts are *blindfold, scary, brave,* and *feelings.*

Setting Community group arrangement

Materials Several blindfolds

Activity **1.** Show the blindfolds to the children and ask them if they know what a blindfold is. Help them learn if they don't know. Try to have them identify the feelings they might have if they were not able to see. Would it be a scary experience? Would it be exciting? Or would it be both?

2. Let volunteers try on the blindfolds. If the children seem interested try a simple game. Make a circle around a "blind" child and have someone call his or her name. The "blind" child tries to go straight to the caller. A more traditional option is to play "Pin the Tail on the Donkey."

3. Discuss the activity and encourage children to identify any feelings or thoughts they might have as a result of the experience.

Suggestion This activity is important as an introduction to blindfolds. Before going on to more difficult blindfold activities, the children should be given the opportunity to repeat this activity until they are comfortable with not seeing. Be sure to respect the right of any child to refuse to be blindfolded. Avoid pushing children into unpleasant experiences.

---

20 Orange Juice Celebration (three years +)

Purpose To promote children's sensory awareness and encourage cooperative behavior. Key concepts are *sweet, sour,* and other sensory concepts.

Setting Small groups of about six children

Materials One orange for the teacher
One orange for every two children
One bowl per group
One paper cup for each child

Activity **1.** Tell the children you have something to show them. See, feel, and smell the orange. Pass it around to each child. When it returns, cut it in half very slowly. Then cut a thin round slice and hold it up to the light so the children can see the design of the fibers. Pass the slice around and encourage each child to examine it closely.

2. When finished, cut the remaining oranges in half and pass out one to each child. With the bowl in front of you, squeeze the juice from your orange and invite the children to do the same. (Encourage them to listen to the sounds their squeezing makes and to look closely at the bubbles in the bowl and at the squeezed orange half.) When the group has finished, pour the juice into individual cups and pass them out to the children. Drink the juice slowly, and after everyone has finished drinking talk about the tastes, sounds, smells, and textures you experienced.

Suggestion Young children may need help in squeezing the oranges. The remaining orange portion makes good eating too.

21 This Apple (three to four years +)

Purpose   To promote children's sensory awareness. Key concepts are *sweet, sour,* and *awareness.*

Setting   Community group arrangement

Materials   One apple for each child (one-half for younger children)
One soft, clean cloth for each child

Activity   **1.** Tell the children that you have something to show them. Take an apple out and hold it up. Ask the children to watch what you do because you want to find out what this apple is really like. Polish the apple, hold it up, and take a good look at it. Feel its texture with both hands and listen to the sounds that result from lightly tapping it. Sense its weight by holding it in the palm of your hand and tossing it from one hand to the other.
2. Give an apple to each child and repeat the above process, asking the children to do the same. Encourage them to explore it in other sensory ways, too. After exploring its external characteristics take a bite of the apple, swallowing it only after you have finished chewing. Continue eating and encourage the children to do the same, taking time to really *taste* the apple before swallowing.

22 Popping Corn (four years +)

Purpose   To promote children's sensory awareness. Key concepts are *salty, bumpy, soft, hard,* and *popping.*

Setting   Community group safely arranged in a semicircle around the popcorn popper

Materials   Popcorn oil, salt, and melted butter (optional)
Popcorn popper (glass top)
Large popcorn bowl
Napkins (or small bowls)

Activity   **1.** While the oil is heating give each child one kernel of unpopped corn. Ask them to find out how the kernel feels, to see how it looks, and to find out what its shape is. Paraphrase comments the children make but do not ask questions at this point. After this exploration ask the children if they know what will happen to the corn when it is put into the oil. Discuss the process.
2. Put the unpopped corn into the popper. Give each child the opportunity to watch the corn popping. Keep your comments to a minimum. When the popcorn is ready put it into a bowl and give one popped kernel to each child.

Ask them to discover how it feels and smells. Encourage them to compare the unpopped kernel to the popped one. Finally, allow children to eat the popcorn and encourage them to chew it.

3. Salt and butter the popcorn in the larger bowl, and then distribute small servings to the children in napkins or small bowls. Discourage talking (without being tyrannical) and encourage tasting while the group eats the popcorn.

Suggestion   You can place the popcorn popper in the center of a large, clean bedsheet and let the popcorn pop without a top. Put less oil in the popper and have children sit safely away from popper around the outside of the sheet. The advantage of this variation is that children will be able to more clearly observe the force of the popping as it occurs. *This activity should be closely supervised to prevent the possibility of serious burns to children. Never leave a popper unattended.*

---

23   Butter Lover (three years +)

Purpose   To promote children's sensory awareness and encourage cooperative skills. Key concepts are *sweet, salty,* and *cooperation.*

Setting   Community group or learning center arrangement

Materials   Whipping cream   Bread or crackers
Salt   Large jar with secure top

Activity   **1.** Show the cream to the children, pass it around, and encourage them to smell it and look at it closely. Following this, pour the cream into the jar, salt it lightly, cover tightly, and demonstrate how it should be shaken.
2. Pass the jar around and encourage children to shake it vigorously (the teacher may have to at times shake it as well). Once it thickens, spread the butter on crackers or bread for a snack.
3. Emphasize the idea that everyone worked together, cooperated, to make the butter. Discuss how it tastes.

Suggestion   Music can be played to enhance the rhythm of the shaking.

---

24   Breaking the Bread (three to four years +)

Purpose   To promote children's sensory awareness. Key concepts are terms related to the whole range of sensory experiences.

Setting	**Community group arrangement**
Materials	**One loaf of freshly baked bread (ready-to-bake loaves are available from your supermarket)**
Activity	**1.** Take a loaf of fresh, *unsliced* bread and pass it around so that each child can touch, feel, and smell it.
	2. When it returns to you, carefully and slowly break the bread in half and pass the two halves so that each child can see, smell, and take a piece of the bread. Ask children to wait before eating until each person in the group has group has a piece.
	3. When all have a piece of bread, ask children to eat slowly so they can be sure to get a good taste. Ask the children to be *aware* of how the bread tastes.
Suggestion	The act of taking a piece of bread while leaving some for others is a nonegocentric, social act. Children who are aware of others are apt to be more careful in selecting their portion.

---

25   **Feel Packages** (four years +)

Purpose	**To promote children's sensory awareness. Key concepts are** *soft, hard, prickly, bumpy, smooth, rough, cold, warm, wet, dry,* **and** *awareness.*
Setting	**Community group or learning center arrangement**
Materials	**Wrapping paper (tissue, wax, butcher, of thin paper sacks)** **Various common objects** **String or tape**
Activity	**1.** Select various objects of interesting size and shape, such as a rope, marble, rubber ball, feather, key, shredded wheat, plastic bottle, wooden toy, etc. Each individual object should be wrapped in such a way as to disguise its actual shape. For example, a feather can be loosely wrapped in tissue paper to make it seem bigger, and a small rubber ball can be wrapped tightly to make it seem smaller. As the children explore these wrapped objects and discover what they are, they will notice that size does not always imply weight. Children can be allowed to hold and handle each package with both hands to try to feel the shape of the hidden object.
	2. A package should be passed around, and, when all the children involved have explored it, they should then begin to list their ideas about what it might be. The package should then be opened and the object revealed. Do this with each package. The children can then pass around the unwrapped objects and compare their sizes, weights, and tactile characteristics. They might also discuss how each object was made, what it is, and what its functions are.

26 Textured Finger Painting (three years +)

Purpose   To promote children's sensory awareness. Key concepts are various textural terms, such as *squishy, gritty, rough, smooth,* **and** *awareness.*

Setting   Learning center arrangement

Materials   Textured substances which can be mixed with the paint (sand, coffee grounds, oatmeal, rice, etc.)
Paper
Aprons

Activity   **1.** Put the finger paint on each child's paper and sprinkle one or more of the textured materials on the paint. Let the children mix them together as they fingerpaint.
2. Briefly discuss the texture of the paint. Is it grainy, rough, smooth, rocky, etc.? Which textures did children like or dislike?
3. Set out each child's work after it is dry to contrast the textures. Encourage children to feel the textures of each sheet.

---

27 Immerse Yourself (three years +)

Purpose   To promote children's sensitivity to touch and temperature. Key concepts are *wet, warm, soft,* **and** *awareness.*

Setting   Community group in a semicircle with a table at the open end of learning center arrangement

Materials   One large bowl about 3/4 full of warm water
Several soft towels

Activity   **1.** Ask the children to do a "wake up" exercise by tapping their faces with their fingers (see *In-Touch Experience*). Then tell the children you are going to give them a chance to see what water feels like. Mention that before you do, you would like to find out for yourself.
2. Slowly dip your hands into the bowl of water placed on the table. Bend over and put your face in the water. Sit up and pat your face and hands dry. Go around the circle and allow children to line up and do the same while encouraging them to be aware of how the water feels. Watch for some overeager child to tip the water over!

Suggestion   The reactions of the children will differ widely. A few refuse to touch the water at all and others will do no more than put their hands in. Other children will bend over and touch the water only with their noses while a few will immerse their face completely. Do not insist that children do more than they want to do.

28 Cold Water—Hot Water (four years +)

Purpose   To promote children's sensitivity to touch and temperature. Key concepts are *warm, cold,* and *awareness.*

Setting   Community group in a semicircle or learning center arrangement. A table is placed at one end with bowls adjacent to each other

Materials   One large bowl about 3/4 full of warm water
One bowl about 3/4 full of cold water
Several soft towels

Activity   1. The procedure is the same as in *Immerse Yourself* except now there are two bowls. The task in this activity is to experience the contrasts between the two different temperatures of the water. Demonstrate the activity for the children by placing one hand in one bowl and one in the other, Then switch hands. Following this put both hands in one bowl then place both in the other. Describe how it feels while performing the actions.
2. Encourage children to try the activity. Discuss the experience when all have had a turn. Sensing two different temperatures at the same time is an interesting experience. Watch out for spilling water!

29 Lotion Motion (three years +)

Purpose   To promote children's sensory awareness and encourage gentle, affectionate behavior. Key concepts are *awareness, gentleness,* and *touch.*

Setting   Partner arrangement

Materials   Hand lotion

Activity   1. Ask the children to form pairs and to sit facing each other. Go around the room and put lotion in each child's hand. Ask the children to find out how the lotion feels by rubbing their hands together. After a few moments ask them to join hands with their partner. Encourage them to explore each other's hands in a massaging, mulching motion.
2. Call the group together and have everyone make a close, friendly circle. Everyone can then put their hands into the middle of the circle and establish contact with others' hands. Pour extra lotion over this group of hands and encourage everyone to explore the different textures of the hands. Emphasize *gentle* contact. Initiate motion by suggesting that the hands on the bottom move to the top in a repeated cycle.

30 Toe-Touch Walk (three years +)

Purpose To promote children's sensitivity to touch. Key concepts are terms related to tactile experiences and *awareness.*

Setting Community group or individual activity in a safe, outdoor location

Materials A variety of natural surfaces

Activity **1.** Take the children on a toe-touch walk. Have them take off their shoes, and allow them to stand and walk about on different surfaces, such as sand, grass, gravel, stones, grating, ribbed surfaces, ropes, textured papers, or marble slabs.
2. Their attention should be drawn to the actual sensations they feel when standing on these surfaces. Is it hot? Cold? Prickly? Does it feel hard or soft? Do their feet sink into it, etc.? They should also be asked to listen to the different sounds their feet make on surfaces when they wear shoes versus when they are barefoot.

Suggestion Check the area thoroughly beforehand for broken glass, metal, etc.

31 In-Touch Experience (four years +)

Purpose To promote children's sensitivity to touch and smell. Key concepts are *soft, hard, prickly, bumpy, smooth, rough, cold, warm, wet, dry,* and *awareness.*

Setting Community group or learning center arrangement. This activity can be done in a safe outdoor location

Materials Blindfolds for each child
Various objects of different textures (see below for examples)
Paper bag

Activity **1.** Talk briefly with the children about the idea that people often do not think about what they feel and often are not aware of what they touch. Tell them that you have some things for them to touch but first you want them to "wake up" their fingers and hands. Ask them to watch and do what you do. Clap your hands together at different rates of speed with various degrees of intensity for 15–30 seconds. Put your hands down and ask the children to be quiet and feel the tingling in their hands.
2. Show the children the paper bag full of objects and tell them that you have some things for them to touch and smell. Blindfold those who are willing and ask the others to close their eyes. Go to the center of the circle,

take objects from the bag one by one and place something in each child's hands. Once everyone has something, moving clockwise, take the object from one child and pass to the child on the left. Continue around the circle until you have made three or four complete rounds (or more, if the children seem interested).

3. Allow the children to look at the object they feel then encourage them to close their eyes and think about what they are touching. Some examples of objects are:

twig	piece of fur, silk, corduroy, etc.
rock	flower
feather	thumbtack
block	sponge

4. When finished go on a touch-and-smell tour of your surroundings. Discuss the various things that are pleasant (and unpleasant) to touch. Identify things that are softer, harder, more bumpy, smooth, etc.

32

Still Water (four to five years +)

Purpose　To promote children's sensitivity to touch and encourage gentle behavior and to help children become more aware of their school group. Key concepts are *gentleness* and *awareness*.

Setting　Small group arrangement of five to ten children

Materials　One blindfold

Activity　**1.** Form a small circle of five to ten children. Describe the activity. Blindfold a volunteer who stands in the center of the circle. The children forming the circle hold hands and begin to rotate while all softly chant, "Around, around, and around we go, where we stop _____ (name of blindfolded child) won't know!" At some point the center child says "Still water!" The other children then stop moving and the center child moves until he or she makes contact with someone in the circle. After exploring this child's face and clothes, the blindfolded child can be encouraged to guess who the individual is.

2. The child who was touched by the blindfolded child has the option to go into the center of the circle to begin the game again. Otherwise, call for another volunteer. When finished discuss the experience.

3. Emphasize the idea of gentle behavior when the blind child touches another. Watch carefully and guide the blindfolded child if necessary. When making contact with others, younger blindfolded children can be inadvertently rough with the children they are trying to identify.

4. Ask the child being touched to talk to the blindfolded child to help him or her make the identification if there is a problem in guessing.

Suggestion   If the children have not had experience with blindfolds they might be uncomfortable in this activity. If so, give them some experience using blindfolds while they are sitting at a table performing some simple activity like *I Cannot See* (p. 65).

33   Silence (three years +)

Purpose   To promote children's awareness of sounds. Key concept is *silence*.

Setting   Community, small group arrangement or individual activity

Materials   None

Activity   **1.** Ask the children to identify any sounds they think are occurring at that moment. Then suggest that if they really want to hear all the sounds everyone should be completely still and totally quiet. Mention that you would like to see how long they can be quiet. While they are quiet ask them to listen very carefully to all the sounds around them.
2. After about three minutes ask them to talk about the sounds. It is more important here for them to describe the sound than to identify its source. For example, "I hear a purring sound, rather than "I hear a cat."

Suggestion   The same activity can be generalized to seeing, feeling, and smelling. With feeling and smelling children can be allowed to move about the room.

34   Listen to the Sounds Around: Part I (three to four years +)

Purpose   To promote children's sensitivity to sounds. Key concepts are *soft* and *loud sounds*, *high* and *low sounds*, and *awareness*.

Setting   Community group or learning center arrangement

Materials   Blindfold for each child
Various objects which create a variety of sounds (see below for examples)
Paper bag

Activity   **1.** Talk briefly with the children about the idea that people often do not think about what they hear. People often are not aware of sounds. Tell them that you have some things for them to hear but first you want them to "wake up" their ears. Ask them to watch and do what you do. With just your fingertips gently tap all around your ears for 15–30 seconds. Take your hands away and ask the children to listen for sounds. For a few moments focus on the sounds that surround you in the room, on the street, the voices of people, and such sounds as body movement, breathing, music, and nature.

2. Tell the children that you have some sounds for them to hear. Blindfold those who seem willing and ask the others to close their eyes. Take objects from the bag, one at a time, and make the noise. Try to make certain that the children do not see the sources. For example:

> Paper being waved, torn, or crumpled
> Musical instruments (bell, horn, etc.)
> Water being poured
> Keys jingling

Sounds may be tape recorded in which case no blindfolds would be necessary. Ask children to listen carefully and notice how the sounds are different from one another. Do not request that children identify origins of sounds at this time, though some may try on their own.

3. Repeat the sounds with children watching (or identify the origins of sounds played on the tape recorder). Explore the room and surrounding area for different types of sounds by listening, tapping objects, or striking them against each other. Establish clear limitations before attempting this latter activity. Identify and discuss sounds that some of the children liked or disliked.

---

35 Listen to the Sounds Around: Part 2 (three to four years +)

Purpose To promote children's sensitivity to sounds. Key concept is *sound*.

Setting Community group or learning center arrangement

Materials Tape recorder

Activity **1.** Record the following sounds (making the sounds yourself if necessary).

dog barking	someone yawning
cat meowing	someone laughing
door shutting	someone crying
clock ticking	someone whistling
water running	glass breaking
automobile starting	fingers snapping

2. Play the sounds for the children and ask them to listen. Play the tape again but stop it after each sound and ask the children to describe and identify that sound. Play the recording again if needed.

Suggestion Children can be included in actually making the tape and suggesting their own ideas for sounds.

36   Who Sounds (three to four years +)

Purpose   To promote children's sensitivity to sounds and to help children become more aware of others in their school group. Key concept is *sound*.

Setting   Community group or learning center arrangement

Materials   Tape recorder

Activity   **1.** Ask the children to come individually to a location where you will record their voice. Have each child and teacher in the classroom make the same statement, such as, "I like you," or "Do you know what my name is?"
2. After everyone's voice has been taped play the tape and ask the children to identify who is speaking. Play the tape for individual children who might be reluctant to make a guess in a large group. Give hints if necessary.

37   Sensory Tour (three years +)

Purpose   To promote children's sensory awareness. Key concepts are terms related to odors, textures, sights, and sounds, and *awareness*.

Setting   Community or small group arrangement or individual activity in a safe outdoor location

Materials   Naturally available odors, sights, sounds, and textures

Activity   **1.** Designate some area to be explored, such as a room, a backyard, or a plot of land. Ask the children if they can discover all of the various smells, textures, sounds, and colors in that particular area. Perform the activity yourself and encourage children to accompany you. In any given area there should be an abundance of different sensory stimuli. Seek them out yourself and let the children share their excitement with you. Allow the children to go barefoot, if possible.
2. Come together as a group and discuss your experiences.

38   Know Hear (four years +)

Purpose   To promote children's sensitivity to verbal and nonverbal communication and to encourage them to offer task-oriented help. Key concept is *hearing*.

Setting   Community group arrangement
Children initially in a circle

Some comfortable device, such as earmuffs, that completely covers the ears.

Activity **1.** Ask the children how they think they would feel if they could not hear at all. Mention that some people really cannot hear because something is wrong with the inside part of their ears. If someone wants to talk to them they have to communicate with their hands or other parts of their body. Ask them, "If you could not hear, how could other people tell you that _____? Some examples are:

> It's time for dinner.
> It's time to go to sleep.
> That they like you.
> Goodbye.

2. Tell the children you would like to find out what it would be like to be in their classroom and to be someone who cannot hear. Ask them about the sounds they hear now. Then ask them to cover their ears with their hands and listen. Talk about their experiences. Tell them you are going to put on ear covers so that you can't hear anything. Put on the ear covers and continue with other activities. When children talk to you say something like, "I know that you are talking to me because I see your mouth moving. I am pretending not to hear you. You will have to show me so I can see what you mean."

3. About thirty minutes (or more) later, reconvene the group, take off the ear covers, and share your experience with the children.

Suggestions **1.** Unfortunately, you will have to pretend not to hear, because no simple device will block out the sound completely. Because of this, the children should not be expected to play the "deaf" role. Also note that this activity may be frustrating to children when they are anxious to tell you something. If this happens try to redirect their comments to another teacher.

2. Ask someone who can do sign language to visit your class and demonstrate the skill. A few simple statements, such as, "I love you," might be taught to the children.

---

39 Know Talk (four years +)

Purpose To promote children's sensitivity to nonverbal communication and encourage them to offer task-oriented help. Key concept is *talking*.

Setting Community group arrangement

Materials None

Activity **1.** Ask the children how they think they would feel if they could not talk. Mention that some people really cannot talk because something is physically wrong with them. Ask how someone who cannot talk tells something to someone else. After this discussion illustrate nonverbal communication (talking with hands and the rest of the body) by asking the children to identify some common signals. Ask what the following mean and make up some of your own as well.

> Shake head yes
> Shake head no
> Shake a tight fist
> Wave
> Extend both arms as an invitation to make contact

2. Tell the children that you want to find out what it would be like to be a person who cannot talk. Tell them that when you finish talking you are going to *pretend* that you cannot talk. If you have something to tell them you will "say" it with your hands or other parts of your body.

3. Following your period of silence, of at least thirty minutes, reconvene the group and discuss your experiences with them.

---

40   Know See (four years +)

Purpose   To promote children's sensitivity to sight and encourage them to offer task-oriented help. Key concepts are *blindness* and *blindfold*.

Setting   Community group arrangement

Materials   Several blindfolds

Activity   **1.** Tell the children that you would like to find out what it would be like to be a pretend "blind" person in their class. Ask them if they know what blindness is, discuss their comments, and clarify any misconceptions. When you are ready, put on the blindfold. Keep it on as long as you can, and, whenever possible, share your thoughts and feelings with the children. Ask for their help when needed. Give them an opportunity to put blindfolds on, too.

2. When you are ready to finish, reconvene the group, take off the blindfold, and share your experiences with the children.

Suggestion   This activity should be initiated early in the day, and there must be other teachers or aids that you can really trust to help you run the classroom. If you aren't comfortable making a commitment to keep the blindfold on, then don't do it.

This experience can provide you with a tremendous learning opportunity. It also puts the children in a position where they have to relate to you differently and develop verbal and tactile communication skills they may not have had to rely on before.

References on body awareness

Brooks, C. *Sensory Awareness: The Rediscovery of Experiencing.* New York: Viking Press, 1974.

Chung-hang Huang, A. *Embrace Tiger, Return to Mountain: The Essence of Tai Chi.* New York: Bantam Books, 1978.

Goodman, M.E. *Race Awareness in Young Children.* New York: Collier Books, 1964.

Kaplan, A., and Bean, J. *Beyond Sex-Role Stereotypes — Readings Toward a Psychology of Androgyny.* Boston: Little, Brown, 1977.

Kübler-Ross, E. *On Death and Dying.* New York: Macmillan, 1969.

Leonard, G. *The Ultimate Athlete.* New York: Viking Press, 1975.

Lowndes, B. *Movement and Creative Drama for Children.* Boston: Plays Inc., 1971.

Mills, G.C., Reisler, R., Robinson, A.E., and Vermilye, G. *Discussing Death: A Guide to Death Education.* Homewood, Il: ETC Publications, 1976.

Montagu, A. *Touching: The Human Significance of the Skin.* New York: Columbia University Press, 1971.

Nickelsburg, J. *Nature Activities for Early Childhood.* Menlo Park, Ca.: Addison-Wesley, 1976.

Rausher, S.R., and Young, T., eds. *Sexism: Teachers and Young Children.* New York: Early Childhood Educational Council of New York City, 1974.

Rudolph, M. *Should the Children Know? Encounters with Death in the Lives of Children.* New York: Schocken, 1978.

Speads, C.H. *Breathing: the A, B, C's.* New York: Harper Colophon Books, 1978.

Spring, B., ed. *Perspectives on Non-Sexist Early Chldhood Education.* New York: Teacher's College Press, 1978.

Stacy, J., and Daniels, B.J., eds. *And Jill Came Tumbling After: Sexism in American Education.* New York: Dell, 1974.

Wilt, J., and Watson, T. *Touch!* Waco, Tx: Creative Resources, 1977. See also the following books from the same publisher: *Listen! Look!* and *Taste and Smell!*

Chapter four
Emotions and empathy:
Discovering inner space

Our quality of life is profoundly affected by how we deal with our emotions. Emotions color our lives, providing us with both a sense of fulfillment and of discontent. Our joy often seems to be balanced by our moments of despair, our sense of well-being contrasted by our experience of fear. Our humanity offers us no escape from emotion.

We ultimately judge our success in life by our emotional experiences. Positive emotions like happiness and enthusiasm provide evidence that all goes well, whereas pervasive negative emotions like fear and sadness may indicate that something is wrong in our lives. For example, how do we feel about teaching children? If teaching contributes to our own sense of well-being then we may have selected a profession which meets our needs for self-esteem. Conversely, if our contact with children seems to bring little more than constant frustration and discomfort, we might consider changing our approach to teaching or switching to another occupation.

We also measure our success by the emotions of others who are significant to us. If children in our class are typically enthusiastic and happy we feel secure with our effectiveness. If they are sullen and withdrawn we may be distressed, and concerned that their negative emotions were influenced by our actions. We may be challenged, for example, by a child who arrives at the beginning of the year lonely and afraid. We sense his fear, try to determine its cause, and do what we can to help. If, later in the year, he appears more secure and happy we might conclude that in some way our efforts have been successful.

What is an emotion?

We often are interested in our own feelings and those of others, but what is an emotion? Robert Plutchik believes that emotion is a chain of events which begins with some stimulus incident and is followed as a chain reaction by cognition, feeling, and behavior.[1] For example, a child sees a spider (stimulus incident), and then thinks, "That bug is dangerous. It might hurt me," (cognition). This decision then triggers the physiological response of fear, heart beating fast, sweaty palms, change in respiration, (feeling) which motivates the child to run away as fast as he or she can (action). The child's experience of fear and the corresponding flight serves as a protective mechanism to deal with a threat.

Plutchik's view of emotion fits well with our social/cognitive approach to personal and social development. From this perspective, emotions are viewed as the result of what we say to ourselves rather than the direct, inevitable result of something that happens to us. We cannot escape responsibility for our emotions or what we do because of them. Yet, even though we sometimes feel we would be better off without them, emotions have functions and are important.

According to Coleman and Hammen, emotions are significant because they are messengers, energizers, and bonders.[2] Emotions are *messengers* because they reveal how we are actually responding to a particular situation. For example, the experience of anger is an indicator that we feel frustrated, attacked, manipulated. Fear is a response to being threatened or to losing valuable sources of physical or psychological support. Sadness may mean that an important source of nurturance is absent or that a meaningful attachment to something is being threatened. All negative emotions tell us that something is wrong, that something needs to be checked out, and that some form of action needs to be taken to resolve the problem. On the other hand, positive feelings alert us to the fact that we feel safe or that a particular course of action needs to be continued for our personal well-being. Each emotion we experience provides us with the opportunity to get to know ourselves better, to become acquainted with a part of ourselves which we may not have been aware of before.

Emotions are also *energizers*. To be alive is to experience feeling, to be affected by events. The word *emotion* is derived from the Latin *e* (out) and *movere* (to move). Emotion initially meant a moving or agitation in a strictly physical way, but it was eventually broadened to include social or political unrest. Finally, the word began to designate any agitated, turbulent, or excited affective state of an individual.[3]

The emotion anger, for example, mobilizes us to overcome restraint or injustice and fear provides the energy needed to escape or protect ourselves. Love and joy, on the other hand, provide us with the energy to approach, maintain contact, and enjoy something. We need all of our emotions, for if we had no fear, anger, sadness, or joy our lack of feeling and energy would paralyze us. We would not commit ourselves to action because we simply would not care.

In addition to providing energy and information, emotions enable individuals to establish closer *bonds* through communication. Sharing feelings with others can help us understand each other better. For example, when a father expresses feelings of anger to a misbehaving daughter, he gives her the opportunity to discover something

Emotions and empathy

about her father she may not have known. Similarly, when the family visits a stranger's house and the daughter reveals her fear and anxiety, the father begins to more clearly understand the kind of person she is and how she views her world.. Emotion is a language which tells others how we view the world.

If emotions are not understood or used constructively, they dominate our lives, or cause us and our children unnecessary pain. If we view emotions as tools we can take time to understand their significance and learn how to use them best. Since emotions begin to affect our lives in early childhood, teaching emotional skills can be a very important part of an educational program.

Education and emotional development

Emotional development is a worthwhile concern for educational programs. The first reason is that emotions can be influenced by education. For example, in the same classroom one child is afraid of spiders because he believes they are threats, and another dislikes herself because she believes she is a failure. Teachers can help both of these children. The first child may overcome his fear if he learns more about spiders, and the second may acquire more self-confidence by experiencing small increments of success and support from her teacher. When children learn something of interest to them, whether it is painting, writing, adding, or speaking, their own feeling of esteem and well-being is enhanced.

Second, by focusing on emotions we can help children better understand themselves and others. They can learn that people have different emotional responses to the same event because they interpret it differently. We can help children explore their emotions. For example, we can ask questions like: "Why are some people frightened of spiders? What do people often do when they are frightened? Are all spiders dangerous? Instead of running away from a spider what can we do?" Education can help children become more sensitive to others and more effective in their emotional problem solving.

Third, education can have an effect on emotional *behavior*. We can help children learn how to express and describe their emotions. Instead of telling children *not* to feel angry, afraid, or sad we might be more effective if we help them learn what to do when they experience the energizing influence of these feelings.

Unfortunately, adults often respond to a child's strong emotion by trying to "turn the feelings off." They may make such familiar comments as "Don't get angry with me! Cool it," "Don't be afraid, there's nothing to be scared of," or "Don't be such a cry baby!" Such critical demands do not make a child's feelings go away. They do nothing to change a child's interpretations of what is happening to him or her and may even contribute to serious emotional problems.

Parents and teachers can touch children's hearts by reaching out to their minds. By helping children understand what feelings are, how emotions originate, and what their consequences might be, we may contribute to their mastery of emotions. By encouraging children to look at situations from the perspective of others and better grasp how they feel, we are nurturing an effective foundation for their social development. **83**

Defining emotional experiences

In this section we consider four issues: (1) What emotions reveal about how children define situations, (2) how these definitions change with age, (3) how children describe their emotions, and (4) the convictions children acquire regarding emotions.

Heart and mind:
Emotions and situational definitions

Robert Plutchik has identified eight basic emotional dimensions which vary in intensiy and can be combined to form additional emotions.[4] At their most intense level these emotions are ecstasy, adoration, terror, amazement, grief, loathing, rage, and vigilance. Each of these emotions reflects a specific cognitive appraisal of a situation.

SELF STUDY 8

Listing emotions

Take a sheet of paper and, in one minute, write down as many emotions as you can. It is important to record the first things that come to your mind rather than pondering what is "right." Do not read further until you have finished this list.

Examine the list. What does it reveal about your attitude toward emotions? Did you have a difficult time writing for a full minute? If so, this may point out that our emotional vocabulary is limited or that we are apprehensive about thinking of feelings.

What emotions first came to your mind? Is there a difference between the first few emotions and the last few? Are the first emotions negative or positive? Does this mean that they are most significant to you?

Count the number of negative (unpleasant) and positive (pleasant) emotions on your list. Which type was named more often? If most of our emotions are negative does this mean that we have had more experience naming or thinking about those feelings?

Compare emotions on your list with the eight emotional dimensions described on pages 84-85. What dimensions did you overlook? Did you leave out any reference to joy, liking, fear, surprise, sadness, disgust, anger, or curiosity? Did you have a difficult time putting some of these emotions into words? Does the omission of any of these affective dimensions have any personal significance?

If possible, compare your list with that of a friend or classmate. Discuss any differences in the total number of emotions, the emotions first listed, the ratio of positive to negative emotions, and the actual emotions identified. Are there any other ways of comparing the two lists?

The *ecstasy-joy-serenity dimension* means that children are defining their situation positively and that they believe there is something enjoyable to be gained from it. The function of this emotional state is to enable children (or anyone else) to reproduce or

Emotions and empathy

repeat this experience. For example, a child who discovers a desired gift on Christmas morning may experience joy. He believes that the gift is important for him and will continue to be so. His happiness draws him toward this experience or similar experiences in the future.

The *adoration-liking-acceptance* dimension means that children define a situation or person as being able to meet their needs. The function of this emotional state is to enable children to *incorporate* or identify with the other. For example, a child who develops strong feelings of affection for a classmate may see something in this person that will nurture her. It might be attention, support and encouragement, or a willingness to make contact such as hugging, holding hands, or playful wrestling. Without being very aware of these motives she is, in effect, saying to the other, "I want to be near you. You can help me." Her feeling of affection is telling her to move toward the other person, to make him or her a part of her life.

The *terror-fear-apprehension* dimension results when children interpret something as a dangerous threat. The function of this emotional state is to help children *escape* or to protect themselves or another. A young child, for example, may be afraid to be left alone at school by his mother. Until now, she has been totally responsible for his protection. Without her, his mind conjures up all sorts of threats and, because of his own insecurity and misunderstanding, he feels afraid. He may tremble, throw up, or try to run away. His fear is telling him to flee from the situation.

The *amazement-surprise-distraction* dimension occurs when children suddenly experience something strange. The function of this emotional state is to help children *orient toward* and investigate an unusual experience. Once recognition is made, surprise is replaced by another emotion. For example, someone may approach a child from behind and suddenly tap her on the shoulder. She is surprised and immediately stops what she was doing to turn around. Her feeling of surprise motivates her to get more information. If the person standing behind her is someone with a frightening mask she may become afraid, if it is father telling her to stop playing she may become angry, or if it is someone to play with she might become happy.

The *grief-sadness-pensiveness* dimension results when children experience a sense of loss. The function of this emotional state is to help children admit and *adjust* to that loss. For example, a child becomes upset and begins to cry after breaking one of his favorite toys. His sadness helps him admit to himself that he will no longer have this toy to play with. Unless this acknowledgement is made and the pain faced, no adjustment and reintegration can be made. Significant loss has to be mourned before we face life again.

The *loathing-disgust-boredom* dimension results when children experience something which is repugnant to them. The function of this emotional state is to help children *reject* and get rid of something unpleasant. For example, a child may avoid someone who is cruel and feel uncomfortable whenever he or she is present. Another may feel nauseous when he sees a dead dog lying in the street. Their disgust moves them to action, to avoid coming into contact with something repulsive.

The *rage-anger-annoyance* dimension occurs when children experience some kind of frustration which prevents them from completing an action they want to take. Anger may help children overcome or *remove* these obstacles. For example, a child is playing with a truck and another child takes it. He becomes angry and pursues the child who has his truck. When he catches up with her, he demands that she give the toy back. When she refuses he forcibly takes the truck from her and returns to his previous play. In this situation anger provided the energy to overcome an unjust act.

Finally, the *vigilance-curiosity-anticipation* dimension is triggered when children encounter something which is novel but likely to be safe. The function of this emotion is to move children to *explore* their unusual surroundings. For example, a five-year-old boy makes his first visit to the county fair. Because his parents are with him he feels safe. He wants to explore the entire area and find out what it offers, but he is somewhat reluctant because he doesn't know exactly what to expect. A child with a new and complex toy may respond in a similar manner. "What is it? How is it used? Will it break?" are questions a curious child may ask.

Plutchik contends that these basic emotions can be combined to form other emotions.[5] For example, love is a combination of joy and liking, disappointment is the result of surprise and sadness, and contempt combines anger and disgust. This blending of emotions results in a complex and rich spectrum of inner experiences.

Fear of ghosts and getting hurt:
Developmental changes in emotional awareness

As teachers, we can help children understand the relationship between emotions and certain situations, particularly if we recognize age differences in the way children define their experiences.

Several research studies have demonstrated that young children do make associations between emotional experiences and certain situations. Helen Borke, for example, identified typical situations for the emotions of fear, sadness, and happiness. After three situations were described three- to eight-year-old children were asked to indicate how the child in each story felt by selecting a fearful, angry, sad, or happy face. In two separate studies she found that happy events were the easiest to identify while angry circumstances were the most difficult. Only half of the seven- to eight-year-olds correctly identified the situations depicting anger. The most pronounced developmental change occurred in the fearful situation. Initially about half of the three-year-olds and over 90 percent of the seven-year-olds correctly identified this emotion in the appropriate situations. Since the researcher did not include in her report examples of the descriptions she gave the children we cannot determine how closely they follow Plutchik's approach. Furthermore, some responses may have been considered incorrect when the children were actually reinterpreting the researcher's situations from their own perspective.[6]

Children's emotional responses change over time because their interpretations of events are also changing. What seemed so upsetting at one age may not affect a child at a later date, and the reverse is also true. For example, a toddler may have no fear of playing in the street but may be extremely alarmed when her mother leaves her at a nursery school. From the toddler's limited perspective each of these situations is interpreted appropriately. The street is interesting and safe but the classroom is unfamiliar and threatening. As she becomes more aware of the threat of traffic and more comfortable with her teacher, her emotional reactions to these situations will change.

The process of developing emotional maturity means learning to evaluate circumstances more correctly and respond more appropriately.[7] Research on developmental changes in children's fears demonstrates such a shift. Between kindergarten and sixth grade there is a marked decrease of imaginary fears (e.g., monsters and ghosts) and a corresponding increase of realistic fears (e.g., bodily injury and physical danger).[8] Additional research is needed to chart developmental changes in other emotions.

In many ways all of us share with children this struggle for understanding. As our emotional development progresses, we may look back to events and recognize that we misinterpreted something or became upset because of lack of experience and good judgment.

CHILD STUDY 7

How do you feel?

Select two or three children of different ages for observation. Watch for an occasion when each child is experiencing a strong emotion of some kind and ask, "Oh, [name] how do you feel right now?" Make notes on their responses. Do they name the emotion, do they simply respond ritualistically by saying "fine" (see Self Study 12), or do they say nothing at all?

On another occasion when each child experiences a strong emotion, make a statement to show you understand *without asking a question*.

You might say something like, "[name] you look so sad, like a person who just broke their best toy." Following your statement simply remain near the child. Make notes on all the children's responses. What do they do this time? Do they respond differently to statements than to questions? Are there age differences in their responses?

Which type of response did you feel most comfortable making? Why? When you experience strong feelings which would you prefer to have others offer? Or is there a third, more effective way you might suggest?

Like a giant feather:
Children's descriptions of emotions

Although research provides us with objective data, descriptions of observation or actual comments by children are not reported. In order to get more personal views, the two children interviewed in Chapter 3, Jason (five years), and Jenny (seven years) were asked for their opinions on anger, fear, love, and happiness.

SELF STUDY 9

Twenty things that nurture positive feelings

On a sheet of paper identify at least twenty things you like to do that bring real happiness, joy, or a sense of fulfillment to your life. Some might be as simple as going for a solitary walk or browsing in a bookstore. Others might be as elaborate as a trip to San Francisco. Do not read further until you have completed this list.

Go over this list. How often do you experience these activities? How many cost money? How many require another person? How many can be done spontaneously without a lot of planning? What does this list reveal about the way you seek happiness?

Somehow we must find time in our lives to treat ourselves with these nurturent experiences. Read *Wishcraft* by Barbara Sher (New York: Viking Press, 1979) to learn how to plan more effectively for experiences which meet your needs.

INTERVIEWS

JASON (five years)

Anger

Jason, what does anger mean? *When someone is mad at another person.* What does mad mean? *That means you might get mad at someone that did something.* What might they do? *If one took away their toy!* How do you feel inside when you're angry? *Feel "jingly," like hurting them, but we won't. We'll tell on them.* Tell me a time when you were angry. *When Jenny kicked me I felt angry.* Is anger good or bad? *I think good . . . cause when you tell on someone and they get in trouble, and no one else would get hurt.*

Emotions and empathy

Sadness

Jason, what does sad mean? *That means someone doesn't like the other person because what that person did . . . he took his toy away from him.* How does it feel inside when you're sad? *Feels sad . . . feels angry.* Tell me a time when you felt sad. *When I first got my garage sale toys Zac* [same-age neighbor] *tried to take my fire engine. That's when I was sad.* Is it OK to feel sad? *Yes . . . cause when a person hurts you that's not OK.*

Fear

Jason, what does fear mean? [shrugs his shoulders] What does scared mean? *When you get afraid of something like a spider. . . when there was spiders on Jenny's bed!* How do you feel inside when you're afraid? *Jingly!* Can you tell me another time when you were afraid? *When I almost fell out of a tree.* Is being afraid bad or good? *I don't know . . . I think it's bad because you have to be brave.*

Love

Jason, what is love? *That's when you like a person.* How does love feel inside of you? *Happy.* Can you tell me a time when you felt love? *When me and Zac needed each other we liked each other.* When did you need each other? *It was way back.* Is love good or bad? *Good, when you love someone they don't hurt you or pick at each other.*

Happiness

Jason, what does happy mean? *That means when you like a person . . . when we moved and I needed a friend — that's when I was happy.* How does it feel inside to be happy? *Happy.* Is being happy good or bad? *Good, because you don't shove or push or hit other people and all that stuff.*

JENNY (seven years)
Anger

Jenny, what does anger mean? *When you're really frustrated.* What does that mean? *When you feel real mad it's like blowing your top!* How else does it feel? *Feel real hot inside and your face turns kind of pink.* When do people feel angry? *Sometimes when they don't get their way . . . if one of your favorite toys gets broke.* Is anger bad or good? *Bad, because sometimes you get real grouchy, and I don't like being grouchy.* Can you think anger could ever be good? *I don't think it's ever good . . . well, sometimes you're glad to get away from all the bad stuff and smooth your nerves out.*

Sadness

Jenny, what does sad mean? *When you're feeling real bad and guilty. Sometimes when Laura* [same-age neighbor] *wants to play with someone else I feel sad, but I also feel mad!* How does it feel to be sad? *Real lonely, like you're in a world of darkness.* How does it feel inside? *Feels kind of ticklish, like you have been tickled by a giant feather.* When do people get sad? *Well, like when a grown-up loses their job they get kind of sad, but they also get mad.* When do children feel sad? *Like if they had a special friend they want to play with . . . and they wouldn't play with her. Is feeling sad bad or good? Bad . . . it feels like you're not wanted. You feel like you want to get away from all of it . . . run away.*

Fear

Jenny, what does fear mean? *When you're afraid.* What does afraid mean? *Means you're scared of something . . . well, if something happens to you, all of a sudden one of your friends wants to play a joke on you, and they jump from behind a large tree with a spooky halloween mask on, it scares you.* How do you feel inside? *Feel real jumpy . . . mostly over here in this part of your stomach.* [she points] Tell me a time when you felt afraid. *When I was in the talent show and I had to play the piano. I was afraid to go up because I knew no one would vote for me.* How did that feel? *I felt like the world was just about to come to an end.* Is feeling afraid bad or good? *Sometimes it's OK because when you get frightened, you sometimes learn that what you were afraid of is really just nothing and then you start laughing.* When might this happen? *When you're in a fun house creatures pop out in front of you, motor controlled bats, things like that . . . what you were afraid of really wasn't true.*

Love

Jenny, what does love mean? [smiles and giggles, then gently slaps the side of her face] *Well, I can't explain how it feels. Sometimes when you love someone you can still be angry.* What does love mean? *Let's see, when you really like somebody a lot. Sometimes they like that person a lot so they become good friends and love each other.* Have you ever felt love for someone? [frowns] *I think I've never had that feeling.* Do you think love is good or bad? *Sort of good and sort of bad.* When is it good? *When you feel you are being loved by someone you sort of feel good inside.* When is it sort of bad? *When you have a boyfriend and he has reckless driving and then somebody gets hurt you get blamed for it, and you feel bad that you once loved him.*

Happiness

Jenny, what does happy mean? *Real glad, glad is real excited.* When do people feel happy? *If they are invited to a birthday party . . . if they get a new purse or a new desk . . . or a new toy.* How does it feel inside? *Ticklish, just plain ticklish.* What's the difference between sad and happy? *When you're sad you're lonely, and when you're happy you're excited.* What's the difference between happy ticklish and sad ticklish? *When you're happy you're ticklish and jumpy, like when you're invited to a party. When you're sad you feel ticklish, and you start crying a little because you feel lonely.* Is happy good or bad? *Good, because it makes you feel real good inside. You feel real happy.*

Although we can't really generalize to all children, these responses reveal a great deal about how these two children define emotions. Anger is associated with frustration, broken toys, and acts of violence. Both children admitted that anger might be good because it could lead to some kind of corrective action. Sadness is associated with loss of a toy or separation from one's friends. Jenny believed that sadness was bad because of how unpleasant it was, but Jason made a positive judgment because

Emotions and empathy

he thought sadness was a reasonable response to a person's unfair behavior. Fear is associated with surprise, loss of face in front of peers, or danger. Jenny thought fear might be acceptable because a person could discover that there really was no basis for their fear, but Jason thought fear was unacceptable because it meant he wasn't brave. Love means that a bond between two people has been formed. Both thought love was acceptable because of its positive consequences, but Jenny could conceive of a situation where such an emotional tie could get someone into trouble. Finally, happy is associated with material or social gain. Both children agreed that this emotion was certainly good.

Several conclusions can be made regarding their responses. Overall, both children made very strong associations between their emotions and their peer relationships. At no time did either child comment about adult influence on their emotions. Although they could probably describe how adults influence their feelings, these two children appeared to be much more conscious of the significance of their friends for their emotional well-being.

Both children also believed that it is possible to simultaneously express multiple emotions, such as, sadness and guilt, sadness and anger, and love and anger. Both thought, for example, that a situation that triggers sadness might also provoke anger if there is a chance to recover what was lost. Jenny asserted that the more pervasive feeling of love may not be dispelled by occasions of anger.

Finally, both children had a fairly well developed mental framework regarding anger, sadness, fear, love, and happiness. They demonstrated an emotional vocabulary which had become associated with certain types of situations. This clustering of ideas about emotions had a logical ordering to it—emotions have predictable causes and consequences. Both children, for example, would find it difficult to conceive of a child who would be happy if someone took his toy away or sad if someone gave him an ice cream cone.

We can now draw two important conclusions from Plutchik's structural theory and our qualitative analysis of children's views of emotions. First, emotions emerge from the way we interpret what is happening around us—our own minds influence how we feel. Second, emotions are *potentially* positive forces in our life which may help us cope with our experiences. Thus, if we define the situation incorrectly it is the definition, not the resulting feelings, that needs to be changed. For example, fear can give children and adults energy to escape or to protect themselves from a threat. But if that threat is not real (e.g., if a child runs away from a toy mouse) the fear is irrational and unnecessary. Irrational emotions can be destructive.

Can "big boys" cry?
Children's beliefs about emotions

In our culture we have four common convictions about emotions which may interfere with personal development: we may blame others for what we feel; we may divide emotions into "good" and "bad" categories; we may equate emotions with behavior; and we may have emotional-role stereotypes. Children learn these stereotypes from adults who verbalize them as they interact with children.

**A difficult
emotion**

Identify an emotion you have difficulty dealing with. Write this emotion at the top of a page and list all the ideas you have about this feeling. How do you think you are supposed to feel? What happens when you have this feeling? How do you think other people might react to you? Think of other questions. In the following example a person who identified anger as a difficult emotion wrote:

> A bad feeling
> Losing control
> Hurting someone
> Breaking something
> Ulcers
> Red face
> Embarrassed
> Must be cool
> Headache
> Fighting others

Go over each item on your list and ask yourself, "Is this really true or is it something that I have been taught to believe is true? Does this item have to be associated with the feeling?" If you decide that something you have written is a misconception, cross it out and write out an alternative point of view. If you think your idea is really an integral part of the feeling, think of the best way you might cope with what you can't change.

For example, the person who made the above list for anger might draw some of the following conclusions: Being cool is not always possible and anger is not always bad; losing control or physical ill effects can be prevented if the anger is described and expressed before it grows; and, though it may frighten others, a disclosure of anger may actually build a stronger, closer relationship.

Who is responsible for our emotions? From a social/cognitive perspective our emotions flow from our own definition of an experience. To that extent we are responsible for our own emotions, but the way we often talk about our feelings contradicts this belief. We may say to a child, "You make me feel so angry!" or "What you did really *made me* feel sad." The use of the word *make* implies that the person who has the feeling has no control over his or her emotions and is not responsible for their occurrence. Children learn this conviction and it is often reflected in their conversations. This passive view of emotions is so rooted in our social beliefs that we may have come to regard it as a self-evident truth.

The alternative view is to assume responsibility for our emotions by claiming them as our own. One way to accomplish this is to replace "you make me. . ." with "I feel. . .." For example, "I feel angry when you talk to me like that," indicates that we believe the feeling is our own response to what the other person is doing. It leaves open the possibility that others may be affected differently. "I feel. . ." is a form of self-disclosure while "You make me. . ." is a confrontation.

Would we be better off without some emotions? Our language sometimes reveals that we put value labels on our emotions rather than directly naming them. When angry, sad, or afraid, we might say, "I feel bad," and if we are happy we might comment, "I sure feel good." When we speak of emotions this way we are evaluating how we feel rather than describing the feelings themselves.

Children often learn to depend on using these evaluative labels. For example, a preschool boy who was quite distraught was asked how he felt. Between sobs he said, "I feel *fine!*" He not only knew how to use evaluative labels in talking about his feelings, but he also learned to respond ritualistically to the question, "How do you feel?" with "Fine!" If we asked one-hundred adults the same question, how many of them would actually say how they felt?

The alternative view is to recognize the value of our emotions by describing rather than evaluating them. When Jenny portrayed her fear as being ". . . like the world was just about to come to an end," she was describing her experience of that emotion metaphorically. Jason identified his emotion by name when he said, "When . . . Zac tried to take away my fire engine, that's when I was sad." In both cases, although they acknowledged the unpleasantness of their emotional experience, these two children affirmed the acceptability of how they felt. They or their emotions were not "bad."

Is there a difference between emotional experiences and behavior? As children begin to learn a vocabulary of emotion they may individually associate emotional terms with certain behavior.[9] For example, a child is frustrated by his mother, becomes angry, and yells at her. His mother responds, "Don't you get angry with me!" Another child sees an unusual bug and runs behind her father. "Why are you so afraid?" he responds. "Don't hide behind me, it won't hurt you." The first child may associate the term *anger* with yelling, and the second may confuse *afraid* with running away.

Our negative view of some emotions may be the result of a rigid association of those emotions with what adults consider unacceptable behavior. When adults disapprove of children's hitting, yelling, crying, or running away and label those behaviors with negative emotional terms, adults may convey to children the idea that anger, sadness, and fear are also "bad."

To some extent this association is likely to occur because adults cannot directly observe and comment on a child's internal private events. This difficulty is minimized, though, if we speak of emotions as internal experiences which can lead to a variety of behaviors, some more productive than others. Thus, we might say to a frightened and withdrawn child on the first day of class, "This is all very new to you, Jamie. Maybe you want to just watch us for now until you get to know us a little better. I can remember how I felt inside when I first started school—I was a little frightened."

Finally, do we associate certain kinds of emotions and emotional behavior with specific roles? Children gradually learn what is expected of them as a boy or girl, brother or sister, son or daughter, first- or last-born, student or friend. Some of these roles may have rigid expectations regarding emotion. For example, boys may learn that fear is an unacceptable emotion for males. Girls may be taught that although aggressive feelings are taboo, feelings of tenderness and affection are socially acceptable. These role demands are likely to conflict with their real experiences. When this occurs children may put up a front in order to receive approval from others.[10] Children who are conscious of these roles may be on guard and self-conscious about their feelings and how they deal with them.

TEACHER: Why didn't the little boy cry when he felt sad?

SCOTT: If the little boy cried people would laugh at him![11]

Children can suffer from these role stereotypes because they have no acceptable way of dealing with those emotions which are inappropriate to their role. They would rather pretend than be rejected.

An alternative to promoting role stereotypes in children is to try to convey the idea that *all* people have feelings. Feelings are a part of being human. No matter what our age, sex, or position in the family, we can still feel sad, angry, loving, afraid, or happy. We are not less of a boy or girl, brother or sister, student or friend because we have emotions. The real struggle is learning how to *respond* to what we feel.

Social perspective taking

We know that children's emotions relate to how they define their experiences, how those definitions can change over time, the meanings they attribute to various emotions, and the convictions they may have about emotions which may promote or interfere with personal development. Emotions are primarily social events through

Emotions and empathy

which children acquire the ability to empathize with others, to take the other's own perspective.

In forming and maintaining relationships, a child may become confused when his or her point of view conflicts with that of another. A two-year-old may be fascinated with his mother's sewing room and may not appreciate her determined efforts to keep him from that area. A four-year-old may completely overlook her friend's perspective while they are quarreling over the use of the tricycle. In both of these situations children are experiencing problems in their relationships because their perspectives conflict with those of others.

Social perspective or role taking involves sensing or comprehending the perspective, attitude, and feelings of another person. Children may not be able to grasp the perspective of another if it is radically different from their own. They are more likely to be successful if they are familiar with the other's experience. For example, a three-year-old might get his teddy bear for a frightened younger sibling or a six-year-old might bring home for her brother a piece of cake from a birthday party.

As they become more skillful in social role taking, children become more competent in their relationships with others. Taking another's perspective can help children who are trying to play, negotiate an exchange of trading cards, or barter with a parent over where the family should go on vacation. The everyday give and take of human relationships is enriched when those involved understand each other's perspective.

Social role taking should be differentiated from *role enactment*, in which a child practices a familiar role.[12] Children playing soldiers, pretending to be teenagers at a dance, or dressing up like their parents are all practicing the actions they think appropriate to the roles they are playing. Role taking, on the other hand, is an attempt to *understand* rather than act out the perspective of another.

According to John Flavell, children learn to synthesize information on other people's intentions, attitudes, emotions, and ideas from two sources: (a) Their knowledge of people and their behavior in various situations and (b) their observations and interpretations of others' behaviors as they interact with them.[13]

Robert Selman and Diane Byrne have identified four stages of social role or perspective taking during early and middle childhood. They labeled these stages as egocentric, subjective, self-reflective, and mutual.[14] They interviewed forty children in four age groups (four, six, eight, and ten) regarding their views on two social dilemmas. Each child's discussion on the perspectives of different characters in the dilemmas was analyzed and categorized into one of the four levels.

My world only:
Egocentric role taking (Level 0)

At this level children can differentiate between themselves and others but not understand that others have different viewpoints from their own. They are not aware of the existence of cognitive perspectives. They may believe that "mommys stay home" not realizing that other children may believe differently. Children are aware of only one reality—their own. In Selman's study 80 percent of the four-year-olds and 10 percent of the six-year-olds were at this level.

Jean Piaget and others have suggested that young children's ability to take the per- **95** spective of others is limited by their own tendency towards egocentrism.[15] They may assume that others think the same thing and the same way they do. They may also be convinced that what they think is always correct. Because of their egocentrism, young children may confuse appearances with reality and generalize their own experiences to everything.

According to Piaget, egocentric thinking can take on several forms. *Realism* involves the tendency to believe that what is imagined is actually real. For example, a child may wake up with a nightmare and insist to his parents that there is a "monster" in his room. No amount of logic will change his mind since, from his egocentric perspective, the event actually occurred. Another characteristic of egocentrism is *artificialism*, the tendency to believe that all objects in the world have been created by human beings for their own purposes. Recall the example of the four-year-old who, after observing the smoke from his father's pipe, may later point out that his daddy "made" all the clouds in the sky. *Animism*, the tendency to attribute life and consciousness to inanimate objects, is another form of egocentrism. Tall trees on a windy evening, for example, may seem especially threatening to young children. They may interpret their movement and creaking sounds as sinister attempts to grab them.

Egocentrism is also characterized by *transductive reasoning*, the tendency to believe one event caused another when the only real relationship is that they occurred at the same time. For example, a young child may think that setting a table will get daddy home from work because he always comes home immediately after this chore is finished. Another illustration is that of a young child who blames himself for his parents' divorce because he was naughty on the day they separated.

To some extent all of us are egocentric and tend to view other people's experiences and problems through our own mental filters. Because feelings, attitudes, and ideas are so private, the best we can do is to estimate these events in others.

Your world differs from mine:
Subjective role taking (Level 1)

Although egocentrism may be most powerful during the period between birth and four years of age, social thinking has its origins in the preschool years. At this level children understand that others may have different interpretations of the same situation. They also realize that people feel or think differently because they have had different experiences or have different goals. However, at this level children are still unable to put themselves in the place of another to understand the reasons for their actions. Nor are they able to evaluate their own actions from another's viewpoint. Among the children in Selman's study, 20 percent of the four-year-olds, 90 percent of the six-year-olds, 40 percent of the eight-year-olds, and 20 percent of the ten-year-olds were at the subjective role-taking level.

In Piaget and Inhelder's classical "three-mountain experiment" of *perceptual* role taking, children were asked to identify the perspective of a doll which was placed in various positions around the model of a landscape by selecting a photo which matched its view.[16] Young children below six years of age were primarily egocentric since they frequently attributed their own viewpoint to the doll. Children between seven and nine years of age could understand more accurately how viewpoints differ.

Emotions and empathy

Children between three and five years of age may be more affected by stereotypes of contexts and emotions than older children.[17] If preschoolers are shown a picture of an unpleasant situation (e.g., doctor with a long needle standing next to a child) in which a child is smiling or a pleasant situation (e.g., birthday party) in which a child is frowning they are less likely than older children to identify the incongruity. They are more likely to mention emotions that are stereotypically associated with pleasant or unpleasant circumstances.

CHILD STUDY 8

Perspective taking

Select two or three children of different ages and observe their social play for evidence of perspective problems, especially in conflict and game play. Do limitations in their social perspective taking influence their relationships with others?

If possible, become involved in one of the children's games and ask them to describe the rules for you. Do their descriptions take your own "naive" perspective into account? Do they disagree over the rules and make adjustments in their perspectives in order to compromise with others? Ask them to demonstrate what you are supposed to do. Are their demonstrations made with your social perspective in mind? Do they give you enough information? Do they check to see if you understand?

Do the children differ in the way they consider others' points of view? Do you think these differences are due to age or to individual personality?

Researchers have also found that four-year-olds tend to regard all acts or movements and their effects as intentional.[18] If they see someone accidentally fall and break a lamp, for example, four-year-olds are likely to say the other actually wanted to or decided to have the accident. Five-year-olds are able, though, to differentiate between intentional and unintentional acts. Also they recognize that although voluntary acts are always intentional, their effects are not always intended. For example, they may recognize that although someone intentionally reached for a glass of milk, the spill that resulted was unintentional. But, unlike older children, they may assume that desirable effects are always intended and undesirable effects are unintended. Although they are beginning to appreciate another's perspective, this viewpoint reveals that young children still do not fully understand the relationship between motives and behavior.

In another study of perspective taking, children between two and six years old viewed brief videotaped episodes (while their mother was in a different room). In them, a narrator pointed out in one segment that the child they saw was entering her grandmother's house and in the other that the child was asking his mother for a cookie.[19] Their mothers joined the children, and both watched the same videotapes with the *sound turned off*. Children were then asked if their mothers knew whose house the child entered in the first segment and what he asked his mother in the second. Children who responded affirmatively were labeled egocentric since they incorrectly assumed that their mothers had the same information they had.

Almost all of the two- and three-year-olds responded egocentrically. Yet 40 percent of the four-year-olds, only 15 percent of the five-year-olds, and none of the six-year-olds were egocentric. Almost all of the six-year-olds could also give reasons why the mothers did not know.

Although they may not be able to coordinate perspectives, young children have been shown to be remarkably sensitive in some circumstances. Children as young as two years of age are able to engage others in discussion and make adjustments in their presentation when listeners did not understand them or were not paying attention.[20] Three-year-olds can rotate a model so they can view it the same way another person sees it,[21] and they can identify positive and negative emotions in others (though they are likely to be confused if the emotions are incongruent with the situation).[22] Four-year-olds can recognize when their mothers or playmates are talking with strangers by interpreting only the videotaped expressions on their faces.[23] Children three to five years old can make adjustments in their descriptions of an object if they know the person they are talking to cannot see it.[24] Kindergarten children can describe how another feels and identify the incident that triggered the emotion.[25] These studies reveal that young children can demonstrate that they understand another's perspective in a limited fashion if the procedure is simple enough.

What do you think of me?
Self-reflective role taking (Level 2)

At this level children are aware that people think and feel differently because they have their own unique set of values or motives. Children may now be conscious of what the other person thinks about their behavior, and they can also recognize that the other person can take their perspective. Among the children in Selman's study, none of the four- or six-year-olds were at this level, but 50 percent of the eight-year-olds and 60 percent of the ten-year-olds were.

Age differences in children's awareness of what others are thinking of them become apparent during observation. Preschool and kindergarten children may be curious about an observer, but they are unlikely to be very self-conscious. For example, a kindergarten girl wearing a dress may not hesitate to hang upside down on the monkey bars. Sometime during the first and second grade, however, children begin to wonder what other people think of them and what they do. An observer in a second-grade classroom will notice much different responses from these children than from preschoolers. At this age, girls with dresses do not usually hang upside down on monkey bars. These children are more self-conscious and more concerned about what an observer notices in them.

This change in perspective has a great impact on children's relationships with others. They may, for example, start being concerned with how their friends view their appearance. During previous levels children may have easily overcome stormy times in their relationships, quickly resuming friendships after arguments. At this level, however, children may worry about whether their friends still like them after an argument. Also, they may hold longer grudges against a wrongdoer.

At this stage children understand the differences between intended and unintended acts and realize that, no matter what a person may try to do, there can be unintended positive or negative consequences.[26] This awareness that "I am thinking of what you are thinking about me" brings about a major change in how children view their relationship with others.

Viewing the total situation:
Mutual role taking (Level 3)

At this level children are capable of looking at what is going on in their interaction with another more objectively, as though they were spectators or disinterested observers. As they continue with an interaction or negotiate a problem, children at this level are able to stand back and view the total situation—how each person views the problem and how each thinks the other views the problem. They can then use these estimates to guide their responses. They understand that people think and feel differently and that differing viewpoints of the same situation can be reasonable interpretations. Thus, one perspective does not make the other incorrect.[27] Among the children in Selman's study, none of the four- or six-year-olds, 10 percent of the eight-year-olds, and 20 percent of the ten-year-olds were at this level.

These four levels of social perspective taking reveal how children gradually become more skillful in understanding the feelings and ideas of others. By understanding the process of this development teachers can help children learn positive, beneficial ways of dealing with emotions.

Emotional problem solving

Intense emotional experiences can make life difficult. Anger may lead to destructiveness, and sadness or fear may result in withdrawal from relationships. In order to gain emotional maturity children must gradually learn how to deal with such strong emotions.

Some children in our classrooms may be especially troubled by their emotions and may be at loss for constructively dealing with how they feel. David, a preschooler, was such a child. He was an intensely angry four-year-old who seemed to take pleasure in hurting others. After hitting or pushing them down he would typically stand back and laugh. A meeting with his mother disclosed that his father frequently spanked him and that David steadfastly refused to cry or show any kind of remorse. This angered his father who then intensified the punishment in order to make David cry. David still refused to break down, but when he came to school he unleashed the rage that he kept so closely guarded at home.

In addition to his frequent use of physical punishment the father encouraged David's physical aggressiveness outside the home. During one conversation the father expressed pride that his son would stand up to and fight with some of the older boys in their neighborhood. David's use of physical aggression to solve his problems was given direct and indirect support from his father.

How did David feel? Anger, rage, revenge, and fear must have simmered below the surface between his violent outbursts. Because of his father's strict control he may have felt powerless, and his cruelty may have been a way of saying, "Hey, look at me! See what *I* can do! See how *powerful* I am! I can hurt you just like my daddy hurt me! I'll *show* you!" Hurting others was the only way he knew how to deal with his feelings.

David's teachers did their best to help him find ways to safely express his feelings, but the efforts had little effect. He continued to hurt others and refused to acknowledge the problem. When he left the class, his behavior was much the same as when he arrived.

About two years later David and his mother visited the school. The teachers were relieved when she commented that David's aggressiveness had dramatically decreased. However, one teacher talked with David, and immediately noticed another obvious change in his behavior, he had developed the habit of nervously blinking his eyes as he talked. Was his rage now being directed toward himself? What price would he eventually pay for this self-destructive solution to his problem?

David's behavior points out two ineffective responses to intense emotions: dealing with the problem by taking it out on others or by directing it against one's self. Some children lose control of emotions and respond by harming others. They may hit, call names, take toys, or destroy property. Other children, instead of attacking, may keep their emotions bottled up inside themselves. This suppression of strong emotions may produce headaches, upset stomachs, nervous habits, or even ulcers. In other words, the energy generated by the emotion is directed toward themselves. Emotional energy *will* be expressed. If not expressed externally, it will be expressed internally.

SELF STUDY II

Feelings about children

On a sheet of paper, list many of the feelings that you have about children and what you experience when you are with them. Do not continue until you have completed your list.

Examine this list of emotions. What does each of them tell you concerning your beliefs about children or the way you interpret them or react to what they do? What kind of information do your emotions provide about your values, your personality, and the ideas you have about yourself and children?

Look at the positive emotions you wrote down. Try to think of ways these might be increased as you work with children. As you consider them, are there others that come to mind? What effect do these feelings have on children?

Go over the negative emotions. In what circumstances do they arise? Can these circumstances be prevented? Is there a way of reinterpreting these situations to reduce the intensity of the feelings? For example, perhaps you feel hassled and frazzled after a busy, hectic day and are irritable over a child's continued requests for help. You might tell yourself something like, "Hey, this has been a hectic day. Getting upset with this child won't help either of us. Reach out to her . . . is she confused, does she

Emotions and empathy

need attention? Maybe if I tell her how frazzled I feel she might even be able to help." This positive "self-talk" might help to transform the negative feeling into a more positive one. Be aware of what you tell yourself when you are feeling afraid, angry, sad, happy, excited, disgusted, or frazzled.

In addition to encouraging them to reflect on the causes and consequences of their emotions, we can also try to help children put their feelings into words. Some of their emotional energy can be channelled into communication.

One group discussion focused on angry feelings. At one point the following exchange occurred:

SIMON: I think Jim is the angriest person in the whole world . . . I think in the whole wide world!

TEACHER: You could ask him.

SIMON: I think Jim is the angriest person in the whole world.

TEACHER: You could ask him.

At that point Simon walked over to Jim who had declined to join the class and was sitting quietly at the table. You could hear a pin drop. Everyone was holding their breath. Simon spoke very gently.

SIMON: Are you angry?

JIM: [looked away then turned back to face Simon to speak slowly and quietly.] You don't play with me . . . and that makes me feel sad.[28]

In this situation both Simon and Jim were struggling to put their feelings into words. Although Jim appeared to place responsibility for his feelings on Simon when he said ". . .and that *makes* me feel sad," his simple, straightforward acknowledgment of how he felt may have contributed to a better understanding between him and his friend.

CHILD STUDY 9

Emotional behavior

Choose two or three children of different ages. Compare the children's behavior when they experience any *two* of the following emotions:

Joy	Sadness
Affection	Disgust
Fear	Anger
Surprise	Curiosity

Do the children differ in the frequency or intensity of their emotional reactions? Do they quickly reveal their emotions or do they seem inhibited? How would you characterize their "style" in dealing with these emotions? For example, does a child always seem somewhat sad and easily brought to tears? Does another basically appear to be a happy-go-lucky person

who rarely becomes angry? How do other children respond to their behavior? To what extent do you think these emotional reactions are influenced by age?

Recall your own childhood emotions. What kinds of changes in your
feelings and emotional behavior did you experience as you grew older?
Are you the same in some ways? Are you still afraid of spiders, for example, or still easily aroused to anger? Why did you change in some ways but
not in others?

Words are very important, but they are not always sufficient to deal with intense
emotions. Thus, we can also explore with children beneficial ways of responding
to emotions. Is crying an effective response to sadness or fear? Is shouting or
stomping an effective way to deal with anger? How about hugging or kissing when
feeling affectionate?

This issue is difficult to resolve because we may be impoverished in our own
thinking about how to express feelings productively. If no one in our past helped
us find acceptable ways of expressing emotion, we may have a better idea of what
not to do than what *to do*. As teachers, however, we are responsible for guiding
children toward positive ends. Somehow we have to help them discover non-
destructive ways of expressing the energy that strong emotion generates.

As we work with children to improve their emotional problem-solving skills, we
should keep in mind that age influences the way they respond to emotion. Both
the *frequency* and *intensity* of emotional reactions may decrease as children grow
older. Mature nine-year-olds, for example, typically do not cry as often as three-
year-olds. They are also less likely to have the intense temper tantrums they may
have had as toddlers. These changes may be largely due to the gradual increase in
children's understanding of situations, their knowledge of alternatives to resolve
problems, and their ability to actually carry out a solution.

Emotional awareness education

The first step in designing an educational program is to decide on the types of
emotional skills we want to emphasize and nurture. Potential emotional development skills are identified in Table 4.1, and the various components of the skills are
defined, examples are given, and related concepts listed. No specific age guidelines are provided, but the skills are defined broadly enough to be adapted to the
abilities of a particular child. Although primarily written for children between three
and eight years, these skills are appropriate for learners of any age.

Our relationships with children

Our relationship with a child may be the most effective tool we have in helping him
or her learn about emotions. The following suggestions can strengthen the impact
our personal contact has on children.

Table 4.1
Summary of emotional skills for children

Skill	Definition	Social/cognitive processes
1. Becoming aware of feelings.	1. The ability to recognize, describe, and accept feelings associated with joy, liking, fear, surprise, sadness, disgust, anger, and curiosity. *Example:* A five-year-old describes sadness as feeling like ". . . there are tears in your heart."	Defining Joy Sad Happy Lonely Like Disgust Affection Bored Fear Anger Brave Curious Surprise
2. Understanding the relationship between emotions and social behavior.	2. The ability to identify experiences which influence emotions, the possible consequences of emotional reactions, and appropriate responses to emotional reactions; to discriminate between potentially harmful forms of emotional behavior. *Example:* A four-year-old says, "When I feel sad sometimes I cry." A seven-year-old comments, "When you get mad it doesn't do any good to hit—they might hit you back."	Deciding
3. Constructively communicating feelings.	3a. The ability to describe how one feels through (a) direct identification, (b) the use of metaphors, or (c) stating the kind of action the feelings urge you to do. *Examples:* A three-year-old announces during a frightening TV sequence, "I'm *scared!*" A five-year-old states after a playground collision with another child, "I feel like a bug that's being squashed!" A seven-year-old describes how she felt during a school play: "I was *so* embarrassed. I just wanted to disappear!"	Acting
	3b. The ability to take action appropriate to how one feels without harming one's self or others. *Examples:* When the TV show becomes frightening the three-year-old changes the channel. When he finds his pet canary dead, a seven-year-old cries.	Acting
4. Developing a sensitivity to the feelings of others.	4. The ability to recognize and describe how another feels; the ability to communicate this understanding to others. *Examples:* A three-year-old points to another child who is angry and says, "He's sad." A seven-year-old approaches his father who is having a difficult time with a woodworking task and says, "You frustrated Dad? Can I hold something for you?"	Sensing

First, our own emotional experiences can provide learning opportunities for children. Without going into unnecessary detail, we can talk about our own sadness, joy, anger, or fear. We can demonstrate that feelings can be put into words and that they do not have to be hidden. When we talk about our own feelings we also point out that these experiences differ from the behavior often associated with the emotions. For example, anger is not the same as hitting, and feeling afraid is not the same as running away.

This does not mean that teachers should indiscriminately reveal how they feel at all times. In some circumstances feelings should not be shared. A three-year-old child who is frightened and anxious on the first day of class might only feel worse if his teacher expresses her own anger following his misbehavior. Later, after a relationship has been established, the same child may be able to respond more positively to such a self-disclosure. Expression of emotion is likely to be more effective if it is done to bring us closer to children rather than to punish them. Knowing when and how to reveal our feelings is difficult, but this skill is also a powerful tool in teaching children about emotions.

Second, we can show respect for the emotional experiences of children and demonstrate our desire to understand by verbally acknowledging their feelings. When we show children we at least partially understand how they feel we help them get to know themselves better.[29]

Our expressions of empathy can also help children differentiate between feelings and behavior. For example, a teacher responds to an angry child who is trying to hit her by restraining him and saying, "Mark, I am *not* going to let you hit me! I know you *feel* angry, and that's OK, but I will not let you hit me. Maybe you could talk rather than hit." The teacher disapproves of the child's unacceptable *behavior,* but also acknowledges his *feelings* and her interest in talking about them to resolve the conflict. This type of firmness in combination with sensitive listening helps children become aware of their feelings and provides them with a clearer understanding of how to deal with their experiences.

Third, we can talk with children and help them explore their own ideas about emotions. By asking children to describe happiness, sadness, fear, or anger, we gain a better picture of how they view emotions. Also, children will be challenged to identify their own ideas about feelings. We can discuss emotions with children any time, not only during an actual experience. The following excerpts from a nursery school teacher's class notes are good examples of discussions about emotions.

> We talked about death and sadness today. Most of the comments regarding this latter feeling involved physical violence. In a very quiet voice Betsy said, "You know what gives me a sad feeling?" I responded, "What, Betsy?" She lowered her eyes and said, "When someone calls me a name."[30]

> The topic for this week is disgust. I introduced the word "disgust," but they didn't comprehend its meaning. This was expected. I then stated that another way of talking about our feelings of disgust is to have a "yucky" feeling. Some of the children understood. Karla said, "I know what gives people a yucky feeling!" "What?" responded Chuck. "When someone lets go with a smelly one!" Karla explained.[31]

We can encourage children who have misconceptions about their feelings to reflect on ideas and consider other points of view (see Table 4.2). For example, a seven-year-old girl points to a boy who is crying after being hurt and says, "Crybaby, crybaby! You're nothing but a crybaby!" We might ask her to talk about her attitudes toward crying. A discussion like the following might result:

TEACHER: What's the problem with crying?

CHILD: Crying's for babies.

TEACHER: What would happen to me if I cried when I felt sad?

CHILD: People would laugh at you.

TEACHER: Maybe. Some people might be surprised or self-conscious if I cried in front of them.

CHILD: I don't cry.

TEACHER: You don't? I remember once when I felt really sad I sat in my car all by myself and cried. I was grown up then, and I was embarrassed to cry in front of others. But when I was all done crying I felt much better. I felt really sad. If we were nicer to each other when we cried, maybe we would all feel better.

CHILD: I don't think so.

TEACHER: OK, maybe you could think about it some more. Will you hold this cloth on Mike's cut while I get a bandage for him?

CHILD: OK.

Table 4.2
Contrasting examples of irrational and rational beliefs about emotions

Irrational belief		Rational belief
• Only sissies and babies cry; big boys don't cry.	vs.	• Crying sometimes helps when people feel sad, tears are like words our heart uses to tell others how sad we feel.
• If someone feels angry with me it means they don't love me.	vs.	• We can continue to love someone even when we're feeling angry with them.
• Many feelings are unacceptable; we shouldn't let others know how we feel.	vs.	• We can talk about our feelings; we don't have to always hide how we feel.
• Fear is a sign of weakness; never admit you are afraid; hide fear as best you can.	vs.	• Sometimes we are afraid of something because we misunderstand it; sometimes, though, we are afraid because something is really dangerous.

There would be many different ways of encouraging this child to reflect on her attitude toward crying. In this situation the teacher presented a different point of view and described a personal experience of crying. The teacher respected the child's idea that crying is unacceptable by listening and taking her seriously. There was no ridicule nor did the teacher insist the child's idea was wrong. The idea that crying may be helpful when we feel sad was presented for the child to accept or reject. Simply telling the child she was wrong would not change her way of thinking.

Fourth, we can encourage children to consider the feelings and ideas of others as they interact with them. We can promote children's social perspective taking by challenging them to investigate how others react emotionally to what they do. In the following conversation a child, Brad, is dressed in his Halloween witch costume. His teacher is trying to get him to reflect on the effect his teasing is having on another child.

TEACHER: What's the problem here?

BRAD: Tell him to stop it!

TEACHER: James, Brad wants you to stop it. What are you doing?

JAMES: I'm a witch! Ha! I'm going to get him!

TEACHER: James, how does Brad feel when you chase him like that?

JAMES: Scared!

TEACHER: Brad, do you want to be scared?

BRAD: No! I don't like it. Stop it, James. That's scary!

JAMES: OK.

TEACHER: James, your witch seems too real for Brad. Maybe you could try to find someone else to play your game or be the kind of witch that's not so scary for Brad.

This brief encounter demonstrates a teacher's effort to help two children focus on their feelings and to be aware of the emotional consequences of their behavior. Of course, there would be many other effective ways to respond to this situation. The teacher here chose to emphasize emotional problem-solving skills rather than to be moralistic ("It's not nice to chase!") or repressive ("Stop that right now or I'll take the mask away!").

Finally, we can take a careful look at how our program is affecting children emotionally. Are children feeling challenged or are they bored? Do we set enough limits to provide a sense of security? Are there so many restrictions that children resent confinement or are there so few that they feel anxious? Do children laugh in our classrooms or do they act reserved and cautious? Each of us will decide on the type of mood we want to nurture in our classroom. Whatever we do will have an effect in the ideas children acquire about their emotional development.

These suggestions for enhancing our everyday relationships with children may have the most impact on what they learn about emotions. This personal contact may be our most powerful teaching strategy, but we can also introduce planned activities which give emphasis to some aspect of emotional development. When these activities are used in concert with the more spontaneous and individualized aspects of our relationships, our overall educational impact may be strengthened.

Activities to promote emotional awareness

The following activities may be helpful to you as you design a program to nurture emotional awareness in children. Please review Tables 3.3 and 3.4 (pp. 53-54) before beginning. For additional activities on emotions see the following:

9 I Like Me
11 Stories with Hands
19 I Cannot See
103 Flower Power
104 Sad Person
107 Won or None

41

Emotion Pictures (four years +)

Purpose   To help children become aware of basic feelings and sensitive to the feelings of others. Key concepts are: *happy, sad, angry, afraid, disgust (yucky feelings), calm, affectionate, and excited.*

Setting   Learning center arrangment

Materials   A collection of pictures cut from magazines, each showing one of the basic emotions listed above.

Activity   **1.** An affective picture collection can be used to create a variety of different activities. They can be placed at a learning center table and the events and feelings revealed in the pictures can be discussed.

2. The teacher can ask the children to find pictures of people who are sad, angry, happy, etc. Children can be asked to group all the sad pictures together, then all of the happy ones, and so on. Also, the teacher can group pictures together and ask the children to identify why they all go together.

Suggestion   Variations in intensity of emotions can be explored by asking children to rank three or more (up to five) pictures from most to least emotional, for example, happy, happier, happiest. If the pictures are available for variations of sad, angry, afraid, and disgust (a more difficult concept), they can be ranked also.

42

Emotion Action Cards (three years +)

Purpose   To help children become aware of feelings and sensitive to the feelings of others. Key concepts are: *happy, sad, angry, afraid, disgust (feeling yucky), affectionate, and calm.*

Setting   Community group or learning center arrangement

Materials	Six cards, each having a face portraying a different one of the basic emotions listed in the key concepts. Pictures can be drawn, cut from magazines, or obtained from commercial sources, for example, TAD pictures from American Guidance Service.
Activity	**1.** Introduce this activity by asking the children if they know what feelings are. Show them the cards, one by one, and ask if they know how each person feels. Point out some of the facial features or other features which suggest the emotion. When finished set the cards up where all the children can see them.
	2. Tell the children that you are going to pretend to feel like one of the people in the pictures and that you would like them to guess how you feel. Choose one of the feelings and make a face which shows the emotion. Repeat this several times with other feelings. Do another round, emphasizing body language. For example, you might shake your fist and stomp your feet for anger.
	3. Let the children have the opportunity to demonstrate feelings by having them take turns choosing the emotion and acting it out while the others continue to guess.
Suggestions	The task can be made more difficult if the action is restricted to the face or hands. In another variation, the emotion to be portrayed can be selected from the "deck" of face-down cards.

---

43 "I Feel" Tags (three years +)

Purpose	To help children become aware of feelings and sensitive to the feelings of others. Key concepts are *happy, sad, angry, afraid, and disgust.*
Setting	No formal arrangement
Materials	Five tags, each having a drawing of a face, which reflect the emotions happy, sad, anger, fear, and disgust. For example:

Happy   Sad   Angry   Afraid   Yucky

Activity	When you are feeling particularly happy, sad, angry, afraid, or "yucky" pin on one of your tags. This sign will encourage your children to talk about emotions. Talk about your feelings if they seem interested. Use simple terms and deal with issues that children can relate to.

For example:

    POOR: I am gloomy because my boyfriend told me he wanted us to break up.

    BETTER: I feel sad because I think someone I really like does not like me anymore.

Suggestion   Make 3" by 5" cards available to your children so they can draw their own "I feel" tags.

---

44   **Feeling Peeling** (four years +)

Purpose   To help children become aware of feelings and the relationship between emotions and social behavior. Key concepts are *afraid, happy, angry, affectionate,* and *sad.*

Setting   Community group arrangement or individual conversation

Materials   **None**

Activity   This activity involves asking questions which encourage children to think about the causes and consequences of various emotions. They are more appropriate for verbal children who are capable of engaging in this type of discussion. Some suggested questions are listed below. Emotions like happy, angry, affection, and sad can be substituted for afraid.

What do you do when you are afraid?

What would you like to do when you are afraid?

What would you like other people to do for you when you are afraid?

What are some of the things that give you an afraid feeling?

What do you think is going to happen when you [see, smell, touch, feel, hear, or taste]

_____ (fill in with response from question four)?

What are some things that people get afraid of? What do they do when they become afraid?

How do you feel when someone is afraid of you?

What feeling is difficult to tell other people about?

This list is only the beginning of a large number of potential questions which will encourage children to explore their emotions. *Remember to respect the child's desire not to disclose how he or she feels. Do not pressure any child to respond.*

45 Face Plates (three years +)

Purpose   To help children become aware of feelings. Key concepts are *happy, sad, afraid, angry,* **and** *disgust (yucky feelings).*

Setting   **Learning center arrangement**

Materials   **Collage materials (yarn, bits of material and paper, etc.)**
Glue or paste
Crayons or paint

Activity   **I.** In preparation for the activity cut out a wide variety of construction paper eyes, eyebrows, noses, and mouths which can be used to reflect different feelings. Place these face parts with the paper plates, glue, and crayons at a learning center table.
2. When the children arrive ask them to identify which pieces might be eyes, eyebrows, noses, and mouths. Give each of the children a paper plate and ask them to make a face on it using the pieces. When they are finished encourage them to identify the kind of feeling the face shows (if they are interested in discussing the idea). Children can then decorate their "faces" with either crayons or paint and the collage materials.
3. Collect all the "face plates" and tape them to a wall. Encourage children to identify the faces that look happy, sad, scared (or scary), angry, and "yucky." Ask the children to try to make the same faces as they see on the plates.

Suggestion   Some children may not make faces at all, preferring instead simply to decorate with available materials. Accept their choice but also direct their attention to the faces other children are making. Tape their efforts to the wall as well.

46 Feeling Face Masks (three years +)

Purpose   To help children become aware of feelings. Key concepts are *happy, afraid, angry,* and *sad.*

Setting   **Learning center arrangement**

Materials   **One large paper bag for each child**
Four bags with happy, angry, sad, and frightened faces drawn on them to be used as examples
Mask materials (e.g., crayons, construction paper, yarn, paste or glue, etc.)
Blunt-end scissors

Activity   **1.** Show all the materials to the children when they arrive at the learning center, but do not set out your examples. Suggest that they try to make masks with either happy, angry, sad, or frightened faces. By cutting out the eyes, you can place the bags over their heads and still enable them to see.

2. Display your own masks if children need help to understand the task better. Do not use your masks as models for the children to copy. Let them make their own creations.

3. Hand out the paper bags and materials and encourage the children to draw their own "feeling faces." While the masks are being made, discuss various feelings, how they originate, and their consequences.

4. When the children have finished have them try to guess what kinds of feelings the others have drawn. Have them try on the masks and encourage the artists to act out how they feel (with safety and reason in mind).

Suggestion   If a particular child wants to draw something nonhuman (e.g., a "monster") suggest that he or she could still give the creature a feeling face. Do not allow children to play with the masks near stairs or outside near a street.

---

47   Contrasting Feelings (three to four years +)

Purpose   To help children become aware of feelings and sensitive to the feelings of others. Key concepts are: *happy, sad, affectionate, afraid,* and *angry.*

Setting   Learning center arrangement

Materials   Emotional picture file (from Activity 48)

Activity   **1.** This classification activity has been commonly used utilizing impersonal objects rather than human feelings. On a large sheet of paper draw a horizontal and vertical line dividing the sheet into four equal parts. In three sections, place pictures which depict the same emotion. Place a picture depicting a much different feeling in the fourth position. For example:

Child crying over spilled ice cream	Child smiling as she plays
Child smiling as he eats ice cream	Child laughing with another

2. Tell the children that three of the pictures go together because in some way they are the same but that one of the pictures does not belong because it is different. Ask them to find the one that is different and to explain their reasons for the choice. Repeat with other emotions.

48 Emotion Photos (five years +)

Purpose   To help children become aware of feelings and sensitive to the feelings of others. Key concepts are *happy, sad, angry, afraid,* and *disgust.*

Setting   Learning center or community group arrangement

Materials   Camera and film

Activity   **1.** Take pictures of individual children acting out certain feelings. For example, you can take four pictures of different children expressing happiness, four of sadness, etc. Each child can have his or her picture taken in the same spot at a time other children will not intrude.
2. All of these pictures can be made into a deck of picture cards and children can try to organize them into emotion categories. The teacher might take each card, one at a time, and ask children what emotion the child in the picture may be trying to communicate.
3. Photos can also be organized into emotional categories and displayed on a classroom wall or bulletin board.

49 The Sound of Feelings (five to six years +)

Purpose   To help children become aware of feelings and sensitive to the feelings of others. Key concepts are *happy, sad, angry, afraid, disgust (yucky)* and *calm.*

Setting   Community group or learning center arrangement

Materials   Tape recorder
"Sound of feelings" tape (see *Activity* below)
Emotional picture file

Activity   **1.** Make a tape which conveys emotions by various types of vocal sounds. For example, make a series of distinct "nonsense" sounds each conveying a specific emotion—a growl for anger, a pleasurable sound for happiness, a moan or cry for sadness, a negative sound of disgust, a shriek of fear (not too frightening), and a calm vocal sound. For the next series of sounds repeat a "neutral" statement but vary the underlying emotion each time. For example, say "Hello, there!" six times conveying a different basic emotion each time. A third round can be recorded using a statement that may contradict the emotion conveyed by the tone of voice. For example. "I like you" can be stated in six different ways to convey the six different emotions.
2. Place the set of emotion pictures where all the children can see them. Begin the tape and ask the children to match the pictured emotion with the sound. Repeat the tape if necessary.

50 Half Feelings (three years +)

Purpose   To help children become aware of feelings and sensitive to the feelings of others. Key concepts are *happy, sad, afraid, angry,* and *affectionate.*

Setting   Learning center arrangement

Materials   Magazine pictures of faces expressing *happy, sad, afraid, angry,* and *affectionate* feelings
Construction paper
Glue or paste

Activity   1. Glue the pictures to construction paper and cut each face in half.
2. Show children one of the two halves and ask them to guess how that person feels. Show them the other half of the picture and see if the additional information makes a difference in their interpretation. Then put both halves together.

Suggestion   1. Make several templates by cutting various size holes in a piece of construction paper. Templates can be arranged in order of least space revealed to most space revealed.
2. Place a template over a whole picture of someone expressing emotion and ask a child to guess what emotion is being conveyed. If the child is incorrect let him or her see the picture with an easier template. Finally, let the child see the picture as a whole.

51 Emotion Drawing (three years +)

Purpose   To help children become aware of feelings and cooperative skills. Key concepts are *happy, angry, sad, afraid, affectionate,* and *cooperation.*

Setting   Learning center arrangement

Materials   A large sheet of butcher paper
A wide variety of creative arts materials (e.g., glue, construction paper, crayons, paint, etc.)

Activity   1. Set out art materials and butcher paper. With your children's help establish a theme, such as, "OK, let's make a *happy* picture!" Distribute the materials and encourage the children to work cooperatively. A single setting, such as a *circus,* should not be rigidly established. Rather, each child can contribute his or her ideas to form a mural effect. Comment on their *cooperative* effort.

2. When finished, tape the emotion drawing to a wall. Examine the picture with the children and discuss the various feelings and creative ideas which are reflected in it.

Suggestion   The specific affective theme in the emotion picture can be prompted by certain classroom events, such as fear for Halloween, sadness for the death of a class pet, affection for Valentine's Day, etc.

52

This Is How I Look . . . This Is How I Feel (five years +)

Purpose   To help children become aware of feelings and the relationship between emotions and social behavior; to help children develop a sensitivity to the feelings of others. Key concepts are *happy, sad, angry, afraid, disgust (yucky),* and *calm.*

Setting   Community group or learning center arrangement

Materials   Six cards, each having pictures of approximately the same adult individual portraying a different basic emotion (see key concepts). Illustrations can be drawn, taken from sets used in previous activities, or obtained commercially (for example, the TAD pictures from American Guidance Service).

Activity   **1.** The idea that people can feel differently than they appear is difficult for children to learn. However, many children who have been involved in education for emotions are ready to explore this more sophisticated principle.

2. Introduce the activity by saying something like, "sometimes people do not want others to know how they *really* feel so they put on a pretend face. They want to hide their feelings. Let's say you called me a nasty name. I could smile and say, 'Now you shouldn't say that,' [demonstrate] when what I really feel deep inside is sadness because I don't like to be called names. Here are some tures of a person who has different feelings. I am going to tell you some stories about this person and then let's talk about how he [or she] really feels."

Story 1:   Put the sad face behind the happy one. Tell the children that this teacher broke a favorite dish when he (or she) was at home. Just then a neighbor knocked on the door. When he (or she) answered the door, this is how the teacher looked (show happy face), but how do you think she really felt? After a discussion reveal the sad face. Explain that the teacher felt very sad because his (or her) favorite dish was broken.

Story 2:   Put the angry face behind the calm one. Tell the children that there was another time when this person had to tell a little boy in his (or her) class that he could not do something. The little boy became very mean and spit on the teacher. Show the calm face and explain that this is how the teacher looked when he (or she) said, "You are not supposed to do that." Ask the children how they think the teacher really felt. After a discussion reveal the angry face. Tell the children that the teacher was really angry because he (or she) dislikes being spit on.

Story 3:   Put the afraid face behind the angry one. Tell the children that there was another time when this teacher was outside watching his (or her) children play. One child climbed up on the very tall slide and began to jump up and down. When the teacher looked over the child almost fell off. The teacher ran over to the slide, looked up at the child, and said, "You get down right now!" Show the angry face and say that this is how the teacher looked. Ask the children how they think he (or she) really felt? After a discussion reveal the afraid face. Explain that the teacher was afraid because this child was almost hurt *very* badly.

Suggestion   Make up additional combinations of hidden feelings. Do not stress this point so much that children conclude that *all* feelings are *always* hidden. Stress the idea that sometimes people think their feelings are bad or they are not aware of a feeling so they do not show it.

53   Orange You Happy? (four years +)

Purpose   To help children become aware of feelings associated with pleasure. Key concept is *happiness*.

Setting   Community group arrangement

Materials   One small slice of an orange for each child and several extra portions
One whole orange
One bowl

Activity   **1.** Take out the whole orange and hold it up to the group. Describe what you like about oranges—their color, texture, aroma, and taste. Mention that the orange reminds you of a happy feeling. Tell the children about a time when you were really happy. Briefly describe what happened, and how you felt.

2. Bring out the bowl of orange slices. Take a portion and give it to one of the children while asking, "Orange you happy? Can you tell us about a happy feeling you once had?" After the child responds and begins eating the orange ask if someone in the group would like to give an orange slice to someone else and ask, "Orange you happy?" Continue in the same manner until everyone has had a turn giving and receiving the orange slices and talking about happy experiences. Every child should receive an orange slice even though some may prefer to remain quiet.

Suggestions   As in other activities of a personal nature do not force or pressure children into revealing how they feel. Respect a child's decision not to talk about his or her feelings. Your support for a child who desires not to talk is a clear example of acceptance for other children.

Some children may receive more than one orange slice. Keep extras available to ensure that all children receive at least one portion.

54 Happy Chalk Drawing (three years +)

Purpose   To help children become aware of feelings associated with pleasure and to develop cooperative skills. Key concepts are *happiness* and *cooperation*.

Setting   An outdoor location which includes a safe, cement area

Materials   Chalks in a variety of colors
Smocks

Activity   **1.** Ask the children if they know what *happy* means. Identify some of the objects or events which nurture happy feelings. Discuss the idea that they can do various things to help others feel happy. Discuss some of these activities.
2. Tell the children that you have some chalk in various pretty colors. Invite them to draw some pictures on the sidewalk which might give them and others a happy feeling.
3. While children create their drawings, offer chalk to observers and encourage them to participate. When finished, take all children on a tour of the "sidewalk mural." Emphasize the cooperative aspects of their task in creating the larger picture.

Suggestions   Try to ensure that none of the children get concentrated amounts of chalk on their clothes. Young children might wear smocks. Also start the mural at a location far enough from the building entrance to prevent any tracking of chalk.

55 The Lonely Star (three years +)

Purpose   To help children become aware of feelings associated with loss or separation; to promote learner's sensory awareness. Key concept is *loneliness*.

Setting   Storytelling arrangement

Materials   One apple for every two children
One knife

Activity   **1.** Ask the children if they know what "loneliness" is. Discuss this emotion. Mention that you would like to tell them a story about the lonely star. (Keep the apples out of sight.) The following brief plot can be elaborated on as much as you want. Use as many simple gestures as possible.

Once upon a time the sky was very dark at night. There were no stars . . . except one, a very tiny star. This tiny star was all alone and felt very lonely all by himself in the sky. One day this lonely little star went to see a very wise, old, old man who lived on the earth on the top of a high mountain. The sad little star asked the old man if he could help. Because the old man loved this little star very much and because he was very wise, he said he could do two things. First, he reached behind him and pulled out a beautiful black shiny bag. He put his hand in the bag, and when he took it out he tossed a sky-full of stars. "There," said the wise old man, "now you have many stars to be your friends. But because you are so special, I am going to do something else for you. I am going to put you *inside* something people like. Now you will be something special." Do you know where that wise old man put that sad little star? [take out the apples.] Why, they are inside apples! Watch, and let's find out if there is really a pretend star inside this apple.

2. Cut the apple horizontally to make two equal portions. Pull the apple apart and show the "star" to the children. Cut the other apples in half and give one half to each child. Encourage the children to explore their apple with all their senses.

Suggestion Pure storytelling without visual aids is a very difficult task with young children. While not overdoing it, be dramatic in both voice and gesture.

While testing this activity with four-year-olds, one little girl said, "I know who that old man is, that's God!" While not our intention, the comment was interesting.

---

56 The Afraid Game (four years +)

Purpose To help children become aware of feelings associated with threats to safety and understand the relationship between emotions and social behavior. Key concepts are *fear, afraid, real,* and *danger.*

Setting Community group arrangement

Materials None

Activity **1.** Talk with the children briefly about the meaning of fear and danger. Try to convey the idea that some of the things we are afraid of are only in our minds and are not really dangerous.

2. Explain that you are going to tell them about several children who are afraid and that you would like them to say if the danger is real or only in the child's imagination.

A boy is crossing a street and hears two cars crashing into each other. Is this really dangerous?

A girl who is helping her father, climbs up a ladder. Suddenly the ladder begins to slip and fall. Is this really dangerous?

A child feels very frightened when his friends shows him her pet hamster. Is the hamster really dangerous?

A child feels afraid when she is chased by a mean bully who wants to hurt her. Is this dangerous?

A child feels afraid when she sees a man with a beard. Is this dangerous?

3. Make up additional situations to illustrate the difference between real and imagined danger.

57

Poor Little Sad Eyes (three years +)

Purpose   To help children become aware of feelings associated with loss, deprivation, or separation; to promote the constructive expression of sad feelings. Key concepts are *sad* and *crying*.

Setting   Storytelling arrangement

Materials   **None**

Activity   **1.** Read and act out the following poem.

Poor little boy with sad eyes	(point to eyes)
See him now how much he cries	(mimic crying)
He tries to stop with all his might	(clench teeth, grimace)
He doesn't know	(shake hand)
That tears are all right.	(nod head "yes" while pointing to "tears")

2. Discuss the issue and ask the children if they think it is OK for boys and daddies to cry. Also ask about mommies and little girls.

Suggestion   Most of the four-year-old boys in our group said that it was not OK for them to cry. This is *their* reality. Most little boys who are punished at home for crying would only be confused by any strong assertive comments that crying is acceptable behavior. Adults, especially men, who talk about accepting their own tears as honest expressions of sadness will help children make their own positive decisions.

References for emotional development

Brown, G.I., Yeomans, T., and Grizzard, L., *The Live Classroom: Innovation through Confluent Education and Gestalt.* New York: Penguin Books, 1976.

Brown, G.I. *Human Teaching for Human Learning.* New York: Viking Press, 1971.

Castillo, G.A., *Left-Handed Teaching: Lessons in Affective Education.* New York: Praeger Publishing, 1974.

Chase, L. *The Other Side of the Report Card: A How-To-Do-It Program for Affective Education.* Pacific Palisades, Ca.: Goodyear, 1975.

Della-Piana, G. *How to Talk with Children (and Other People).* New York: John Wiley and Sons, 1973.

DeMille, R. *Put Your Mother on the Ceiling: Children's Imagination Games.* New York: Penguin Books, 1976.

Harmin, M. *Better Than Aspirin: How to Get Rid of Emotions That Give You A Pain in the Neck.* Niles, Ill.: Argus Communications, 1976.

Jensen, L.C., and Wells, M.G. *Feelings: Helping Children Understand Emotions.* Provo, Utah: Brigham Young University Press, 1979.

Jourard, S.M. *The Transparent Self.* New York: D. Van Nostrand Co., 1964.

King, N. *Giving Form to Feeling.* New York: Drama Book Specialists, 1975.

Lederman, J. *Anger and the Rocking Chair: Gestalt Awareness with Children.* New York: McGraw-Hill, 1969.

Chapter five
Affiliation: The child's emergence
into a social world

I n every classroom and neighborhood, on every playground or street corner, and indeed every place they can possibly meet, children engage in an intense struggle for social recognition. At stake is the need for self-worth and the precious benefits of group membership. Success in this contest demands quick thinking, sensitivity, compromise, and sharing. The struggle to gain social respect and acceptance from their peers is important to children because they share a common future.

Contact with adults can never be a satisfactory replacement for involvement with peers. No matter how kind they might be, adults represent authority to children because of the limits they must impose and the skills they have acquired. Also, due to differences in perspective, adults may not always understand or make themselves understandable to children. So, for children, adults will always be different. An adult is someone to observe and learn from, someone who represents an ordered social reality in an adult-dominated world.

With their peers, however, children are free to establish relationships based on *mutual* respect and cooperation. This is possible because children can relate to each other as equals. They think similarly, they share similar problems and experiences, and they are not tainted with adult authority. Children feel free to disagree, to discuss, and to negotiate with their peers because they feel as though they can contribute to the outcome of the engagement.

After reviewing the work of Jean Piaget on cognition and that of Harry Stack

Sullivan on social behavior, James Youniss concluded that children experience two very different forms of socialization.[1] Youniss asserts that children's relationships with adults are characterized by *complimentary reciprocity*. This means that during interactions children primarily respond to the initiatives or directives of adults. They are more likely to follow than to take the lead. For example, a preschooler who is typically self-confident and assertive may become passive and compliant when his mother visits his school. However, Youniss states that relationships with peers contribute to *symmetrical reciprocity* in which all are equally free to contribute their ideas. When children resolve disputes among themselves, they are forced to make concessions and cooperate because no one can claim ultimate authority. Both forms of socialization are critical. Adults guide children to understand the social constraints and expectations which exist in society, and peers nurture creative thinking and social sensitivity.

Children can afford to "learn by losing" when they are with their peers. They are more likely to experiment with different social behaviors among their peers than when they are with parents or teachers. Children may find their peers more accepting of failure, and they can seek new friends if they are rejected. Jason, for example, was a quiet well-mannered child with a bossy older sister. During the middle of the school year, though, he began to assert himself more with his peers. He became bossy when he tried to assume a leadership role. To the surprise of his teachers, he was even involved in a few minor fights with his peers. As a result of his experimentation with more outgoing, socially assertive behavior, Jason's peer group changed. Some children drifted away to other close friends while others became more attracted to him. Thus, his peers provided him with the opportunity to test himself socially and discover new skills.

The significance of the peer group

The peer group provides opportunities which are not available from relationships with adults. According to Zick Rubin the peer group can nurture social skills, self-understanding, and a sense of group belonging among children.[2] *Social skills* refer to a variety of strategies children use to effectively initiate and manage social interaction. Within the peer group children learn, for example, how to make, keep, and break friendships. To survive within the group, they may master such skills as the art of negotiation and conflict resolution. Because their relationship is based on equality, only peers can teach these skills to each other. The struggle to overcome and survive isolation and rejection can be a harsh but necessary way to learn the skills of affiliation. To be successful children have to face their peers alone, without adult interference.

The peer group can have an educational impact on children. Although they are rarely "instructed" by their peers, children learn by observing what they do. Young children have overcome their fears of dogs after observing other children playfully interact with them.[3] Peers have also contributed to the acquisition of sharing skills,[4] and the Harlows' research on social deprivation of monkeys has demonstrated that contact with peers can offset some of the damaging effects of problems in parent-child relationships.[5] These investigators discovered that, even though they were deprived of mothering, infant monkeys developed normally if they had sufficient playful contact

Affiliation:
The child's
emergence into
a social world

with other young monkeys during their "childhood" and "adolescence." Other researchers have discovered that third graders were very accurate (much more than their teachers) in identifying peers who were going to have psychiatric problems.[6] The peer group can be a sensitive and powerful teacher in children's lives.

Self-understanding by means of social comparison and confirmation is another important function of the peer group. In order to better understand their own skills or traits, children compare themselves to their peers. Am I really a fast runner? Am I tall? Will others listen to my ideas? Children are able to make decisions about themselves by contrasting what they do with the actions of their peers. Children are also likely to solicit comments about their behavior from others. Comments like, "You sure are a fast runner, Sarah!" and "Bill, you are my friend," are especially significant when children hear them from their peers. They will actually seek a comparison with and the confirmation of their peers to check the truth of what they believe and feel about themselves.

Children also seek a sense of *belonging* in their peer group. No matter where they are or how old they may be, children are drawn to each other. This recognition and acceptance is vitally necessary to facilitate their separation from adults. Shunning, a form of isolation in which a group pretends that one of its members does not exist, is one of the most powerful and bitter punishments a person can possibly experience. As Eric Fromm has stated, "Man finds his fulfillment and happiness only in relatedness to and solidarity with his fellow man."[7] This acceptance is important among children because they consider each other to be equals. Adults are too different, and too psychologically distant to satisfy children's needs for belonging. After all, a child's future is with the peer group.

Peer groups are important because they teach skills, provide support in identity formation and offer a sense of belonging. Thus, it is important to understand how these relationships begin and develop and how they change over time. According to Will Schutz, all social relationships develop in three stages. When two or more people encounter each other, the first issue that emerges is *inclusion*, the need to be recognized as a person by others and to be accepted into the group. The problem at this stage of a relationship is being "in or out." When children begin school, for example, inclusion or affiliation is the first social task they try to resolve. They ask themselves, "Who is in my class? What are their names? Will they appreciate what I do?" Children reveal their desire for inclusion by seeking attention.

Once children feel recognized and included, *control* issues will begin to appear. Children need to feel as though they have influence in their relationships and that others will listen to them and include them in their decision making. The problem at this stage of the relationship is "top or bottom." In regard to their school mates children may ask themselves, "Will they do what I want to do some of the time? Will someone try to boss me around? Will we be able to get along or will there be a lot of fighting?" Children reveal their desire for control when they confront their peers, when they give or are given orders, and when they offer to help another.

When children feel respected they can begin to develop social bonds which include *affection*, the need to feel loveable and loving and the need to develop strong emotional ties with others. The problem in this more advanced stage of relationships is "near or far." Children begin to develop these bonds of affection by sharing objects and information with each other, by telling each other their little secrets, and by making sacrifices for each other. What they want to know is, "Do my friends really like me? Are they happy when they're with me?"

Children's feelings about themselves have important effects on how successfully they deal with relationships. A feeling of personal *significance* is necessary for children to reach out to others with confidence; believing in their own *competence* enables them to resolve social problems; and feeling *loveable* makes affectionate ties more likely.

Affiliation is the first step in forming relationships. Children's views of friendship, how they actually imitate social contact with their peers, and how they make and keep friends help us understand the development of affiliation. The social/cognitive process of defining, sensing and problem solving apply to each of these three areas.

Children's *peer* relationships can be examined much more effectively by our educational programs than parent-child or sibling (brother-sister) associations. Children are present in the classroom and their peer relationships are of immediate importance. Because of this unique opportunity, school can be an excellent social setting where children can get to know themselves and others better.

Children's ideas about association

Every child has questions about approaching people. Are others safe or dangerous? Will they be fun to be with? Will they accept or ridicule me? A system of beliefs about people provides the answers to these questions and is a very useful tool which children can use to predict their relationships with each other. A child may observe a new child in his school and say to himself, "I don't know him—he looks mean so stay away!" Another child may see a police officer approach him and conclude, "Oh, a police officer! She's important so I have to use good manners." Other children might have radically different reactions to these same individuals because of their different assumptions about the nature of the other person. These *theories* about others are useful because children use them in guiding how they should respond and what they might expect in a social encounter. Every relationship children have begins with their image of who the other person is.

When they encounter strangers, children consciously or unconsciously calculate an *estimated relationship potential* (ERP) which is used to evaluate whether a relationship is possible and desirable.[8] These assessments of others are influenced by children's own degree of self-esteem and self-confidence as well as their views of the various social situations.

In their assessments of a social situation children evaluate both the social partner and the context of the encounter.[9] For *social partners* children may monitor others' physical characteristics, what they are doing, how they are feeling and what their role relationship may be (e.g., mother, father, brother, friend, doctor, stranger). In terms of the *context* of the encounter children consider the setting (e.g., school, home, park, doctor's office) and the occasion (e.g., birthday party, picnic, girl scout meeting).

Affiliation:
The child's
emergence into
124   a social world

SELF STUDY 12

Strangers

Take a few moments in a quiet place to think about your emotions and behavior when you encounter strangers. How do you respond to a group of strangers? How comfortable are you and what do you do? What kinds of thoughts run through your mind? Does the situation make any difference? Is there anything about your reactions to strangers you would like to change? Try to imagine a situation in which you respond ideally to strangers. How different is this ideal from what you really do?

How did you react to unfamiliar people when you were a child? Were you frightened of strange adults and other children, or were you confident when you met them? How did you typically respond when you were faced with a novel situation?

If you could go back into time, what would you want to say to this child who was once you? Imagine the conversation that might take place. Does it reveal anything about your attitudes toward affiliation?

Very young children initially react to only a few of these cues. They may respond only to physical characteristics. A toddler, for example, may run gleefully to a familiar male neighbor but hide behind his mother when a bearded stranger tries to strike up a conversation. As their social experiences continue these children are likely to become more conscious of others' behavior and feelings. For example, a child may try to approach and reassure a friend who is crying or may run away if another child shakes her fist in anger.

During the later preschool years children also begin to conform to social roles and the expected demands of the setting and occasion. For example, there may be an obvious difference in the way preschoolers and first graders relate to others at a birthday party and during a church service. Older children are more likely to recognize that different contexts make different demands on their behavior.

During the early grade school years, changes in cognitive development allow children to pay attention to and simultaneously evaluate multiple social cues.[10] Thus, a second grader might observe another child crying (cue 1) with his hands in his face (cue 2) as others are attempting to comfort him (cue 3) and conclude that this child does indeed feel sad. Another second grader may notice that although her teacher is smiling (cue 1) her hands are clenched (cue 2) and her voice has a sarcastic tone (cue 3). Because of the last two contradictory cues, this child may discount the obvious sign of happiness and decide that the teacher is actually angry. A younger child may focus exclusively on the smiling and misinterpret the teacher's real feelings. This shift in children's sensitivity to multiple cues has a significant effect on the way they relate to each other.

Children's ideas about friendship

Children's theories of human relationships include firm convictions about the nature of friendship. Children are, as Robert and Anne Selman describe them, "friendship philosophers." They have their ideas of who friends are, how friends are supposed to behave, and how friendships begin and end.

Researchers like Robert Selman, James Youniss, and William Damon have documented that children's reasoning about friendship is dramatically different from that of adults.[11] Children seem to have their own expectations and rules of friendship which make sense to them but may be different from the way adults think about friendship. If we want to help children with friendship-making skills, we can begin by trying to understand what they think of that relationship.

Robert and Anne Selman interviewed over 250 children and adults (from three to forty-five years of age) and identified five separate stages in the way children and adolescents think about friendship.[12] During the earlier stages children reveal a logic which closely parallels such social/cognitive skills as perspective taking (see pages 94-97). Although the ages are only rough guidelines, the first three stages help us understand how to be more effective in helping children develop friendship-making skills.

Friendship as momentary playmateship (three to seven years)

During their early years children initially view friends as interesting people who may live close to them or enjoy similar activities. Friends are valued for material resources or important physical skills, such as the ability to run fast or throw a ball. If you ask a young child what a friend is, he or she may mention someone who has interesting toys or is fun to play with. At this stage children have no concept of being attracted to another's stable personality or behavioral habits like friendliness or cheerfulness. Enjoyable social play is their primary concern.

Children cannot conceive of any psychological basis of friendship during this period because their perspective-taking skills are so limited. They are preoccupied with their own needs and beliefs and assume others want what they want. They also have a difficult time grasping other people's intentions. This may explain why play among friends during these early years may suddenly explode with conflict and just as easily resume its previous tranquility. At this stage children move to another activity or find a different toy, but they do not prolong a disagreement by brooding and nourishing the bitterness.

Friendship as one-way assistance (four to nine years)

In this stage children become more aware of the psychological and emotional benefits of friendship. They now view a friend as someone who will do what the other person wants. Their concept of friendship deals only with the needs and experience of one person in the relationship. Friends are considered worthwhile if they meet the other's wishes.

Affiliation: The child's emergence into a social world

Jason (five years old) responded to my questions regarding friendship and this interview illustrates the type of ideas children have at this stage.

INTERVIEW Jason, what is a friend? *Friends are one person who likes another person.* Do you have any friends? *Kathy — she invites me to her house, go to the park, eat lunch at her house.* How do you make friends? *When a new person lives in another house, you shake their hand and that will make you a friend.* How can you help a friend? *Asking if she could play outside.* What can happen to make your friend not a friend anymore? *If you don't shake their hand, if you get into a fight they won't be your friend either.* What kind of people make good friends? *People that be very nice to friends get the friends more often.* What does nice mean? *Nice means you are being good to each other.* How do people show they are friends? *Show by being good to their friend.*

In his description of friends, Jason recognizes that friendships can be beneficial. Note, however, that the direction of the friendship is from one person to the other. "One person likes another person," he points out. "She invites *me* to her house . . . you shake their hand." Jason is not clearly aware of the reciprocity in the relationship. He overlooks the more sophisticated conviction that friends benefit from *each other*, though he does point out that people get friends by being nice and that "nice" means people are being good to each other. This comment reveals that he is beginning to think of friendship as a rewarding twosome.

During this period children can differentiate between each others' perspectives, but they have a difficulty realizing that effective relationships involve give and take between two people. In their actual relationships they may be able to compromise in their play, but they experience difficulty in describing this social strategy.

Friendship as two-way assistance
(six to twelve years)

During this stage children think of friendship as a special relationship which should benefit both parties. They may insist that friends may drift apart if they do not respond to each other's interests.

This concern for the other's experience is due to a change in the way children think. They now may be concerned with making an impression in the minds of others regarding their worth as friends. In this interview Jenny (seven years old) comments about friendship and reveals an awareness of this exchange of benefits.

INTERVIEW Jenny, what are friends? *Two children who like each other a lot and play together.* What do they do? *Help each other.* How do people make friends? *Well, you find one kid that doesn't have anybody to play with, then you talk together, then you kind of join together.* Join? *They just get together.* What sorts of people make good friends? *People you can trust — you know — they can keep a secret or people won't run off with somebody else.* How do people show they are friends? *They protect you and you protect them.* What does that mean? *If one person started a fight and said something mean and then the other person starts defending and talking back for you.*"

Jenny's description of friendship puts emphasis on the responsibilities friends have for each other and the shared benefits of friendship. Friends "help each other," they "join together," and they "trust" and "protect" each other. By emphasizing the need for trust, Jenny is beginning to key on the psychological dimensions of friendship rather than just the observable or physical dimensions of earlier stages.

The limitation of this period is that children typically see friendship as meeting separate self-interests rather than mutual, shared goals. They do not yet have a clear idea that friendship is a collaboration, a relationship which simultaneously nurtures both parties.

In the last two friendship stages children are able to view friendship more objectively and consider the common interests between friends. Friendship may become more intimate as children describe such benefits as sharing feelings and secrets, talking about their problems, and offering helpful suggestions.

SELF STUDY 13

Three words describing friendship

Choose three words which best portray your concept of friendship. After doing so, reflect on the meaning these terms have for you. If possible, order them according to which is most important. Contrast these concepts with the types of ideas that children have about friendship described on pages 127-128. Do you remember how you felt and what you believed when you were a child? Have you changed your views since then?

Talk to at least two other people (children or adults) and ask them to identify their three words for friendship or to simply describe what it means to them. Are their views different from your own? If they are interested, share your ideas with them.

Where did you acquire your ideas about friendship? Did adults or peers teach you? Did you form them on your own in response to your experiences with friends?

Based on this analysis of your definition of friendship, what conclusions can you make about how teachers might respond to children's relationships with each other?

Developmental changes in concepts of friendship

Zick Rubin has identified three dimensions of social understanding which are gradually transformed as children progress along these stages of friendship.[13] As teachers, being aware of these dimensions can help us understand the role of friendship in children's lives.

First, children shift from a preoccupation with themselves to an awareness of the other person's thoughts and feelings. A three-year-old sees friendship as a means of self-gratification. A friend is someone who will give them toys to play with. Four or five years later, however, this same child is likely to insist that friends look out for each other's welfare. "We are friends," he may say, "because we both like to play baseball. We help each other learn how to play."

Second, children shift from a focus on observable or physical qualities to an awareness of their friends' more subtle psychological characteristics. A young child may describe his friend as having, "red hair, cowboy hat and boots, and a sandbox in his back yard." Later this description will include such behavior as, "He can be trusted. He's funny and smart."

Third, children shift from the view that friendships are brief interactions to a belief that these relationships will endure over time. Young children may be less selective in choosing friends and may make and break friendships more often than older children. The child who offers another a toy may become a "friend" immediately, but he may lose that favored status just as quickly if he refuses to share. Older children are more aware of the depth of social ties and are more likely to realize that friendship can survive disagreements and conflict.

CHILD STUDY 10

Images of friends

Select two or three children of different ages and record their responses to the following: (1) "Tell me about your friend" and (2) "What is special about you and your friend?" In the first response do children include descriptions of psychological characteristics like "He's smart" or "He's funny," or do they only use observable traits like "His name is John and he's big"? In the second response do children view their friendship as *one directional* (e.g., "He let's me play with his toys.") or *reciprocal* (e.g., "We have fun together.")? Are there any age differences? How do their responses compare with those of Jenny and Jason on pages 127-128? How do their views of friendship affect their actual relationships with others?

We cannot accelerate children's movement through these stages by trying to teach them how to think about friendship. They will mature in reasoning about friendship relations as changes in their cognitive abilities make it possible and as they gain more experience with their peers. However, by showing sensitivity to the way children view their associations with others, we are more likely to establish our own credibility and better understand how to be more effective in helping them in their struggles to become integrated into their social world.

Learning the rituals of social performance

Every social engagement makes three successive demands of children. Initially, they must gain access to the ongoing social activity of another. Next they must actually manage the engagement while it occurs, and finally they must learn to withdraw gracefully.

One of the greeting rituals we have in our society when familiar people pass each other is the sequence, "Hi, how are you? — I'm fine, how are you? — Fine, see you later." No matter how terrible either person feels, they are both likely to insist they are "fine." Instead of being a sincere request for revealing feelings this exchange is actually a greeting ritual.

The next time someone approaches you and says, "Hi, how are you?" do not answer the question (that is not really asked) but respond by simply saying, "Hi!" What will the other person do? Quite likely he or she will complete the ritual by saying, "Fine, thank you."

Make the opening moves of the "Hi!" ritual with children of various ages. At what age do children learn this habitual pattern? Do you think it will have any effect on children's attitude toward sharing feelings?

To successfully initiate relationships with others, children gradually learn to adopt what sociologist Erving Goffman calls *presentation* or *access rituals*.[14] Children use access rituals to gain entry into another's ongoing play. Young children between two- and four-years-old will typically try to gain entry by combinations of such nonverbal appeals as smiles and gestures, engaging in a similar activity, circling the other's play, being disruptive, or making a claim on the area. Older children may use words to gain involvement. For example, a child may approach another and ask, "What are you doing?" or "Can I play?"

William Corsaro observed that the most successful strategy employed by preschool children to gain access in others' play was to display a similar activity.[15] Thus, if one child is playing in the dress-up area another child may initiate contact by trying on clothes and setting a table. The second child would blend into the activity as it proceeded. The least successful response was being disruptive. Children who simply intrude into the ongoing play of others are not likely to be accepted.

Children who feel inadequate and are either rejected or overlooked by others do peculiar things just to get the attention of their peers. For example, one teacher recalled an unhappy second-grade schoolmate who gained instant notoriety by squeezing ink from his fountain pen into his mouth and eating dog biscuits. However, the applause he gained one moment was quickly replaced by contempt and ridicule from others. Even during the laughter, the other children realized that his clowning revealed a desperate effort to be recognized, and his unusual behavior only served to isolate him further from acceptance. In such circumstances children often sense that something is seriously wrong but lack the maturity to provide others with what they need.

CHILD STUDY 11

Rituals of engagement

Select two children from the same age group and observe how each gains access to interaction and how each makes a farewell when they separate. When your target children want to become involved in the play of others, how do they gain access? What do they say and do? How do others respond? Pay close attention to such signs as eye contact, body position, and hand movements that children might use to convey interest and acceptance. Similarly, what do these children say and do to indicate that they are no longer going to play? Are these rituals of engagement different from those you have observed in younger or older children?

From the same group of children choose either a popular or rejected child and compare their access and farewell styles with the two children you originally selected. How are they similar or different? Do you think teachers can influence the acquisition of these behaviors? If so, how would you go about organizing your program to accomplish this?

Children try to demonstrate through access rituals that they are interested in engagement and are worthwhile playmates. The ritual of displaying a similar activity may be successful because it accomplishes two tasks: (1) By doing something similar children demonstrate that they are interested in playing, and (2) they can prove their value by successfully engaging in that play. In using effective access rituals children make positive statements about both themselves and their peers.

Once they become involved, children must *manage* the ongoing interaction.[16] They must convey that what they are doing is playful. If they are playing a monster "chase and capture" game, for example, both children must agree that the chasing is only pretend. If the game becomes too real to the child being chased, he or she may become frightened. They also must agree on the theme of the play, the kind of action they are to portray. In the monster game, for example, one child becomes "the monster" while others are supposed to be frightened and run away.

Sometimes it is necessary to negotiate the theme. Is the person doing the chasing a "monster" or a "bad guy"? Does the action take place in the water or on land? What kind of props are needed? Is there more than one monster? Once the theme is selected, subtle rules must be followed. For example, if you are a "monster" you are supposed to growl and chase others, and if you catch someone you must let them escape after pretending to hurt them. Children who cannot maintain the distinction between play and reality, who disrupt play by making abrupt changes in play themes, or who cannot follow the rules will not be successful in maintaining social contact with peers.

Finally, children will gradually learn to use some form of farewell display to ease the transition from playing to not playing. Children use such farewell displays as waving goodby, kissing or hugging, or explaining why they have to leave. A child who must leave an activity may say something like, "Bye, I have to eat," while maintaining eye contact with the child who has the most significance for him or her. Some children have elaborate farewell displays involving a sequence of hugs, kisses, waves, and goodbys when their parents leave for work in the morning or when they leave for school. A farewell display allows children to demonstrate their interest and commitment and calls attention to the fact that there is a separation in the relationship. Children seek recognition by presenting access rituals when they begin their play with others and by offering farewell displays when they or others leave.

The genesis of social engagement

Children's peer relationships begin during infancy and gradually become more complex during their early years. Changes in their relationships are partly due to changes in the way they define others. As children learn to take others' perspectives and to understand the psychological basis of friendship, their methods of reaching out to others change similarly. As they grow older they may listen more, their friendships may last longer, and they may be more helpful to others. At each step of the way children must translate what they know into effective action.

The beginning of social contact

During the first year of life infants learn to become socially responsive in their relationship with others.[17] By two months of age children can differentiate between people and objects and by five weeks of age eye-to-eye contact elicits their smiles. Beginning at about four months children show attentive interest in another's cry and soon learn to smile and reach out to another in a nearby crib. Near the end of the first year, they begin to imitate each other.[18] For example, after watching another child scooping up sand at the beach, an infant may try to repeat those actions with his own toy shovel.

Infants' first encounters with each other are likely to be limited to mutual inspection or exploration.[19] Although they may be socially responsive to adults who know how to draw them into a social engagement, infants are unfamiliar with the give and take necessary for successful contact with their peers.[20] They may perceive other infants as fascinating toys. Their behavior is novel and their reactions to being pulled, poked, or pushed can be dramatically unpredictable.

Mueller and Lucas suggest that infants first peer social contacts are "object centered."[21] Most of their experience during their first year is with objects. Because they are more familiar and skillful with things than with people, their first social contacts may centered around toys. A group of one-year-olds, for example, may cluster around one child's toy, or they may engage in a similar activity with a toy of their own. This "parallel" play occasionally may be disrupted by a child who takes an interest in another's toy. Their preoccupation is more with the object than with the effects of their actions on each other.

During the first half of their second year, children demonstrate dramatic growth in

**Affiliation:
The child's
emergence into
132   a social world**

sensitivity to peer play and in ability to resolve peer problems. Toddlers are now able to engage in what Mueller and Lucas call "simple and complex interchanges."[22] Although during the previous period their emphasis was on things, children now demonstrate the ability to engage their peers in a sustained social interaction. Mueller and Lucas give the following example of this type of contact:

> Larry sits on the floor and Bernie turns and looks toward him. Bernie waves and says, "da," still looking at Larry. He repeats the vocalization three more times before Larry laughs. Bernie vocalizes again and Larry laughs again. Then the same sequence of one child saying, "da" and the other laughing is repeated twelve more times before Bernie turns away from Larry and walks off. Bernie and Larry become distracted at times during the interchange. Yet when this happens the partner reattracts the attention either by repeating his socially directed action or by modifying it, as when Bernie both waves and says "da," reengaging Larry.[23]

By waving and saying "da," Bernie (thirteen months) elicits a laugh from Larry (fifteen months). Larry's laughter encourages Bernie to repeat his action. There is a cycle of action-reactions which form the basis for their playful game. Both children share the responsibility for maintaining the interaction.

In the second half of the second year children begin to demonstrate "complementary interchanges."[24] During the previous period any contingent action would have been appropriate to maintain the interaction. Now children formalize their play by acting out certain roles and expecting certain roles to be fulfilled by others. They try to elicit responses from peers that are complementary to but different from their own actions. For example, two children may play a game in which one runs and the other pursues or one throws a ball while the other catches and throws it back. In the first **133** instance the one running away expects to be chased. No other response, such as laughing or showing a toy, will be as satisfying. In the second situation the one who throws the ball expects the other to catch and return it. If the receiver catches the ball and throws it in another direction or decides to keep it, the child who initiated the activity will be disappointed. In a complementary interchange each child expects the other to respond in a coordinated manner.

Toddlers are able to initiate these complementary interchanges only in their one-to-one (dyadic) play.[25] They lack the social/cognitive underpinnings and the experience to coordinate roles in a threesome. If more than two children are involved in play, the group will subdivide into dyads which are likely to change as the play session continues.

Barbara Davis Goldman and Hildy Ross obtained similar results in their examination of the structures of spontaneous game interactions among unacquainted toddlers.[26] They documented a variety of social skills children demonstrate in coordinating their play with others. *Alternation of turns* involves the ability to indicate to a partner that it is his or her time to act and to wait for the partner to start and complete that turn. *Nonliterality* means that toddlers are able to communicate through smiles, laughter, silliness, and other nonverbal messages that what they are doing is really only a playful game. Thus, when a child throws a ball to another and laughs, she may be trying to invite the other child to play. She is not really giving him the ball to keep. The *spontaneous creation of game content* is another skill which involves the ability of toddlers to select a theme or concept for their play. Thus, even unacquainted toddlers can spontaneously create games with such play equipment as balls and blocks, animated with their own vocalizations and body movements.

The research clearly indicates that even infants and toddlers are beginning to become skillful in their social involvement with peers. They are beginning to form ideas about play and about how others can become involved. They are learning to use their own sensitivity and imagination in maintaining play, and they are able to deal effectively with simple disruptions in their games. Although they are not able to describe their ideas about social engagement, infants and toddlers demonstrate by actions that they are social thinkers. In the remaining years before school children build on these foundations as they acquire even greater social maturity.

Expanding social relationships

During the years before grade school three trends emerge in the way children relate to each other. First, children become more sensitive to their partners. Second, they begin to use language more effectively in their interactions. Third, cooperative play increases as parallel play decreases.

Beginning at about two years of age, children gradually become more aware of their social partners. Although during their toddler years they could coordinate their activities with only one child at a time, children are now able to direct social acts to two children at once.[27] This is a significant step in social development because it increases the complexity of play and makes *group* interaction possible. Between three and five years children also are able to make adjustments in their behavior to better suit the age of the child with whom they are playing.[28] In mixed-age play younger children act slightly older, and older children act somewhat younger. As they play together both

**Affiliation:
The child's
emergence into
134   a social world**

the older and younger children strive for a more compatible common ground. For example, a three-year-old may become more verbal and demonstrate more self-control in her play with a five-year-old than what she would ordinarily do if she were with other three-year-olds. The five-year-old also changes his style of play by talking more simply and making the rules of play easier to understand for the younger child. By doing so, these children are able to involve each other in their play. The ability to orchestrate involvement with more than one peer and make changes in style of play to become more compatible with a peer demonstrates a remarkable sensitivity to a social partner.

CHILD STUDY 12

Play themes

Select two or three children of different ages and observe them during a period of time when they can play together freely. When they play cooperatively with one or more peers, determine what play theme or "focus" they have. For example, the theme may be:

Monster chase
Cowboys and indians
Hospital
Building with blocks
Dancing to music

The play theme is the shared emphasis of the activity, and all must agree to it in order to be accepted in play. How do children demonstrate that they are appropriately involved in the play theme? How do they show that they can do what others expect them to do? Are differences in the children's ability to cooperate in play due to age or individual background?

The growth of language skills during this period also increases the complexity of children's play.[29] The social play of infants and toddlers is limited to simple nonverbal behaviors like smiling, giving, receiving, and taking. These actions have a powerful impact on peers but, because of their ambiguity, can be misinterpreted. The addition of verbal skills changes the nature of children's interactions by making them more clearly defined. When children can talk about what they are doing, they can strengthen social bonds by using each others names and by commenting on what is happening as the interaction unfolds.

Mueller and his associates found that the period between two and one-half and three years of age is a time of rapid growth in spontaneous peer verbal interactions.[30] Children have to learn the skills necessary to carry on a conversation. They are gradually able to select message content more appropriate to the listener and to maintain eye contact when they speak. They also learn to listen and to watch speakers more often. Mueller concluded that *reply elicitation*, a speaker's ability to draw out some form of recognition by a listener, helps to sustain verbal exchanges. Children who fail to adjust the content of their conversations so they can be understood by another or who fail to maintain eye contact with another during conversations are likely to be spurned by their peers.

Children's relationships with their peer group also changes in the years before school. Parallel play, in which children play beside but not with each other, can be observed throughout the preschool period in two- to five-year-old children.[31] It predominates in the play of two-year-olds or younger three-year-olds and gradually decreases with age as it is replaced by cooperative play.

Sometime between the third and fourth year, as children become more involved in cooperative efforts, the nature of solitary play becomes more complex. During the toddler period children are confined to playing alone, playing next to someone, or interacting with a single peer. With the addition of cooperative group interaction, however, solitary play may occur for one of two reasons: (1) It may be a sign of independence and constructively active involvement or (2) it may reveal passive flight from any effort to make contact with peers.[32] Solitary play is not necessarily a sign of immaturity.

No matter how socially skillful they may be, children need a break from social involvement. Quiet contemplation and diligent work on a personal project are examples of worthwhile activities that require working alone. They provide an important contrast to the intensity of play with peers. Many children are happy to work at solitary activities. Others may be eager to be accepted by the group but are forced into solitary activities because no one will play with them.

From play group to clubs

The importance of the social group to individual children becomes even more critical during the early elementary school years. During the early grade school years children's relationships with their peers are influenced by changes in their cognitive development and in their attitudes toward the peer group. As their egocentrism diminishes, children become more self-conscious toward their peers. They are more aware now that others are thinking about them and evaluating what they do. Conformity is one strategy children use to gain approval from their peers. They may try to impress the group by the way they dress or behave. Children become more urgent in these efforts because of their greater awareness of how they and others think.

During this period the peer group gradually increases in size and status. Children move from parallel play to cooperative play in pairs, and then to involvement in small, informal groups which eventually become more cohesive or "official" in children's minds. Children may form "clubs" that have well-defined memberships and titles. These self-generated groups may not endure for long, but they do provide an excellent opportunity for children to practice leader and follower roles. They are formed because during this period children begin to perceive the group as a collective entity. They are not just friends to several individuals, but they *belong* to a group. Within this group children begin to maneuver for recognition and continued acceptance. Although its influence may be more predominant during adolescence the peer *group* begins its significant role in the lives of children sometime during the first several years of elementary school.

Affiliation:
The child's
emergence into
136   a social world

The significance of friendship

Young children may use the term *friend* to refer to any child they may enjoy playing with, but older children use the term to refer only to someone who has special significance. Adults may misinterpret young children's casual use of the word "friend" and conclude that they do not really form close attachments with others. Children do form strong emotional bonds with some of their peers, but they simply do not have the words to differentiate between playmates and real friends. Friendship is a special emotional attachment two people, adults or children, have for each other which promotes a continued association and the loss of which would produce distress. Playmates can be replaced, but friends cannot.

SELF STUDY 15

Your childhood friend

When you were five, six, or seven years old and someone asked who your "best friend" was, whom would you have mentioned? Can you picture this person? What she or he looked like? How did this person dress? Did she or he have any particular mannerisms you can recall?

What did this person have to offer you as a friend? What emotional need was fulfilled for you? What, if anything, could you put into a thank-you note if you could send one to this person now? What would you think he or she would write in the return note?

Remember the good times with this person . . . where you were, what you did . . . the sounds, sights, and smells associated with your play. In your imagination relive some of these experiences as vividly as you can. How do you feel?

What happened to the relationship? How did you feel about this change? Did your needs change or did you form a friendship with someone who met them even better?

Can this recollection of one of your early relationships help you relate to children more effectively as they experience the jubilance and misery of making and keeping friends?

The emphasis on *attachment* makes friendship difficult to assess. Most researchers have used sociometric techniques and observation to measure popularity or likeability, which are not necessarily the same as friendship. We can only assume that well-liked children are those who are able to make friends more quickly. Craig Perry has developed a sociometric technique which differentiates between different types of social status.[33] He asked four-year-old children to nominate peers that they like and do not like to be with. The *social impact* of a specific child could be measured by adding positive and negative votes they received from others. A high score indicated that a child was on the minds of many while a low score would mean that few, if any, peers thought of him or her. The *social preference* status for a child was measured by subtracting the negative from the positive votes they received.

In Perry's study, a high score meant that a child was liked and a low score meant the others would prefer not to play with him or her. Social impact and preference scores were combined to form four different types of status profiles (see Table 5.1). Children who were well liked and named by many were categorized as *popular*; those who were well liked but named by few peers were *amiable*; those who were

Table 5.1
Four categories of sociometric status

		Social impact	
		High	Low
Social Preference	High	Popular	Amiable
	Low	Rejected	Isolated

Affiliation:
The child's
emergence into
138   a social world

disliked and named by many were *rejects* while those who were disliked but named by only a few were *isolated*. Popular children were more likely to have many friends while amiable children were likely to have only a few. The process of differentiating between children on the basis of their being preferred and having an impact on others begins during late infancy.

SELF STUDY 16

Your early peer group

Your first peer group may have been composed of children in your neighborhood or classmates at school. Can you remember their names? What did they look like? How did they behave toward you? How did you feel about your involvement with this group?

How would you categorize the sociometric status of the members of this group and those who wanted to be included? During these early years who were the popular, amiable, rejected or isolated children with whom you came in contact (see pp. 138-139)? How would you rate yourself?

What happened to this group? What caused it to break apart? Can you remember how you felt about this change?

If you could go back in time and give the child you once were a message, what would you say? Is there any way of communicating this type of idea to children in your classroom?

By choosing playmates, children as young as eight to fourteen months of age begin to express their preference for others.[34] Preferred infants may be different from others in terms of a "personal style" which is more responsive and adaptive to their partners.[35] They may react more positively to another child's overtures and be less aggressive in their play. Research has also demonstrated that preferences for certain others continues in a moderately stable manner throughout the preschool years.[36]

Several research studies point out that children's style of play is different among friends than with non-friends or strangers. One-year-olds are more likely to engage in activities which involve proximity and touch with familiar, well liked peers than with strangers.[37] Among three-year-olds the presence of a familiar peer increases the amount of social interaction and the complexity of their play with toys.[38] Four-year-olds show more positive affect, are more animated in their behavior, and are more verbal when they play with a friend.[39] They also receive more positive reactions from those they like.[40] Seven- to eight-year-olds laugh, look, and smile more often at each other when they view a comedy film with friends.[41] The results of these studies clearly indicate that friendship influences the quality of play during early childhood.

Affiliation education

Many affiliation skills can be considered in our educational programs for young children. In Table 5.2, six possible skills are listed, and they are specific enough to give a sense of direction in teaching but sufficiently abstract to apply to a broad range of children. These skills are intended to be beginning points from which more specific goals for individual children can be developed. For example, a three-year-old is likely to be simpler in his or her description of human interaction than a child who is six years old.

Table 5.2
Summary of affiliation skills for children

Skill	Definition	Social/cognitive processes
1. Understanding the basics of human interaction.	1. The ability to identify behaviors approved or disapproved of by one's self and others; the ability to describe the causes, consequences, and alternative solutions to social isolation. *Examples*: A four-year-old says, "I think Sammy doesn't like it when I push him off his bike." A seven-year-old states, "When they won't let me play with them, I just find someone else to play with."	Defining *Rejection/acceptance* *Like/dislike* Sensing Deciding
2. Understanding the concept of family life.	2. The ability to identify the various types of families people live in and the significance they have for personal development. *Examples*: A four-year-old comments, "In Jamie's family there is a mommy, a brother, and a sister. In my family there is a grandma, a daddy, a mommy, and me." A five-year-old points out that, "My family is important because they take care of me and love me."	Defining *Families* *Neighborhoods* Deciding
3. Understanding the rudiments of friendship.	3. The ability to identify one's friends and the reasons for the attraction; the ability to describe qualities that promote friendship and reasons that friendship may end. *Examples*: A kindergartener points out that "Joanne is my friend because she invited me to her house." A seven-year-old concludes, "Laura used to be my friend but not any more. She took the money from our lemonade stand. I can't trust her any more."	Defining *Friends/enemies* Deciding
4. Eliciting and holding the attention of others in socially acceptable ways.	4. The ability to attract and hold the attention of another in an acceptable nonverbal or verbal manner. *Examples*: A four-year-old taps another child on the shoulder and asks her a question after she turns around. A five-year-old calls to another child, "Jamie, look at this. Do you like it?"	

Skill	Definition	Social/cognitive processes
5. Achieving social contact.	5. The ability to develop and maintain satisfactory and comfortable relations with others with respect to interaction and association. Ideally, children would interact widely and frequently with other children and take an active interest in their activities. On the other hand, they would also be comfortable away from interaction with others. This may involve participating in a group depending on their needs and preferences at a particular time. On an affective level these children would feel that they are worthwhile and significant. They are capable of being genuinely interested in others and confident that they will be included in other's activities.	Defining Sensing Deciding
6. Establishing significant, emotionally satisfying relationships with peers.	6. The ability to initiate and maintain satisfying friendships. Ideally, the child demonstrates the capacity for forming close relationships without overwhelming or being entraped by the other. What is significant is that the child can form relationships rather than acquire a large number of friends.	Defining Sensing Deciding

Our relationships with children

Helping children learn social skills, such as making friends, is a troublesome effort for many adults. Ultimately, every child is alone in the social arena. We can stand by the sidelines and cheer their efforts, but they must be the ones to act. By becoming too involved in manipulating a social situation, we take the risk of alienating children from their peers. Yet, by doing absolutely nothing for them we may contribute to their own confusion and sense of isolation. These two extremes can be avoided by becoming involved without being oppressive, and detached without being aloof.

First, we must recognize that there is a wide range of individual differences among children in their sociability. Some children are very outgoing and interested in frequent social contacts, whereas others are more shy, preferring the occasional company of a small number of friends. Suzanne was a shy child in preschool, and her socially outgoing parents were concerned about her lack of peer involvement. Suzanne was a delicate looking child who preferred quiet activities with a small number of children rather than very active, rough-and-tumble play. When her parents realized that her shyness was really just a style which best suited her own personality rather than a defect, they were more accepting and supportive of her relationships with her peers.

Second, we must recognize that fluctuations in the intensity of children's peer relationships are a part of a natural social rhythm of involvement and withdrawal. There are instances when children need to become involved with their peers; for example, they may want to observe others and test their own social problem-solving skills. During these occasions we may be surprised by the intensity of their reaction to rejection or the depth of their devotion to a friend. However, children may just as quickly reveal a need to withdraw from contact and be alone. These moments can be opportunities for heightened self-awareness and reflection which may later make their relationships with others even more satisfying. This social ebb and flow may occur from year to year or even day to day.

Third, we can talk with children to explore their ideas about association and friendship. By becoming more familiar with how children view their peers, we can more clearly understand their behavior. To illustrate, a newcomer to a school may withdraw from contact because she cannot predict what constitutes acceptable behavior by either the teacher or other children. By standing back and observing she may begin to recognize what is expected.[42] Her teacher might help by talking with her about her discomfort, by explaining the classroom limits, and by giving her time to blend into the play of others at her own pace.

In some instances we may have to gently confront a child's misconceptions and encourage him or her to consider other possibilities (see Table 5.3). We should remember, though, that many misconceptions are related to a child's developmental level. A preschooler who thinks egocentrically may believe that "a friend is a person who always does what I want." For a child who has a difficult time understanding the perspectives of others, this type of belief is not unusual. Regardless of their developmental level, though, we can help children examine their ideas. In this instance, if a four-year-old boy becomes angry when another does not give him a truck, we might engage him in a conversation similar to the following one:

CHILD: He's not my friend. He won't give me the truck.

TEACHER: Are friends always supposed to give you what you want?

CHILD: Yes! Give me that truck!

TEACHER: Are you her friend?

CHILD: Yes.

TEACHER: What does she want?

CHILD: The truck.

TEACHER: Maybe she thinks you are supposed to let her play with what she wants.

CHILD: I don't care. Give me the truck!

The teacher does not say that what the child thinks is wrong. Instead, she attempts to help him examine his own convictions about the matter and change his beliefs on the basis of his own conclusions. Although in this instance he apparently retains his self-serving belief, this four-year-old may begin to consider what his teacher said. Gradually these gentle confrontations may begin to dissolve the child's egocentrism, but we should not expect young children to acquire beliefs that are beyond their intellectual grasp. We may get them to parrot back what we say, but they won't really believe something until they are capable of understanding the issue.

Fourth, we can provide opportunities for children to become acquainted and to relate to each other. We can help children learn each other's names, backgrounds, likes, and dislikes. For example, during lunch a group of kindergarteners might begin to talk about what they like to eat. The teacher can take advantage of this situation by suggesting a game in which children try to identify the food preferences of others. As

Affiliation: The child's emergence into a social world

Table 5.3
Contrasting examples of irrational and rational beliefs about affiliation

Irrational beliefs		Rational beliefs
• I must be liked by everyone; if someone dislikes me then that means I am not OK.	vs.	• I am still OK even if some people dislike what I do.
• A friend is someone who always does what I want.	vs.	• Sometimes my friends do what I want; sometimes I do what they want.
• Other people are not OK; they are all going to hurt me.	vs.	• Some people are friendly and are nice to me; but some people are mean sometimes so I have to be careful of them.

far as their cognitive limitations will allow, children can be encouraged to talk about themselves and consider other's comments about them. Familiarity may strengthen children's bonds of friendship.

We can provide opportunities for children to relate to each other in an enjoyable, safe way, such as play with older and younger peers as well as with playmates of their own age. Research by Willard Hartup and his colleagues demonstrated that socially isolated preschoolers benefitted from one-on-one play with *younger* children. For example, a child who has poor social skills may not be as threatened by play with a younger child because it provides an opportunity to be socially outgoing more successfully than with children his or her own age. In Hartrup's study, when such children returned to their same-age peer group, their social activity was found to increase.[43]

Fifth, when children are rejected we can provide understanding and support. A child who has been shunned by his or her peers can experience a heartache that only loneliness can bring. To get the recognition they so desperately need, these children may turn to aggression, or they may protect themselves from painful rejection by withdrawing into their own protective shell. During these difficult moments we can reach out to children and offer encouragement and affection. This nurturance, however, should encourage children to resume their efforts to find a place among their peers rather than create a dependency on the teacher for attention.

After being rebuffed by a group of kindergarten peers, for example, Jason withdraws to sit alone near his locker. This rejection has been a recurring problem, and recently he has been complaining of stomachaches. When he sees what has happened, Jason's teacher quietly walks over and sits next to him. "It's difficult not having friends sometimes," he comments. Jason sighs and the teacher continues, "I remember when I was little and some boys called me names and wouldn't let me play with them. I remember how I felt then. I felt like crying." Jason begins to move closer and the teacher puts his arm around him. "Jason, I really like you. You give me good hugs, and I think you have neat ideas about insects, too. I think some of the children would like to see your bug collection if you bring it to school. Could you?" When Jason nods the teacher continues, "I think you can be a good friend to someone. You will find a friend if you try." This encounter illustrates the principle that support should encourage children to renew their efforts to make contact with peers. The emphasis in the teacher's comments was on the child's relationship with others.

Finally, we can recognize the value of classroom activities which bring the group together for an enjoyable experience. Storytelling, singing, lunch time, and games are examples of opportunities for children to become involved with each other. If these occasions become a regular and predictable part of a classroom program they will have a cohesive effect on the group.

Activities to promote affiliation

The following activities may be helpful to you as you design a program to nurture affiliation in children. Please review Tables 3.3 and 3.4 (pp. 53-54) before beginning.

---

58   Name Game (three years +)

Purpose   To help children achieve social contact by becoming more aware of each other's names. Key concept is *name*.

Setting   Community group arrangement

Materials   None

Activity   **1.** This activity involves chanting and associating group members with their names. The teacher begins by making the following chant and encouraging others to join in. In this example, the teacher's name is Ann and the first child to be selected is Sue.

Ann, Ann look at everyone—
Point to *Sue,* and then you're done.

2. Then, in this example, Sue becomes the subject and is asked to point to someone else selected by the teacher.

Sue, Sue look at everyone—
Point to *Bill,* and then you're done.

3. Bill then becomes the subject and the procedure continues until all children have been named. The last child to be named can be asked to point to the teacher to complete the activity.

Suggestion   This activity is especially useful early in the year when children are first getting to know each other.

59 **Name Fame** (three years +)

Purpose   To help children achieve social contact by becoming more aware of each other's names. Key concept is *name*.

Setting   Community group arrangement

Materials   None

Activity   **1.** This activity involves chanting and associating group members with their names. The teacher should move around the outside of the circle while the entire group chants:

Think real well
We hope we don't miss
Think real well
Now who is THIS?

2. Just before the word *this*, the teacher moves directly behind one of the children in the group. After the chant is finished the group shouts the child's name in unison. This procedure can be repeated until everyone is named.
3. Once they are familiar with the "rules" of the game, children can be selected to take turns moving around the circle.

Suggestion   This activity is less difficult than *Name Game* because the group, rather than a specific child, is asked to respond.

---

60 **Child in the Dell** (three years +)

Purpose   To help children achieve social contact by becoming more aware of each other's names.

Setting   Community group arrangement
Children standing in a circle.

Materials   None

Activity   **1.** This activity is patterned after the traditional "Farmer in the Dell" game with children's names substituted for *farmer, wife, nurse,* and so on.
2. The group forms a standing circle, and one child is selected to begin. This child goes to the center of the circle, and the others sing while they move in a circle around him or her. For example,

Sarah in the dell,
Sarah in the dell.
Hi ho the dairy-o,
Sarah in the dell.

3. The song continues in its familiar manner with the center child being asked to choose another child. For example,

Sarah picks Michael,
Sarah picks Michael.
Hi ho the dairy-o,
Sarah picks Michael.

4. The song continues until approximately one-half of the group is chosen. In the traditional manner the last child chosen is asked to stand alone while the others return to the group.

Tom stands alone,
Tom stands alone.
Hi ho the dairy-o,
Tom stands alone.

5. This activity can then be repeated with the other half of the group being named.

---

61 Name Chanting (three years +)

Purpose   To help children achieve social contact by becoming more aware of each other's names. Key concept is *name*.

Setting   Community group arrangement.

Materials   None

Activity   **1.** This activity can be used as an introduction to other activities or as a means for settling children down at the beginning of a group activity. Make up a brief rhyme for each child's name (nonsense rhymes are sufficient). For example:

Anne, Anne bought a pan.

Peter, Peter pumpkin eater.

Sarah, Sarah fe fo farah.

Bill, Bill climbed a hill.

2. Chant each rhyme twice and clap your hands to the beat of each syllable as it is spoken. For example:

Peter, Peter (four claps) pumpkin eater (four claps).

3. Look directly at the child whose name is being chanted. The speed of the chant and clapping can be varied. As children listen and clap in unison to the beat of each other's names, they also begin to develop a sense of community.

62

Double the Fun (Or How to Find a Partner) (three to four years +)

Purpose   To help children achieve social contact by forming partnerships. Key concept is *partner*. Many activities for children involve working in groups of two. If they are free to pick their own partner, those children who always choose each other will be limited in their opportunities to relate to others. On the other hand, if the teacher does the choosing some children may resent being told whom to be with. Two methods which enable children to find partners for an activity on a chance basis are described below.

Setting   Community or small group arrangement

Materials   One four-foot length of yarn for each pair of children (all same color)

Identical pairs of construction paper in various colors and shapes (one pair for each pair of children)

Activity   **1.** *Untangling yarn:* The four-foot lengths of yarn are arranged side by side and gathered up (by the teacher) so that all of the ends protrude about four inches from the teacher's hand. Each child then selects one end of a string, the teacher lets go, and each individual tries to find his or her partner at the other end of the string. The situation can be made more complicated by overlapping the yarn when it is first arranged.
2. *Matching shapes/colors:* Take each pair of shapes cut from construction paper and shuffle them with all other pairs. Distribute one to each child and, at a given signal, have the children look for the person who's shape matches theirs. This activity can be made more difficult by making the shapes more complicated.

63

Missing Person (four years +)

Purpose   To help children achieve social contact by becoming more aware of the presence of others in the group. Key concept is *group*.

Setting   Community group circle

Materials   One large bedsheet

Activity   **1.** Briefly discuss the idea that although sometimes people have problems with each other everyone in the *group* is important. Sometimes the group misses someone when he or she is not there. Going around the circle, identify who is (and is not) present. Tell the children that you would like them to do an activity with you in which someone in the group will hide and the rest will try to guess who is missing.
2. Take out the blanket. Tell the children that you will first ask them to close (or cover) their eyes. Then you will go around the inside of the circle

and tap someone on the shoulder. That person should open his or her eyes and crawl under the sheet. Explain that when the selected child gets under the sheet, you will ask everyone else to open their eyes and guess who is the missing person.

3. Begin the activity by crawling under the sheet yourself and allowing the children to identify you as the missing person. Following this warm-up, select children who are self-confident and are not likely to feel too uncomfortable under the sheet. This procedure may encourage less confident children to participate. If the group is unable to identify someone, ask the person under the sheet to say something. Children can use this clue to make their guesses. When children make a correct identification, show your approval by clapping and cheering their success.

Variation   The difficulty of this activity can be increased by putting two or more children under the sheet (probably no more than five). Children who are identified should remain under the sheet until all are named.

Suggestion   *Do not force* any child to go under the sheet if he or she is hesitant to do so. Be supportive and encouraging, but at all times respect the child's feelings.

    This activity should provide interesting feedback regarding the degree of awareness the group has for its members. Some children are, unfortunately, "missing" even though they are present in the group.

64

What You Wear (four years +)

Purpose   To help children achieve social contact by becoming more aware of each other's presence in the group. Key concepts are *individual* and *group*.

Setting   Community group arrangement

Materials   **None**

Activity   **1.** Talk with the children briefly about how important everyone, each *individual* person, is to the *group*. Point out that being noticed helps individuals feel comfortable with their group. Tell the children you have a "what you wear" game for them to play.

    2. Stand up and ask the children to take a good look at you because in a moment you are going where they cannot see you and change something that you are wearing. Tell them to remember as much as they can about you because when you return they will have to guess what is different. After leaving, alter something about your clothing. If the children are very young, do something obvious like taking your glasses or your shoes off. If they are older, do something more subtle like switching your watch to your other wrist, untying a shoe, or removing a small item of jewelry. Return to the children and have them guess what is different about you. Give them clues if they find the guessing too difficult.

**Affiliation:
The child's
emergence into
148 a social world**

3. Let other children take turns being the center of attention. You may have to help them select what to change.

Suggestion   This activity can be made more difficult by increasing the number of items that are changed or the number of children making changes.

---

65   People Memory (four years +)

Purpose   To help children achieve social contact by becoming more familiar with the characteristics of individual group members. Key concepts are *group* and *individual*.

Setting   Learning center arrangement

Materials   One picture of each child in the group (each one mounted on a sheet of construction paper)

Activity   **1.** Display all the pictures so the children at the learning center can examine them easily. One at a time, show the pictures and be certain that everyone can identify each child's picture. Discuss briefly the idea that all of these children are, as *individuals*, very important to the group.
2. Stack the sheets together so that no one can see the pictures. Tell the children that you are going to show them one of the pictures for a very short period of time. When you turn the picture over you will ask them to recall who they saw. Select one of the pictures, show it to the children for three to five seconds, and then turn it over. Ask the children to identify whom they saw.
3. Increase the number of picture sheets you show at one time to two, then to three, four, and finally five. When using more than one picture, the sheets should be turned over in the same order they were shown (or a cover sheet could be lifted and immediately put down).

Suggestion   To reduce the possibility of one or more children dominating responses, this activity can be done at a learning center with only one child at a time.

---

66   Who Is This? (three years +)

Purpose   To help children achieve social contact by becoming more familiar with the characteristics of individual group members. Key concepts are *group* and *individual*.

Setting   Community or small group or learning center arrangement

Materials   One picture of each child in the group (each one mounted on a separate sheet of construction paper)

149

Several "screens" cut from a piece of construction paper (see activity directions)

Activity   **1.** Make the screens by cutting holes in a piece of construction paper. A screen is then placed over a child's picture. The children are then asked to guess who the child is, examining only what they can see through the screen. Some examples of screens are shown below.

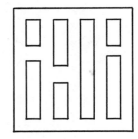

Suggestions   This activity can be made more difficult by placing more than one screen over a picture and removing them one by one as a child tries to guess who it is. If photos are not available, children can draw self-portraits.

---

67   Getting to Know You (four years +)

Purpose   To help children achieve social contact by becoming more aware of each other's presence in the group and more familiar with the characteristics of individual group members. Key concepts are *group* and *individual*.

Setting   Community group or learning center arrangement

Materials   Tape
Tape recorder

Activity   **1.** Over a period of several days (or even weeks) and in a quiet setting, tape a brief, private interview with each child in your group (about five minutes for each child). Ask such questions as:

> What is one of your favorite foods?
> What is one of your favorite toys?
> What is one of your special places to visit?
> Name something that gives you a sad (happy, angry, or scared) feeling?

Be sure not to mention the child's name in the interview. Once all of your interviews are completed select one of the discussions to play for the group.
2. Call the children together (or make the tape available at a learning center) and tell them you would like to play one of the interviews for them.

**Affiliation:
The child's
emergence into
150   a social world**

After the tape is played ask the children to identify who was interviewed. Also, go over the main points made in the interview. Emphasize the idea that now the group knows more about that child than they did before. Ask the children to identify other important comments the child made.

3. Introduce the other interviews on other days, focusing on no more than one on any particular day. Contrast (do not judge) each interview with those previously played. Emphasize the idea that differences in opinions and feelings are acceptable.

68

True for Who? (three years +)

Purpose   To help children achieve social contact by becoming more familiar with the characteristics of individual group members. Key concepts are *group* and *individual*.

Setting   Community group arrangement

Materials   **None**

Activity   **1.** Tell the children that you are thinking about someone in the group and you would like them to guess who it is. Also, in order to help them make a better guess, you would like to give them a clue.

2. To demonstrate the activity use yourself as the first person to be guessed. Your first clue might be something obvious to the children. For example, "I am thinking about someone who is tall and has a beard." Give additional clues if needed. To increase the level of difficulty, give clues that involved preferred activities such as "someone who likes to play with puppets" or nonphysical characteristics such as "someone who is a college teacher." Try to get various children to take your place as the individual who makes the selection and gives the clues.

Suggestions   You can encourage and allow children to play a type of "is it bigger than a breadbox" game in which those who are doing the guessing ask direct questions regarding the person they are trying to identify (e.g., "Is it someone who has red hair?").

This activity might be more effective if it is initiated after the children have been involved in several discussions of *Getting to Know You.*

69

Say Day (four years +)

Purpose   To help children achieve social contact by becoming more familiar with the characteristics of individual group members. Key concepts are *individual* and *group*.

Setting   Community group or learning center arrangement

Materials Tape recorder
Tape

Activity **1.** Take each child in the group separately to a quiet room to record his or her voice, asking each child to repeat the same sentence. When finished, play the tape to the group and encourage them to identify the child who is talking. Decrease the possibility of learning the names in order by skipping around on the tape. The playback unit can also be set up as a learning center for use with individuals or small groups.

2. The activity can be made more difficult by asking children to repeat only one word instead of a sentence or to make a very simple sound.

70 My Family (three years +)

Purpose To help children understand the concept of family life. Key concept is *family*.

Setting Community or small group arrangement

Materials Pictures of each child's family
Bulletin board space

Activity **1.** Contact parents directly or send notes home requesting pictures of everyone in each child's family (either individual or group pictures). Pictures of family members can be drawn by children who cannot get photographs.

2. Tape the pictures to a bulletin board or wall in clusters so that each child's family stands alone. After all the pictures have been put up, have a discussion about their families, the size, number of brothers and sisters, age differences, etc.

3. Discuss the special contributions each individual can make in his or her family. Try to convey the idea that children contribute to their family's well-being (e.g., by giving older members an opportunity to feel proud about their ability to teach and care for someone younger).

4. Discuss some of the important functions of families. For example, you might ask, "Why is your family important to you?" "What would it be like if you didn't have a family?" "Did you ever miss your family when you had to stay with someone else?"

71 Classmobile Pictures (three years +)

Purpose To help children achieve social contact by becoming more aware of their school group. Key concept is *group*.

Setting Community group arrangement

Materials One picture of each child and teacher in the group

Hole puncher

Various lengths of yarn, one for each picture

Coat hanger

Rubber cement

Activity **1.** Before the group actually meets, select pictures of similar sizes and glue them together. Punch a hole in the top of each picture or picture set. (Be sure the hole is centered.) Insert a single piece of yarn in this hole and tie securely. Also, hang the coat hanger from the ceiling where the group will meet.

2. Call the children together and briefly discuss the idea that they all belong to the same group. Tell them that you would like them to help you make a mobile to hang in the classroom for everyone to see. The mobile will be made of the pictures of themselves.

3. Take out the pictures and ask the group to name those you hold up. Than take each picture (or picture set) and tie them to the hanger. When finished, encourage the children to discuss the creation. Hang the mobile at a height and location which will enable all children to make a close examination.

Suggestion If photographs are not available the children can draw self-portraits. The teacher should draw pictures of those children who are unable or unwilling to make their own.

Instead of a mobile, the class can make a wall chart with the pictures.

---

72 Classy Tree (three years +)

Purpose To help children achieve social contact by becoming more aware of their social group. Key concepts are *group* and *individual*.

Setting Community group and learning center arrangement

Materials Several different colors of construction paper

Scissors

Crayons

String

Tape (or stapler)

Large branch

Bucket of sand

Activity **1.** Find a moderately large branch on the ground in a nearby wooded area (take the children with you, if possible). Strip all dead leaves from the branch and insert the base in a bucket of sand for support.

2. Gather the children together around the "tree," and ask them if they think anything is missing. Suggest they make some leaves for the tree and mention that these leaves can be very special because they could be cutouts of their hands. Explain that the tree is like their class *group* and that the leaves are all the *individuals* in the group. Ask the children to go to a nearby table where construction paper and other materials are available.

3. Trace around the children's hands, using as many colors of construction paper as possible. Have each child write his or her name on the "hand," and tape a piece of string on the middle finger of each cutout. The children can then bring their "hands" over to the tree and, with the teacher's help, tie them to the branches. Gather everyone around the tree again to admire the group creation and to determine who belongs to each of the hands.

Suggestion In one variation of this activity a tree is painted on a large piece of butcher paper which is then taped on a wall or a bulletin board. Children can then put their hands in finger paint (spread on a sheet of fingerpainting paper) and leave their hand prints as leaves on the tree.

73

Secret Friends (four years +)

Purpose To help children establish significant, emotionally satisfying relationships with others by developing friendships. Key concept is *friend*.

Setting Community group and learning center arrangement

Materials Paper
Crayons
Paper bag
A sheet of paper for each child (with his or her name written on it)
Envelopes or folders

Activity **1.** Tell the children that you have an activity in which they each draw a picture for a "secret friend." Briefly discuss the concept of *friends* and the idea of keeping a secret.

2. Place the sheets of paper with the names of the children into the bag. Have each child draw a name. (The teacher can whisper the name of the child.) Emphasize the idea that the children should not tell the name of their secret friend.

3. Tell the children that you would like them to draw a friendly picture of any kind for their secret friend. They will have an opportunity to exchange drawings later. Ask the children to move to nearby tables where crayons and paper will be available. As children finish, place their artwork in individual folders or envelopes with their names on the outside. Be sure the slip of paper with the name of the secret friend is placed inside.

**Affiliation:
The child's
emergence into
154   a social world**

4. As the day progresses talk about friends, being kind, and keeping secrets. At a convenient time ask the group to reconvene and form a circle. Move clockwise around the group and ask each child to take the drawing from the envelope and give it to his or her secret friend. Discuss the concept of friendship and the idea of making new friends.

Suggestion   When this activity was done with a group of four-year-olds, one child did not want a secret friend. He wanted to draw a picture for a specific friend. After briefly talking to him about the fact that someone in the group needed him to be a secret friend, he was allowed to draw two pictures.

Some children may not want to choose the "bully" or some other disfavored child. If this occurs, the teacher should choose the neglected child as his or her secret friend. During the final part of the group activity, discuss the possibility that ". . . sometimes people do not want others for friends. I wonder why? Why should a child say to another child, 'No, I don't want you to be my friend!'?" Do not hide antagonisms in the group, but try not to alienate anyone either.

74

Win In (four years +)

Purpose   To help children develop an understanding of social isolation and achieve social contact by asserting themselves within the group. Key concepts are *individual, group,* and *rejection*.

Setting   Community group arrangement preferably in a safe outdoor area

Materials   **None**

Activity   **1.** This activity involves acting out or role playing responses to problems related to social exclusion. Ask the children to form a circle, and lead a brief discussion about how someone may feel if he or she is not allowed to join a group. Tell the children that you have a game in which they will have a chance to try to get into the group. In this game, the group makes a circle, and those wanting to get in have to break through the circle to get inside. Ask for someone to volunteer to get into the group.

2. Ask everyone to stand and hold hands while facing the inside of the circle. The child who wants to get into the circle stands outside. The teacher could say something like, "OK, now you try to get into our circle. Although we will try to keep you out, please do not hurt anyone when you try to break through. If you need help getting in you can ask someone to work with you." The circle can then begin to move slowly while the group chants:

Hello there, please don't pout
Though we'll try to keep you out.
Do your best to get in
'Cause when you do you win.

3. Repeat the chant until the "excluded" person gets through. Ask for others who want to try. To reduce the time involved, more than one child can try to break in at the same time.

Suggestion This activity is symbolic of the kind of effort an individual must make to break into a group which excludes him or her. *Do not force* any child to participate. The purpose of the activity is to encourage social involvement and not to reward or encourage exclusion.

---

75 Out Rout (four years +)

Purpose To help children achieve social contact by asserting themselves with the group. Key concepts are *individual, group, friends, alone,* and *together.*

Setting Community group arrangement preferably in a safe outdoor area

Materials **None**

Activity **1.** This activity involves acting out or role playing responses to problems related to social entrapment. Children who are popular are sometimes "trapped" by their admirers. They may find it difficult to engage in solitary activities and become tired of continually adjusting to the needs and demands of others.

2. Ask the children to form a circle and begin a brief discussion of *friends*. Try to introduce the idea that although sometimes it is great to be with friends, *individuals* in the *group* often would prefer to be *alone* too. Tell the children that in this activity they will have the opportunity to get out of a group. To do this, the group will make a circle, and the person who wants to get out will have to break out from the inside. Ask for someone to volunteer to break out of the group.

3. The group should then stand and circle the volunteer. The teacher should then say something like, "OK, now you try to get out of the circle. Although we will try to keep you in please do not hurt anyone when you try to break through. If you need help getting out you can ask someone to help you." The circle can then begin to move slowly around the middle child while chanting:

Hello there! Would you like to win?
We'll try our best to keep you in.
Get out, get out, get out right now.
How to get out? You'll find out how.

Repeat the chant until the person in the center of the circle breaks out. Cheer them on! Ask if anyone else would like to try. To reduce the time involved, more than one child can try to get out at the same time.

Affiliation:
The child's
emergence into
a social world

156

4. When a child breaks out he or she can immediately join the circle and another child can have a turn. If a child has difficulty breaking out, ask him or her to select someone to help or offer your own assistance. When finished have the group applaud everyone's effort.

References for affiliation

Goffman, E. *The Presentation of Self in Everyday Life.* Garden City: Doubleday and Co., 1959.

Rubin, Z. *Children's Friendships.* Cambridge, Mass.: Harvard University Press, 1980.

Zimbardo, P. G. *Shyness.* New York: Jove/HBJ Books, 1977 (see pp. 81-107).

Chapter Six
Conflict resolution and cooperation:
The child's pursuit of influence

Five-year-old Paul, struggling to make a tinker toy truck, is totally absorbed in his activity. He is excited about completing his task, but just as he puts two critical pieces together his older sister arrives, grabs his arm, and tries to pull him away from his project. "Stop it, Sharon!" he shouts, but his sister continues with her teasing. Paul demands even louder, "I said *Stop it, Sharon! Stop it!* You're ruining my truck!" Following this outburst, Sharon stops pushing and pulling, looks at her brother with a grin, and runs from the room.

During the bus ride home from second grade, Sarah turns to a friend and says, "Michelle, can you come over to my house and play? I have a new music box. I want to show it to you." Michelle nods affirmatively and says, "Yea! I want one, too." Sarah then responds, "Ask your Mom when you get home and come over right away, OK?"

What do these two situations have in common? In both circumstances the children successfully established their influence in a social encounter. Paul was able to stop his sister's playful interference, and Sarah convinced her friend to visit her home. To some extent each child made an effort to control the behavior of another. This desire for social influence is an important element in children's relationships.

A sense of affiliation helps children feel recognized as worthwhile and significant individuals, and once recognition is gained children will pursue *influence* in their relationships. When children have influence, others will listen, respond to what they say, and involve them in decision making. Influence can give children a sense of power for influencing events which shape their lives.

Social influence and competence

Will Schutz has suggested that relationships develop progressively along a continuum from inclusion, to control, and finally to affection.[1] Control, or social power emerges only after the affiliation or inclusion issue is satisfactorily resolved. An acceptable balance of control is necessary before a relationship can progress toward affection.

Schutz believes that a central issue affecting control is an individual's feeling of self-competence.[2] Children who feel incompetent or incapable of influencing others will resort to extremes in control behavior. They may shrink from any responsibility and remain exclusively in subordinate relationships to others, or they may attempt to dominate others and assume more responsibility and independence than appropriate. Thus, children who cannot make decisions, who constantly fight, and who consistently order other children around, may be doing so because of their own sense of powerlessness.

On the other hand, children who believe in their own competence are more confident of their decision-making ability and are not overwhelmed by fears of helplessness or stupidity. They may also feel no need to withdraw from responsibility or to dominate others. Depending on the circumstances, they are comfortable in either leader or follower roles. For example, a child who believes in her own competence will be comfortable showing a friend how to build with tools and will just as easily follow another's directions in playing a game. Children who believe in themselves are able to be democratic in their use of influence.

Children's attempts to influence or control others will inevitably clash with the intentions of their peers and adults. For example, a child may refuse to go to bed, but his parents insist that he do so. Another may want to play with the truck that her friend is using, and two sisters may disagree over the selection of a television program. In each of these situations a conflict emerges because of the opposition of wills.

For children who are attempting to resolve control issues in their relationships with others, conflict is not only inevitable but necessary. According to Piaget, conflict with peers contributes to diminished egocentric thinking.[3] Disagreements can force children to reexamine their own ideas in light of the viewpoints of others. Through repeated disagreements with others, children may eventually discover that not everyone thinks as they do, that others often have quite different ideas and goals. Children who are prevented from engaging in conflict may remain egocentric and insensitive to the perspectives of others because they do not have to resolve the differences.

Conflict can also strengthen the emotional ties between people. Disagreements are opportunities to be understood and to understand another's perspective. If those in conflict stand up for their ideas without ignoring or harming the other person, mutual respect and close, affectionate ties become possible.[4] Feelings of love and aggressiveness are not necessarily contradictory. Even close friends will have their differences, but over time they can begin to accommodate to each others perspectives.

From violence to cooperation: the use and abuse of influence

The pursuit of social influence can be expressed in two ways. First, influence is expressed in relationships. Children use their emerging sense of power and competence to make contact with others. Influence in such relationships can occur along a continuum from the "*power-to-be*," a basic will to live, to *violence*. Second, influence is exerted in the pursuit of goals. Children use their power and energy to get what they want. Achievement influence can occur along a continuum from *cooperative helpfulness* to *competitive rivalry*.

Power: from being to violence

In his book, *Power and Innocence*, Rollo May reflects on the constructive and destructive uses of power in human relationships.[5] May believes that power is energy, fortitude, and strength of will rather than force and domination alone. He suggests that there are five levels of power, gradually increasing in force, which may emerge in our relationships: the "power-to-be," self-affirmation, self-assertion, aggression, and violence.

The *power-to-be* refers to the strength of will necessary to maintain life itself. Every living thing needs this power to maintain its very existence. This life force is reflected in the energy of an infant's determined crying and in the emerging curiosity of young children as they explore their surroundings and learn new skills. The power-to-be is evident in all children who celebrate life by playing, exploring, and investigating everything they possibly can. When this energy and interest in life is missing children may become listless and withdrawn like the children Rene Spitz once observed in an orphanage.[6]

The second level of power described by May is *self-affirmation*, a ". . .quiet undramatic form of self-belief. It arises from an original feeling of worth imparted to the infant through the love of a parent or parents in the early months, and it shows itself later on in life as a sense of dignity."[7] Dignity means that we believe in our own intrinsic worth, that we can stand up and say, "This is who I am and I am OK." For example, a young child who bursts into the kitchen shouting, "Mommy, Mommy, *see me, see me, see me* jump! Look!" is affirming his worth and self-confidence. Children demonstrate self-affirmation by showing pride in what they do and accepting their limitations.

When self-affirmation is insufficient to gain influence, *self-assertiveness* emerges. Self-assertiveness is an active reaching out to achieve a goal, a way of calling out to others and *demanding* attention. Assertiveness is speaking up for oneself. Children demonstrate self-assertiveness when they say "No!" and when they make requests and offer suggestions.

Assertiveness has a positive orientation. By being assertive, children reveal their priorities and demonstrate their own self-respect.[8] When a six-year-old says, "*I* want to ride my bike around the block. I can do it!" she is standing up for her own self-belief and clearly advocating a specific action. Unlike aggression, she is not directly trying to intervene in another's priorities or change another's behavior.

Select two children from the same age group and have them participate as a pair in Activity 94, Won or Two (p. 194)? Record their reactions to the task and how they proceed to solve the problem. Who took the initiative? How assertive (e.g., "I want that.") or aggressive (e.g., "You give that to me!") were they? Did they use competitive or cooperative approaches to solving the problem? Were both parties satisfied? If not, put another item in the bowl and give them another chance. What happens then?

Do their responses in this situation reveal how these children typically use influence in their relationships? If possible, observe their social play and record any incidents of affirmative, assertive, and aggressive behavior. If you were their teacher would you like to see any changes in their influence style? If so, what kinds of goals would you set and how would you go about changing them?

The fourth level of power, *aggression*, can emerge when neither self-affirmation nor self-assertiveness is successful. For example, a child who is physically threatened by a peer may assertively insist that she does not want to fight, but if attacked she may aggressively reach out and push the other away. Aggression is confrontation, ". . .a moving out, a thrust toward the person or thing seen as the adversary. Its aim is to cause a shift in power for the interests of one's self or what one is devoted to. Aggression is the action that moves into another's territory to accomplish a restructuring of power."[9] With aggression, conflict emerges in an overt and direct manner.

May believes that aggression can be constructive. One child, for example, may actively try to break through another's passive barrier to form a relationship, and another may try to defend herself when attacked. A child who speaks louder to get others' attention and one who stops two peers from fighting are additional examples of constructive aggression. In these instances aggression is used courageously and compassionately to bring about positive changes.

Terry Orlick has identified four types of aggression: accidental, instrumental, expressive, and destructive.[10] *Accidental* aggression is unintentional. For example, a child twirling around in dance may may accidentally hit another or knock over another's block structure. *Instrumental* aggression is goal oriented because the objective is primarily to achieve a goal rather than to hurt another. A toddler may push another child to get a toy but have no intention of actually harming his playmate. *Expressive* aggression is self-oriented. The act of interference is pleasurable rather than the outcome. A child, for example, may knock down another's block tower to experience the actual pleasure of a well-placed kick. In a play fighting situation a child may toss a playmate to the ground simply to experience the pleasure of a "good" toss. *Destructive* aggression is an antihuman effort to actively or passively inflict harm on another. Satisfaction is experienced because of the other's physical or psychological pain. A child may, for example, push over another's tower to see him cry or another may steal a peer's toy in order to cause him sadness. Another type of aggression that can be added to these four is *defensive* aggression, a self-protective response to perceived threat or intentional frustration.[11] A child pushing away her attacker is demonstrating this form of aggressive behavior.

Because of these intentional differences, aggression can be misinterpreted easily. A parent may see a child responding defensively and interpret his behavior as destructive. A child may experience another's accidental aggression and respond as though it were intentionally destructive. These misunderstandings, to some extent, may be due to our inability to discriminate among the various forms of aggression.

May suggests that in our culture we have overlooked the positive aspects of aggression and emphasized the negative aspects. ". . .we have been terrified of aggression, and we assume—delusion though it is—that we can better control it if we center all our attention on its destructive aspects as though that's all there is."[12] Our wish to exclude any form of aggression may foster such unreasonable messages as "Nice people don't fight."[13] This illusion of innocence is dangerous because it may actually nourish violence.

May's primary thesis in *Power and Innocence* is that the roots of *violence* are found in the conscious denial of our own power and the pseudoinnocence that follows. Powerlessness is the source of violence. Power is not the same as force or competition—it is the ability to make a difference in our own self-realization. When we fail to gain influence through self-affirmation, self-assertiveness, and aggression, we may mask our weakness by the pseudoinnocent claim that power is insignificant but then resort to active or passive violence to establish influence.

If we continually frustrate children's desire for influence, we may unwittingly contribute to the very expression and acceptance of violence which we are trying to prevent. As May states, "As we make people powerless, we promote their violence rather than its control. Deeds of violence in our society are performed largely by those who are trying to establish their self-esteem, to defend their self-image, and to demonstrate that they, too, are significant."[14] If we celebrate with children their own love of life, accept their self-affirmation, and help them learn how to be assertive and deal with aggression, we may contribute to their self-belief and reduce their need to resort to violence.

Power: from cooperation to competition

In addition to viewing power as influence in relationships, we can examine how it emerges in the way children try to achieve their goals. Strategies for achieving power and influence can occur along a continuum of cooperation to competition.

Make arrangements to have a group of children play a traditional game of musical chairs. Observe them and record their reactions to the game. Do not forget to include the children who must drop out. What is your impression of the mood and intensity of the group as a whole?

Immediately afterwards, play a game of Cooperative Musical Chairs (Activity 89, p. 191). What changes do you observe in the group with this game? Do the children act differently? Is the mood and intensity different for the second game? Which did you enjoy more?

What do children learn from participating in these activities? What is the most central idea being transmitted by the game? Does each have its advantages and disadvantages?

Terry Orlick has identified six variations of the cooperation-competitive theme: Cooperative helpfulness, noncompetitive cooperation, cooperative competition, individualism, competitive competition, and competitive rivalry.[15]

Cooperative helpfulness is an altruistic orientation toward helping others achieve their goals. A child who retrieves a toy for a friend who cannot reach it himself is demonstrating this type of power.

Noncompetitive cooperation is a collaborative effort which involves working together to achieve common goals. Two children who cooperate to build a sand castle at the beach are demonstrating this form of influence.

Cooperative competition means that two or more individuals are pursuing a similar competitive goal but show concern and support for each other's efforts. Competition in this sense may enhance performance because those involved urge each other to do better and praise their accomplishments. Two small groups of children playing a lively game of "Red rover, red rover" and cheering each other on demonstrate this "caring" form of competition.

Individualism is a self-oriented pursuit of an individual goal. The emphasis is on personal accomplishment without reference to others. A child who works alone at a puzzle and refrains from comparing her performance to that of others is emphasizing individualism rather than interpersonal competition or cooperation.

Competitive competition emphasizes goal achievements without regard to the welfare of others. Winners are clearly rewarded while losers are considered failures. Concern for self dominates and respect for competitors is overlooked. A group of children playing a game of musical chairs, in which success is possible only when someone loses and is forced to drop out, is an example of this noncaring competition.

Competitive rivalry is a destructive form of winning in which satisfaction is the result of denying others their goals. A child who resorts to this type of behavior finds pleasure in another's loss. Under these circumstances an older child may steal another's project simply to prevent her from winning a ribbon at the county fair, or an adolescent may let the air out of a classmate's tires immediately before his big date. Young children are

not likely to engage in competitive rivalry because they lack the perspective-taking skills necessary to envision how to interfere in another's goals.

Orlick's differentiation between cooperative and competitive competition may be one of the more significant aspects of this continuum. When we think of competition among children, we must consider *how* they are relating to each other. Are they showing support and expressing pride in each other's accomplishments, or are many of their efforts directed toward belittling or humiliating their opponents? Competition is not necessarily bad, but what is important is the way we encourage children to relate to each other as they challenge their skills.

Defining the use of power and influence

Children's ideas about power and its limitations can affect the way they relate to others. For example, if violence is the only alternative children can envision to resolve a conflict, then brute force can be expected when problems occur in their relationships. If they believe that everyone else is out to shame and defeat them, they may try to reach their goals by becoming intensely competitive or by withdrawing to avoid conflict.

But others have tender skin:
The child as a philosopher of power

Jason and Jenny were asked how they might go about resolving conflict with another in four different situations. In the first two circumstances they were asked how they would respond to another's aggressive interference, and in the last two situations they described their reactions to a competitive challenge.

The Block Tower
JASON (five years)

Jason, let's say you're building a tower with blocks and someone comes over and knocks it down. What would you do? *I'd go tell their parents.* What do you think would happen then? *He'd be sitting in the room.* What if he knocked them down again? *He would stay in for the whole day.* What would you do if his mommy and daddy did not do anything, and then he knocked down your blocks again? *Oh, I'd take all of my blocks back inside, then I could build my building inside instead of outside.* Would you say anything to the person who knocked them down? *I just wouldn't pay attention to him.*

JENNY (seven years)

Jenny, let's say you're building a tower with some blocks and somebody comes up to them and knocks them down. What do you think you would do? *I'd yell "Stop it!" and then go tell my mother and father what they did.* What else could you do, something different? *Well, I could just run ahead of him and tell his mother and father. But that would be tattling!* What would be something different? You could think of something nice or something not nice. . .what could you do? *If he was bigger it wouldn't be very wise to do something not nice.* What would happen then? *He could beat me up, that's easy.* What if he was smaller than you? *If he was smaller than me I'd tell him not to do it* again. What would happen if you hit him? *You'd probably get into trouble. . .I don't dare hit anybody smaller than me. . .because they have tender skin. Little children can get hurt easier.*

The Push
JASON

Jason, let's say you are walking outside, and there are no grown-ups around. Someone comes up behind you and pushes you. What would you do? *I'd tell their parents.* Can you think of something different you could do? *Oh, I would just go somewhere else. . .or I could turn to them and say, "Stop pushing me."* What do you think would happen if you hit them? *He'd hit me back.* And then what would happen? *We'd start a fight. . .I don't like fights.*

JENNY

Jenny, what if you are playing outside, there are no grown-ups around, and someone pushes you from behind, what would you do? *Go after his parents, that's what I would do! It's better than hitting him. That would solve the problem.* What if *you* wanted to solve the problem. . .what would you do? *Walk away from him.* What else could you do? *Plop "dead" and pull out his feet, pull his feet down.* What would happen if you hit him? *I'd get into trouble, most likely.*

The Argument
JASON

Jason, let's say you and a friend are having an argument over playing with a toy. What would be a way you might solve the problem? *What toy was it?* Oh, you think of one. *I don't know.* Let's say you're arguing over a hat. *One of those kind of army helmets. And I think maybe whose ever toy that was, he could play with his toy and the other boy could get his own toy. Or they could share it—why don't they share it?* How would they do that? *Well, if there was two men, he might think of another person who has the toy—maybe he could tell the other person, "I could get another truck, another thing and they could play together."* Can you think of another way they could solve this problem? *Nope.*

JENNY

Jenny, let's say you and one of your friends are having an argument about one of your toys. How would you solve that problem? *I'd solve it by telling her "Go get an alarm clock—if you don't have one I'll go get one—and we can set you for half an hour, then I can have half an hour."* That's one idea. Can you give me another idea about solving the problem? *We could take the stick like this [motions as though gripping a stick] then whoever got to the top first would win the toy to play with.* What would be another way? *Go get a second best toy for the other person to play with. If they didn't want that then they could have just gone home and bring back one of their toys.* Can you think of another idea? *Nope.*

The Race
JASON

Jason, let's say you are running a race with one other child and the prize is a toy space ship. Who would win? *How old is he?* Same age as you. *I should win.* Why? *That's tough, 'cause if the boy has been in lots of races that wouldn't be fair to me—he would have lots of toys.* Is he a new person or an old person; he lived here for long? Let's say he's a new person. *Let him win.* Why? *'Cause then he could play with his new toy with the children that didn't go in the race.* How would you feel? *Sad.* Would we change it if I win? What would happen? *He'd feel sad. . .if it was a tie what could we do with the prize?* What do you think? *The other person could get another's toy, 'cause I would let him get another toy and I would have the toy space ship.* What if he has no other toys? *Well, I could trade all of my space ship things so I could have another one.* Trade with whom? *Trade with the person who lost. . .he'd get my other space ship toys.*

JENNY

Jenny, let's say you're in a race with another child and the prize is something you both want. What do you think that would be? *A new bicycle!* What would happen if you were in that race? *If I was in a race I would have two prizes, a new bicycle for first prize and a new doll house for second prize . . . because maybe the person I was racing against really wanted a new doll house and I wanted a new bicycle so we could both get what we really wanted.* Let's say in this race there is only the bicycle. What would happen? Who should win? *Whoever wanted the bicycle most.* Let's say you won. How would the other person feel? *Sad.* Would you do anything? *We would take turns riding the bicycle until it was time for her to go home . . . unless it was Diane. I would be glad if she's sad!* Why? *Because she's so bossy.* What would happen if the other person won? *Probably ride it home.* How would you feel? *Maybe lonely and sad . . . and embarrassed.*

Of course, not all five- and seven-year-olds are the same as Jason and Jenny, so we cannot say all children would respond as they do. Also, ideas expressed to an adult may be quite different from the ideas that occur to these children during actual conflict with another. Despite these limitations their responses do reveal some interesting, though subjective, views about influence.

In the first two situations, "The Block Tower" and "The Push," both Jenny and Jason mentioned adult intervention as a prominent solution to the problem. Jenny, however, expressed some reservation in approaching an adult for help since ". . . that would be tattling!" Both children gave strong disapproval to physically aggressive or violent responses to the conflict, although to what extent this response was made to elicit adult approval is not known. In addition, both children completely overlooked the motive of the person starting the conflict and appeared to assume the act was intentional.

The most prominent difference between Jenny and Jason in these situations was in the alternatives they gave other than requesting adult help. Jason preferred to avoid the problem by taking his blocks to another area and ignoring the provocation. As an afterthought in the push situation he identified a verbally assertive alternative, "Stop pushing me." On the other hand, Jenny's style was more assertive, "I'd yell, 'Stop it!'. . . I'd tell him not to do it again . . . Plop dead and pull out his feet." She also mentioned withdrawal as an alternative in the push situation, however. This difference in preference for either withdrawal or aggression appears to carry over to Jason's and Jenny's peer relationships. Jason typically avoids serious conflict while Jenny rarely retreats from a confrontation.

Jason and Jenny described their ideas about cooperation and competition in "The Argument" and "The Race." Both children were very concerned about the reactions of another child to being deprived of a toy or losing a race. Their ideas for resolving this conflict were primarily cooperative. Because of the other person's anticipated distress, each wanted to establish a reasonable form of equity in the situation. Jason's suggestions included sharing, getting another toy, and even giving away some of his own toys to the loser in the event he won. Jenny suggested sharing by time, resorting to chance, and obtaining another toy as ways to resolve the conflict. In the race situation she suggested that *two* toys be given away so that both she and the other child could be winners, "so we both could get what we wanted." If her competitor was someone she disliked, however, Jenny became much more callous to the other's feelings. "I would be glad if she's sad!" she said, savoring the thought of her adversary's distress.

Conflict resolution and cooperation: The child's pursuit of influence

Overall, though, both children tried to resolve their conflicts by creating a situation in which both could emerge as winners.

SELF STUDY 17

Your style of seeking influence

Sometimes, when we do not get what we want, our responses reveal how we feel about influence. If we feel powerless we may either withdraw or overreact by being destructive. If we actually feel influential we might try to convince the other person of our need or insist that what we want is necessary.

Think back to the time you were a child. How would you have reacted if one of your friends refused to do something you wanted him or her to do? Would you have reacted differently if the other person was someone of authority, like a parent or a teacher? How do you react now when someone disagrees with you? How have you changed since you were a child?

How assertive are you when you feel wronged? If a product you have purchased does not live up to your expectations, what do you do? What do you do if your food is cold or prepared improperly at a restaurant? Do you have difficulty asking a stranger for directions or the time of day? When you talk about your feelings do you say, "I feel . . . !" or "You make me feel . . . !"?

Do your answers to these questions reveal any consistent style in the way you feel about your own ability to influence events? Try changing your style a little bit. If you are shy, see if you can be a little more bold when you ask a stranger for the time. If you are already a brash, pushy type, try to be a little more mellow. Experiment with these changes until you find a style of seeking influence which you believe fits your needs.

Robert Selman's study of children's social thinking helps us put these ideas in a broader developmental perspective.[16] Selman contends that children's ideas about how conflict can be resolved progresses along five levels. The first three relate primarily to the age group that concerns us in this book.

At the most basic level (level 0) which Selman calls *Physical Solutions to Conflicts,* young children suggest either retreat or force as likely solutions to resolving conflict. For example, Jason seemed to favor physical separation when the conflict involved direct aggression by another, but he preferred other alternatives in less hostile situations. Children who reason at this level may disregard the emotional effect of their withdrawal or the use of force for either person. Their ideas about resolving conflict are simplistic, emphasizing force for gain and flight for avoidance.

At the next level (level 1), *Unrelated Solutions to Conflicts,* children between five and nine years old ". . . view conflict essentially as a problem that is *felt* by one party and *caused* by the actions of the other."[17] Their resolutions for conflict emphasize that the other person must assume responsibility for reversing the effects of what he or she has done. This unilateral solution is stressed because at this stage children assume that the origins of the conflict reside in the misbehavior of one person rather than a coordinated, mutual disagreement. Both Jason and Jenny's comments regarding the block-tower and pushing situations overlooked the motives and feelings of the transgressor. Because these two solutions involved physical aggression, they may have overlooked how the other person felt. In the competitive conflicts both children were much more concerned about the other's welfare.

CHILD STUDY 15

Responding to provocation

Select two children and interview them separately about their ideas for resolving conflict. Ask them to describe their views in response to the block tower situation (p. 166). Ask each child, "Let's say you're building a tower with blocks and someone comes over to you and knocks it down. What would you do?" Engage the child in a conversation to draw out his or her thoughts as much as possible about this problem. You may wish to tape record their comments.

How do their reactions compare to those of Jenny and Jason? Do they advocate aggression or threats, withdrawal, or more peaceful negotiation to resolve the conflict? Do their responses involve a mixture of these three general types?

About one week later ask each child to build a block tower in the middle of a high traffic area in their classroom during a period of free play. Tell each child you would like to see how tall he or she can make a tower. How do they protect their towers from being knocked over? Do they use threats, force, withdrawal, or negotiation to deal with the problem? Do they involve other children? Is there any comparison between what they do in the actual situation and what they advocated during the interview?

In Level 2 reasoning, *Cooperative Solutions to Conflicts,* children between seven and twelve years old typically recognize that both parties are psychologically involved in the conflict and that both must participate in its resolution. They may suggest a "time out" for both parties to calm down, offer sincere apologies, or appeal to the other person's logic. In "The Argument" and "The Race" Jason and Jenny both described alternatives which were primarily cooperative. This is a remarkable outcome since Jason is five years old, and we would expect his reasoning to conform to the previous two levels.

In the final two levels described by Selman, older children and younger adults first reason that "*each side must feel that both he or she and the other are truly satisfied with the resolution and would be satisfied if in the other's place.*"[18] This idea may progress toward concern for autonomous growth of individuals within the relationship and the responsibilities each party can have toward the other in resolving a conflict.

Selman's interviews demonstrate that children's reasoning about conflict can gradually change over time. Because of such age differences additional stress can exist if a

Conflict resolution and cooperation: The child's pursuit of influence

teacher attempts to resolve a conflict by reasoning at a level beyond a child's progression of understanding. Much more research is needed for us to understand how children change in their thinking about conflict and the impact their reasoning has on behavior.

James Youniss interviewed children at three age levels to determine how they viewed unkindness and how they would respond to another's misbehavior.[19] The youngest group (six to seven years of age) identified not sharing, not being generous, taking or breaking things, and fighting as examples of unkind behavior. Interviews with six- to fourteen-year-old children indicated six different patterns of victim reactions following peer offenses of unkindness. The three most frequent patterns for the youngest age group (six to eight years) were Pattern A (transgressor offends — victim reciprocates — transgressor offends again — victim reciprocates), Pattern C (transgressor offends — victim reciprocates — transgressor undoes offense, e.g., asks to play or offers toys — victim accepts), and Pattern D (transgressor offends — victim reciprocates — transgressor apologizes — victim apologizes or accepts). Each of these three responses includes an immediate negative reaction to another's unkindness with resolution being dependent on the transgressor making the first move to reestablish equity in the situation. Apparently young children believe that victims have the right to reciprocate unkindness, although a smaller number of children did suggest nonconfrontation as a response.

Roger Jensen and Shirley Moore demonstrated that adult comments about children's cooperative and competitive behavior can influence how those children actually work together on a task.[20] One group of seven- to twelve-year-old boys were told by an adult, "You really get along with others. You play fair. You are willing to share, and you don't get pushy with others. You work well with others." Another similar group of children were told "You are real winners. You don't settle for second best but climb right to the top. You also go out and get things done. You could be the best at things you do." Children who were told they were cooperative were paired as were the children who heard competitive comments. These pairs were given fifteen seconds to build a single block tower and were told that each child would receive awards according to the number of blocks he or she put on the tower. Children who were told they were cooperative typically encouraged and supported their partners and averaged thirteen blocks in each tower. In contrast, the children who were told they were competitive appeared jealous of their partner's rewards and typically interfered with his efforts to place a block. The result was that these children averaged only five blocks in each tower. When assuming a competitive posture toward each other, these children performed significantly poorer than children who assumed a cooperative attitude toward their task.

George Spivak and his associates have taken a different approach to children's reasoning about conflict.[21] They believe that children who can envision a wide range of solutions rather than one specific outcome are likely to be more effective in resolving conflict: "Apparently youngsters who can think of only a few ways to obtain what they want from others think the fastest and surest way is through some kind of attack."[22] In one of their studies they discovered that elementary school children who had social problems were significantly more likely to suggest physical retaliation, such as fighting or kicking, as the *only* responses to a nasty remark.[23] Although they might also mention these alternatives, more adjusted children are also likely to describe nonphysical responses to the provocation. The child who can think of many potential solutions to a problem will have more available options in actually responding to conflict.

An eye for an eye:
Is aggression justified?

Research has revealed that children as young as kindergarten age accept the *reciprocity norm* in evaluating the aggression of another.[24] The reciprocity norm is a conviction that another's kindness or unkindness should be repayed. At about this age children begin to consider the intentions of wrongdoers in judging their behavior. They may point out that hitting in response to being mistreated is more justified than hitting for selfish reasons or for no gain at all.

In one study both kindergarteners and adults rated a character who pushed another down because he was either refused a legitimate turn on a piano or was ridiculed for doing a puzzle incorrectly. Their responses were less negative than those for a character who pushed someone who was trying to be helpful.[25] In another study children in kindergarten through sixth grade were asked to evaluate the naughtiness of children who hit another child either to get candy for themselves or to secure and return the candy to its rightful owner. Regardless of age, children viewed altruistic reasons for physical aggression as more justified than the personal reasons.[26] Both studies demonstrate that children as young as five or six years can discriminate between different intentions in evaluating aggressiveness.

Staub has suggested two significant sources for the acquisition of the reciprocity norm.[27] First, children may be taught to retaliate by adults or peers. For example, a parent may tell a child who complains about being hit to retaliate against his attacker. In this instance the parent implies that the child must use force to save face and maintain respect. This invitation may remove whatever restrictions of authority the child has that inhibit aggression. Second, the concept of reciprocity may emerge naturally as the logical conclusion of a child's view of interpersonal conflict. Wrongdoing creates an imbalance in a relationship which can be resolved by punishment. A child who hits another child in retaliation "evens the slate" and reestablishes the balance in the relationship. Unfortunately this "eye for an eye" position can escalate the intensity of the conflict.

But boys cannot be nurses?
The limits of influence

Underlying the norm of reciprocity is a child's beliefs about the types of rules that govern behavior. Although they may seem totally undisciplined to some adults, children have a very strict set of rules which govern their behavior. Nancy Much and Richard Shweder observed a group of nursery school and kindergarten children and were able to classify the 630 situations they recorded into five rule types: regulations or laws, conventions or customs, morals, truths or beliefs, and instructions.[28]

Regulations or *laws* are established by authority and are maintained by the threat of

Conflict resolution and cooperation: The child's pursuit of influence penalty. They can also be changed by those in authority. Children evaluate their behavior by deciding if what they have done is legal or illegal. A child who tells a newcomer to the class, "You can't go outside without a teacher—that's the rule," is describing a regulation.

Conventions or *customs* are established by social consensus and are maintained by the threat of criticism. Some typical conventions are that boys should wear pants but not dresses, and that children must say thank you when someone gives them something. Conventions can be changed, but the procedure for doing so is ambiguous.

Morals are considered necessary and unalterable beliefs about right and wrong. Their origins are intrinsic in the world and are not the result of decisions made by authority. Avoiding physical harm and respecting another's ownership of property are examples of moral rules.

Truths are laws, in a scientific sense, which are derived from logic and experience. Differentiation between rational and irrational convictions can encourage children to reflect on the logic of their beliefs. A child who says, "Anger is bad!" or "Boys are stupid!" is making a statement of truth from his or her own perspective even though this truth may be irrational and conflict with the beliefs of others.

Finally, *instructions* are ". . . recipes for achieving results."[29] Instructions are descriptions of behaviors which are associated with predictable results. For example, "If I share my toys she will be my friend," or "If I hit him he will be hurt," are instructions. This rule type is concerned primarily with the causes and consequences of actions.

In their study of children's speech behavior, Much and Shweder discovered that kindergarten and nursery school children were different from adults in their sensitivity to the five rule types. Young children were more likely than adults to judge behavior in moral terms, suggesting that they are very aware of the difference between right and wrong. Also, children understood the concept of justice regarding such things as physical or psychological wrongdoings. Unlike adults, children were likely to overlook breaches of regulations, failing to remember such rules as, "Shut the door before you go outside," or "Wipe your shoes before you come in." These researchers also found that both children and adults had a high awareness of conventional rules but low concern for violations of truths or instructions.

This analysis of children's awareness of rules means primarily that children tend to view rules as either moral or conventional demands. This view is supported by the research of William Damon and Elliot Turiel, who attempted to demonstrate that even preschool children are very aware of the differences between moral rules (which cannot be changed), and social conventions (which can).[30] In one study, for example, preschool children judged moral transgressions to be wrong even if there was no school rule against it.[31] Thus, stealing would have been considered wrong even if a teacher tried to legalize it with a rule. On the other hand, they considered that social-conventional violations were wrong only if a school rule had been made. According to this reasoning, failure to wash hands before lunch would be wrong only if there was a rule stating that hands must be washed before eating.

Elliot Turiel examined the developmental course of social-conventional concepts by interviewing children and young adults about such issues as styles of clothing, sex-appropriate occupations, and modes of eating. Analysis of their responses indicated that social-conventional concepts show clear age-related changes in a gradual progression along seven levels.[32] In the first level, children up to seven years of age form convictions associated with observed consistency in the appearance or behavior of others. For example, based on his observations, a child may reach the conclusions that "all nurses wear dresses" and "all men are not supposed to wear dresses." Once these conventional rules are determined by a child, we can understand why he or she might argue that "men cannot be nurses." After all, men would look silly in dresses. At this level children are simply commenting on what *appear* to be the conventional rules governing social behavior.

Eight- to nine-year-old children gradually begin to use second level reasoning and insist that these conventions are not absolutely true. They may point out that although these rules are uniformly followed by others they are not absolute, necessary guidelines. One eight-year-old boy responded to this issue in the following way.

Why do you think his parents believe that job is only for women? *Because most women do it. But on my baseball team there is a girl. So you can't say she can't. She is a good player in fact.*[33]

The remaining five levels describe how older children and young adults view conventions. Although beyond the scope of this book, they basically follow the pattern which affirms that a particular approach to conventions is followed by a negation and reexamination of the validity of that construction. Each negation on one level provides the basis for beginning the next level.

This pattern of oscillation explains why children, adolescents, and young adults go through periods of questioning and doubt regarding the propriety of social conventions. For example, parents may have become accustomed to having their children wearing "nice" clothes to school only to discover that these same youngsters have reevaluated this expectation and have decided to dress unconventionally. This cyclical change in ideas related to conventional rules is an important aspect of social cognition.

This research helps us understand that children view their attempts to gain influence as being affected by their beliefs about rules. They have a well-defined concepts of right and wrong, but their ideas about morality and conventions do not necessarily conform to adult concepts of these rules. Also, children's behavior is not always influenced by what they *say* is important. Children may not be able to clearly describe the ideas which actually guide their actions. The research described in this chapter is, at best, only an estimate of what children think about conflict and rules.

The genesis of social influence

Conflict resolution and cooperation: The child's pursuit of influence

As children gain a clearer appreciation of others' perspectives and acquire more effective language skills, their ability to solve problems is also enhanced. Unfortunately, these strengths may be neutralized by the threat and pressure of competition. The struggle for a sense of power takes a different form as children mature and face different types of personal and social demands.

The emergence of assertiveness

During the second year of life, two developmental milestones have a decisive effects on the emergence of influence in young children. The first is the use of the words, *I* and *me* in reference to themselves, and the second is the declarations, *Yes* and *No* in response to conflict.

Self-reference is a necessary step in self-affirmation. In order to get what they want, children must learn to refer to themselves when making requests. This effort begins during infancy as children learn to point to what they want and to cry in protest when they are frustrated. Language makes this effort clearer to both children and adults. "Me! Me! Me wants to go too!" is a very clear statement conveying a child's self-awareness as well as a desire to favorably influence the actions of another.

These attempts to exert influence inevitably bring children into conflict with others. When this occurs children have two options, they can either withdraw or confront. Children who consistently withdraw from such conflict are likely to lose confidence in themselves and in their ability to get what they need. They may begin to believe that others know them better than they know themselves and that meek submission and loss of self-belief is the price for acceptance. In contrast, assertive confrontation, in which children insist "Yes!" or "No!" or "Mine!" emerges during the second year as an expresion of self-awareness and belief in their own power to influence others.[34] Even though authority figures may need to be equally assertive in setting limits, they should recognize that a toddler's negative expressions are ways of saying, "Hey, I'm important. I know what I want. Listen to me!"

Very young children have limited strategies for dealing with the failure of their self-assertiveness. They may resort to crying or using force to get what they want when assertion does not work. Although infants may be indifferent if a toy is taken from them, toddlers typically respond with aggression.[35] They do not have the language skills or the intellectual capability to explore other alternatives to resolving the conflict. Overall, though, toddlers get along remarkably well with each other and do more sharing than hitting.[36]

SELF STUDY 18

Dealing with threats

How you respond to another's aggression may reveal your attitude toward influence and power. For example, recall a time during your childhood when you fought with another child or when someone tried to hurt you. Sit back, close your eyes, and try to remember as much as you can about the incident. Where were you? How did you feel? How did the other person seem to feel? What happened?

Does your response to this incident reveal your childhood beliefs about the use of power and influence? How do those ideas fit into your present view? How do you respond now to two young children fighting? What ideas do you emphasize by the way you choose to become involved?

The beginning of instrumental aggression and competition

During the years immediately before elementary school, children begin to acquire a style of influence which may endure well into middle childhood and adolescence. An emerging sensitivity to others' perspectives combined with increasingly sophisticated language skills allows them to begin to negotiate and cooperate to get what they want.[37] From two to six years of age the use of language increases as a way to register protests with others rather than physical aggression.[38] Even so, some children still seem to prefer force rather than negotiation, and others choose to avoid conflict by meek submission to the demands of peers and adults.[39]

Instrumental aggression is the most common type of aggression observed during early childhood years. These young children typically argue or fight over material goods, territory, or privileges. Conflict over the use of a truck, the distribution of balloons, or who gets to sit next to the window in the car are examples of instrumental aggression.[40] During this period, children do not frequently target other children as the specific objects of their aggression.

Early in this period children are primarily "self-gain" oriented when they try to achieve their goals, and they will try to gain as much as they can without reference to the success or failures of others. At about five years of age, however, children become more aware of potential competitors and many will actually prefer less gain for themselves if that option provides them with more gain than their competitor.[41] For example, children who have this view would prefer to have ten marbles rather than thirty marbles if it meant that the other person would gain only two marbles instead of twenty-five marbles. This sense of rivalry increases during the elementary school years as children begin to compare themselves more intensely to their peers.

The emergence of hostile aggression and rivalry

During the early elementary years, children continue to change in the ways they seek influence and respond to frustration. Because they better understand cause and effect, children at this age frequently direct their anger toward a specific source of frustration rather than exploding in a temper tantrum. They can stand back and more clearly identify the cause of their frustration, but they also sulk and hold resentment longer after angry or aggressive encounters.[42]

Response to threat also changes because these children can express themselves more effectively than before. Physical aggression continues to decline and is often replaced by verbal displays.[43] In grade school there is relatively little physical fighting, but minor conflicts and misunderstandings often escalate into heated exchanges of insults and ridicule. These children often talk about their disagreements, offer suggestions, and make compromises. However, some children will continue to use violence as a response to conflict despite the fact that they have the potential to use words to resolve the problem.

Willard Hartup has noted that elementary school children are more likely than their younger peers to use language as an expression of hostile aggression.[44] He noted that when young children are insulted they hit back about one-half of the time, but during

Conflict resolution and cooperation: The child's pursuit of influence

middle childhood they hit back only about one-fourth of the time. These older children are much more likely to follow the offense with insults of their own. Instead of using aggression directly, their intent is indirectly hostile, to demean or belittle the other person. Young children do not use hostile aggression because they do not understand how and when to use language to threaten another person's self-esteem.

In the early elementary years, children become more conscious of competitors and their gains during a conflict. They may be so preoccupied with comparing themselves to their competitors that "they learn to pursue personal ends and block opponents in conflict-of-interest situations, even when mutual asistance is required for personal goal attainment."[45] Imagine a game in which two ten-year-old children are asked to pull strings of blocks through the same small opening. If there is a prize for the winner, the ten-year-olds spend much more time blocking their opponent than younger children do.[46]

Instead of being self-gain oriented, elementary-age children may prefer the other's loss. One study described by Nelson and Kagan revealed that "given a choice, Anglo-American children took toys away from their peers on 78 percent of the trials even when they could not keep the toys for themselves. Observing the success of their actions, some of the children gloated, 'Ha! Ha! Now you won't get a toy.'"[47] In contrast to

Mexican children, American children are apparently more willing to reduce their own rewards in order to reduce the reward of a peer. In boys, this competitive stress is related to being less empathic and kind.[48]

Elementary school children are more capable than preschool children of understanding and responding to the need for mutual assistance. If the situation does not involve conflict of interest, cooperation is more likely to occur. In the block game described above the older children were more successful than younger children when *both* had to pull their blocks through the opening in a short period of time before a prize would be awarded. Thus, children are capable of cooperation, but conflict of interest interferes with their ability to work together.

SELF STUDY 19

Winner-loser

When you were a child how did you feel about competition? What memories and feelings does the word "competition" evoke in you? How did you feel about your opponents? Did adults ever influence your attitudes toward winning or losing? Recall an incident during your childhood that conveys how you felt and how you once responded to competition.

Ask a friend to arm wrestle with you. Be aware of how you feel before, during, and after the match. Were you afraid of winning or losing? How did the other person react to your request? How did you feel during the match? Were you surprised at the other person's strength? How did you respond to each other after you were finished?

Tell the other person that the match was a way to help you better understand your feelings about competition. Talk with your partner for a few minutes about his or her reaction to the match.

How do your beliefs about competition affect how you react toward competition in children? Do you see a difference between cooperative competition and competitive competition? If so, how might these two types of competition occur in a classroom? What would you look for if you wanted to observe them in children's relationships?

Children in our culture may learn to perceive that winning requires a conflict of interest. For example, "For me to win, you have to lose." They overlook the potential for mutual gain that can occur with cooperation and cooperative competition. This emphasis on being an exclusive winner is especially evident in boys.[49] If children learn to disregard others, they may never learn how successful they might be if they could count on other's help.

Competition and aggression can merge together into what is called *Type A* behavior—a blend of extreme competitive achievement striving, a strong sense of time urgency, impatience, and easily aroused anger. This behavior may be associated with heart disease in adults. Karen Matthews and Julio Angulo explored the developmental antecedents of Type A behavior in kindergarten through grade six.[50] In the first study, teacher evaluations revealed that Type A behavior was more prevalent among males than females across all age levels. In the second study, second-and fourth-grade children who were identified as Type A by teachers were actually more aggressive, impatient, and competitive under some conditions than other conditions.

In a related study David and Louise Perry found that among third, fourth, and fifth graders competition led to aggression even if the competitor won the contest.[51] Apparently competition which stresses conflict-of-interest outcomes encourages both insensitivity and hostility in peer relationships.

Education and influence

If we would like to help children acquire a sense of influence which promotes their relationships with others, our educational programs must focus on specific skills. In Table 6.1 eleven potential skills are identified for consideration. They are identified at a level of abstraction which allows them to be applied to both early and middle childhood. More specific adaptations of these skills can be identified for specific children. For example, our expectations for how well a four-year-old might negotiate conflict would be quite different from our expectations of a seven-year-old.

Table 6.1 Summary of conflict resolution and cooperation skills for children

Skill	Definition	Social/cognitive processes
1. Identifying the regulations, conventions, and moral beliefs which may restrain behavior.	1. The ability to differentiate between regulations, conventions, and morals; to describe the reasons for limits and discuss the potential consequences of violation; to describe values which guide one's own behavior. *Examples*: A five-year-old says, "My school has a rule—no running inside." A seven-year-old comments, "No, I don't want to hit him. He's too little, and I don't want to hurt him."	Defining *Rules* Sensing Deciding
2. Describing the antecedents of conflict and alternatives for its resolution.	2. The ability to identify the characteristics of conflict; to discriminate between necessary/productive and destructive forms of conflict; to identify the antecedents of conflict; to describe the various alternatives and their consequences, including *violence*, that can be initiated in an attempt to resolve conflict; to describe nonviolent, minimally hostile forms of conflict resolution, including sharing, mediation, third-party judgment, and compromise; to evaluate the relative productiveness/destructiveness of conflict resolution strategies. *Examples*: A four-year-old states, "Let's share the truck, OK?" A six-year-old says, "We all want the balloon. Let's take turns for about ten minutes. You go first, then me, then you, OK?"	Defining *Conflict, Agree* *Disagree,* *Arguments* *Fighting* *Sharing* Sensing Deciding

Skill	Definition	Social/cognitive processes
3. Describing cooperation.	3. The ability to identify the characteristics of cooperation; to identify circumstances in which cooperation would be a constructive alternative; to describe the consequences of cooperation. *Examples*: A four-year-old comments while he and another child are building a tower, "We're cooperating, Sammy!" A seven-year-old states, "Cooperation—that's when two people work together to do something."	Defining *Cooperation* Sensing Deciding
4. Affirming one's self.	4. The ability to make requests and show pride in one's accomplishments. *Examples*: A three-year-old says, "Daddy, look at ME!" as she begins to climb on the outdoor play equipment. A five-year-old asks the teacher, "Can I get out the tinker toys? I want to build a spaceship."	Defining Sensing Deciding Acting
5. Asserting one's self.	5. The ability to reasonably affirm what one wants after being denied; to oppose any unreasonable intrusion on one's personal domain including (a) the resistance to demands, orders, or physical coercion and (b) the protection of property. *Examples*: After being ridiculed by two older children for the way she talks, three-year-old Sarah says, "Stop that, you meanies." When he is told that he cannot spend the night with his friend, the seven-year-old responds, "Please Mom! I really want to!"	Defining Sensing Deciding Acting
6. Offering protection and assistance when needed.	6. The ability to verbally defend another; to physically defend another without victimizing the offender; to give warning of danger. *Examples*: A four-year-old takes a pin away from an infant. A six-year-old tells other children to ". . .stop making fun of my friend."	Sensing Deciding Acting
7. Leading and following peers.	7. The ability to assume control (to give suggestions, to orient and direct, to set one's self up as a model for imitation in peer activities); to follow the lead and suggestions of others. *Examples*: A five-year-old suggests, "C'mon let's play soldiers. Follow me!" A six-year-old agrees to play the table game suggested by a peer.	Sensing Deciding Acting

Skill	Definition	Social/cognitive processes
8. Cooperating	8. The ability to work with others in order to solve a problem or complete a task. *Examples*: Two four-year-olds work together in picking up and shelving the blocks they played with. Two eight-year-olds work together to complete a class project.	Sensing Deciding Acting
9. Engaging in cooperative competition.	9. The ability to participate in a prosocial contest, match, or other trial of ability; to focus on doing one's best while confirming the efforts of others involved; to celebrate the efforts of opponents whether they win or lose and take pride in one's performance regardless of the outcome. *Example*: A group of kindergarten children cheer *each other* on in a game.	Sensing Deciding Acting
10. Negotiating a response to conflict (four years plus).	10. The ability to seek nonviolent resolution of conflict. (This response can involve deferring the problem and identifying its causes, sharing feelings, generating possible alternatives, and identifying a mutually acceptable solution which is implemented and evaluated. The types of constructive alternatives available to young children are taking turns, sharing, resorting to chance determination, and bargaining.) *Examples*: A five-year-old finds another toy for his friend to play with when they begin to argue over one toy. Seven-year-olds take turns on a swing.	Defining Sensing Deciding Acting
11. To protect one's self from harm.	11. The ability to initiate a constructive response to physical or psychological attack. (This may involve confronting the attacker directly without resorting to excessive counterforce.) *Examples*: A four-year-old grabs a child who is trying to hit him. A seven-year-old wrestles with a child who is trying to hit her with a stick.	Defining Sensing Deciding Attacking

Our relationships with children

First, by encouraging children to be reasonably self-assertive, we can help them develop a sense of competence which contributes to their self-esteem. Although we may have to be firm in maintaining our classroom limits, we can invite children to "speak their mind" without being disregarded or criticized. For example, after telling his preschool class they cannot go outside, the teacher listens to one of his children say, "But teacher, Jamie and I *want* to go outside and play pirate!" The teacher then responds, "I know you want to go outside, and I'm glad you're telling me what you want. Let me show you the mud out there. What would happen if I let you play there?" The teacher in this situation is trying to tell the children that he is interested in what they want and what they feel and that he wants to listen and talk with them about those things. This kind of message conveys to children that they are important and that they have influence.

Second, we can share power with children by giving them a voice in many of the decisions which affect them. Although we may have to make decisions entirely on our own, we can allow children to be responsible for much of their own behavior and classroom routine. Children can choose what books they would like their teachers to read, what games they would like to play, and the extent of their involvement in many classroom activities. Sharing of power can be quite subtle, and we can show respect for children by listening to them, by responding to what they say, and by encouraging them to contribute their ideas. Children who feel that they are worthwhile and important and can influence their lives will have no need for aggressive violence.

Third, we can examine and eliminate potential causes of violence in our classroom.[52] We can try to reduce the amount of frustration children experience by setting reasonable classroom limits. We can respond to children not only when they misbehave but also when they solve problems. We can encourage and reward children's efforts to resolve conflict nonviolently and to cooperate with others. We can expose children to influential, nonviolent role models in classroom visits, literature, mass media. Peacemaking and cooperation can be conspicuous values in a classroom.

Fourth, we can talk with children and explore their ideas about conflict. Conflict provides an excellent opportunity to work on problem-solving skills with children. A variety of nonviolent alternatives to resolving conflict can be examined and evaluated in a problem-solving encounter. In addition to *sharing* or *taking turns*, children can utilize *chance* in making decisions. The most common example of chance is flipping a coin. Children often accept a chance decision because they do not really "lose face" to any other person.

Children can also settle their differences by *bargaining*. In this alternative each child is offered something worthwhile. For example, an older child who wants to read a book that a younger child has might say, "Look, if you let me have this book right now, I will read it to you later." Children learn this strategy early in life, offering friendship, attendance at birthday parties, and the use of other toys as rewards. Bargaining resolves conflict by establishing mutually acceptable and appropriate rewarding consequences. For example, a child might offer his friend another toy if she shares her toy with him. As long as all parties in the conflict are pleased with the agreement, the bargain is effective.

In some instances we may have to gently confront children's misconceptions and encourage them to consider other possibilities (see Table 6.2). We must remember to consider the developmental limits in children's thinking when we talk to them. There is no way we can force young children to overlook their own desires and focus on the needs of the other person in a conflict. However, we might expect an older child to begin thinking more about another's perspective.

Fifth, we can allow a reasonable amount of play fighting among children in game activities and free play. Rough-and-tumble play is natural for children, and it may strengthen their relationships with others and lead to cooperative behavior.[53] As long

Table 6.2
Contrasting examples of irrational and rational beliefs about influence and conflict

Irrational belief		Rational belief
• Hitting is the best way to solve a problem with another child.	vs.	• There are lots of ways to solve a problem with others, many of them are better than hitting.
• I must always win. Losers are failures.	vs.	• I can't always win but I can do my best. Even if I lose I can learn how to do better.
• Other children always have to do what I want.	vs.	• I want others to listen to what I have to say, but they don't always have to do what I want.

as roughhousing is playful, children can enjoy the contact and match their strength and physical ability to that of others. The opportunity to display strength safely and to experience the strength of others may build mutual respect. Willard Hartup has noted that if we deprive children the opportunity to display playful aggression, we may actually contribute to aggressive problems in children, especially in boys.[54]

Sixth, we can explore with children effective responses to the aggression and violence of others. What should children do if someone tries to hit them or take away their toy? What happens to children's sense of power and self-confidence if we teach them the rule, "Always ask a teacher for help"? What if no adult is around? Should they run away, fight back, or simply sit and cry? We can give children confidence in taking care of themselves without giving them permission to engage in violence. Many of us may remember discovering that the neighborhood bully was really a fraud who backed down after we stood up to his threats. Of course, since some of us may have been soundly thrashed when we tried the same thing, a good message for children is, "Take care of yourself. Don't let someone hurt you or destroy something you own. Sometimes you may have to fight, but make them stop with words if you can. Other times running away is the best thing to do. You must decide." This approach allows children to make decisions based on their values and feelings about power and force, and each of them will address it differently.

Seventh, we can establish cooperative goal structures in our classrooms by emphasizing working together to accomplish tasks. David and Roger Johnson have suggested that we might present goals as *group* goals, encourage sharing of ideas and materials, invite a division of labor where appropriate, and reward the group for the successful completion of the task.[55] Elementary school children in cooperative learning environments have been observed to more actively encourage and support the efforts of their peers than children from competitive or individualistic learning environments. They also feel more accepted and supported by peers in their efforts to learn.[56]

Cooperative and noncompetitive games help establish a cooperative learning environment by emphasizing the uncertainties of the nonhuman aspects of the game, for example, the placement or speed of a pitched, kicked, or batted ball. These games differ from more traditional, competitive games in the following ways:

1. All participants work together toward a common goal.
2. All participants win if the goal is attained or all lose if the goal is not attained.
3. All participants compete against the nonhuman aspects of the game rather than against their peers.
4. Participants do not necessarily play identically, but their actions are coordinated in a united effort to reach the goal.[57]

Cooperative games may reduce interpersonal hostility and nurture group cohesiveness, fostering the types of skills identified in this chapter.

Finally, we can emphasize cooperative forms of competition. We do not need to avoid all forms of competition because children want to compare their skills with those of others. In some situations, when risk of failure is not too intense, they may accomplish more if competition is a part of the activity. Two guidelines should be considered for making competition effective: first, it should not overshadow cooperative activities and, second, children should be encouraged to respect competitors as persons with feelings. Instead of finding pleasure in defeating others, children can view competition as an opportunity to do their best and to encourage and bring out the best in others. With this kind of support, competition can be enjoyable and rewarding.

Activities to promote conflict resolution and cooperation

The following activities may be helpful to you as you design a program to nurture conflict resolution and cooperation in children. Please review Tables 3.3 and 3.4 (pp. 53-54) before beginning. For additional activities on conflict resolution and cooperation see the following:

4 Stick Together	54 Happy Chalk Drawing
6 Frankenclass	99 Arm Lifting
20 Orange Juice Celebration	100 Body Lifting
23 Butter Lover	106 Being Generous
51 Emotion Drawing	

---

76 Group Pass Pictures (four years +)

Purpose   To help children learn how to cooperate. Key concept is *cooperation*.

Setting   Learning center arrangement

Materials   Paper   Crayons

Activity   **1.** This activity gives children an opportunity to create and receive a drawing composed by the entire group. Give each child a sheet of paper and at least four or five crayons. Ask the children to write their names at the top, and tell them that you will give them one minute to draw what they want. When you give the signal they pass the picture to their right. As the pictures circulate, each child will contribute something to each drawing. Each child will receive a drawing after they have been passed around the circle.

2. When finished, take all of the pictures to the wall and encourage the group to discuss what they see and what they drew. Comment on the cooperative nature of the task.

---

77 Picture Descriptions (four years +)

Purpose To help children learn how to cooperate. Key concept is *cooperation*.

Setting Small group or learning center arrangement

Materials Ten simple pictures (found in children's books)

Activity **1.** Briefly discuss the concept of cooperation. Tell the children that you have a cooperative activity for them to try.

2. Select a picture and *describe* it to the children. Immediately following this, show this picture and another picture at the same time, and ask the children to point to the one you described. If they identify the correct one, discuss how the pictures differ. If they identify the incorrect picture, point out the features you described.

3. Ask a volunteer to come forward. Secretly show the volunteer two pictures and ask him or her to describe one to the group. Then show both pictures to the group and ask them to point to the one the volunteer was trying to describe. This process can be repeated with other pictures.

Suggestion The activity can be made more difficult by increasing the number of pictures shown to the group and by making the central characters in the paired pictures similar or identical (e.g., a monkey in a zoo and a monkey in a tree).

---

78 Card Partners (five years +)

Purpose To help children learn how to cooperate. Key concept is *cooperation*.

Setting Learning center with children arranged in pairs

Materials Several three-card sets, each set having two identical pictures and one different (pictures may be hand drawn or photocopied)
A barrier for each pair which will allow children to see each other when seated (e.g., a feltboard sandwiched between two blocks)

Activity **1.** Tell the children you have a game for them to play in which they will have to work together to solve a problem.

2. Have partners assume positions on opposite sides of the barrier. Give the "tellers" one of the two identical pictures, and give the "showers" the remaining two different cards in the set. The tellers then describe their card to the showers. The showers then select one of the two cards, show it to their partners, and ask "Is this it?"

3. If the showers make a wrong choice ask the tellers if they know what they forgot to tell their partners. Try to help them understand how they can make more accurate descriptions. If the choice is correct, have the partners switch roles and continue with another set of cards.

Suggestion   The activity can be made more difficult by increasing the number of cards the showers have to select from.

---

79   Team Puzzles (three years +)

Purpose   To help children learn how to cooperate. Key concept is *cooperation*.

Setting   Small groups of three children

Materials   One puzzle set for every three children (see activity instructions)

Activity   **1.** Make puzzles of varying difficulty out of construction paper. The least difficult puzzle can be divided into three simple sections (one for each child). One simple division might look like illustration A. To make a more difficult puzzle, the pieces can be cut abstractly as in illustration B. Even more difficulty can be built into the activity by doubling the number of pieces (two for each child) as in illustration C. Put the pieces of each puzzle into an envelope.

2. Tell the children that you have an activity for them to do in which they will have an opportunity to solve a problem together. Break them up into groups of three and give each group an envelope. Tell them that each envelope has puzzle pieces in it that can go together to form a rectangle. Explain that you would like them to work together to solve the puzzle. After asking them to open the envelopes, encourage their efforts and help them resolve any conflicts they might have. Groups who finish early can, by invitation, help those who have not.

3. After all have finished, briefly discuss the various types of responses which occurred during the activity.

Suggestion   This activity can be made easier if the puzzles are divided into only two pieces and the groups composed of only two children. Each puzzle can be a different color to make distribution and collection easier.

80

Three-Leg Shuffle (three years +)

Purpose   To help children learn to cooperate. Key concept is *cooperation*.

Setting   A large open space to allow for movement

Materials   Rope, twine, or old ties (of sufficient length to tie legs together)

Activity   **1.** Ask the children if they know what *cooperation* means. Briefly discuss this concept and then have the children choose partners. Tell them you are going to tie two of their legs together because you want to see how well they can work together and cooperate. Have a pair stand side by side and tie their two adjacent legs together. Ask them to walk together to a certain point (e.g., across the room, to another teacher, etc.).
2. Cheer the children on and encourage their efforts. Praise them for their attempts to cooperate.
3. To make it even more difficult, tie the legs of three children together (or four, or five, . . .

Suggestions   The emphasis of this task should be on cooperation rather than competition. The activity should not be set up as a race. Rather than having them moving at the same time the pairs can take turns walking.

Do not tie their legs too tight. Materials that stretch slightly, such as old ties or scarves, work best.

Set out large blocks, chairs, tables, balance beams, ropes, or sawhorses, as obstacles for the children to navigate. Supervise closely for safety.

81

Carry-Board Teams (four years +)

Purpose   To help children learn to cooperate. Key concept is *cooperation*.

Setting   A large open space to allow for movement of children in pairs

Materials   Long, flat boards (light enough so that two children can carry them)
Objects that can be placed on the boards with various degrees of stability

Activity   **1.** Briefly discuss the concept of cooperation and then ask the children to choose partners. Ask each pair to pick up a board with one child at each end. Place an object on the center of the board and ask the children to move from one end of the room to the other.

2. During the activity, comment on the children's ability to consider the actions of their partner. Encourage and praise their efforts. Time them as they move across the room and encourage them to improve their score the next time they try.

3. This activity can be made more difficult by setting out obstacles over the path.

---

82 Dough It Together (three years +)

Purpose	To help children learn how to cooperate. Key concept is *cooperation*.
Setting	Learning center arrangement
Materials	3 cups of flour
	¾ cup salt
	powdered tempera paint
	½ cup of water
	(Increase proportionately to make the necessary amount for all children involved.)
Activity	**1.** Divide all materials (flour, salt, water, tempera) into proportions which can can be given to children. Briefly discuss the concept of cooperation.
	2. Pass out the materials and have the group of children seated at each table work together to make the dough. Encourage all children to become involved in its preparation (e.g., one child adds the water to the bowl, the next mixes in one portion of flour, the next adds the salt, etc.).
	3. When finished, the group can divide the dough into portions for each child. Following this period of play the dough can be returned to a container designated for the group and refrigerated for later use.

---

83 Back-to-Back Lifts (four years +)

Purpose	To help children learn how to cooperate. Key concept is *cooperation*.
Setting	Learning center arrangement
Materials	None
Activity	**1.** Tell the children that you have an activity for them to do which involves their cooperation. After the children have selected partners, ask them to sit back-to-back with their legs outstretched. They should then interlock both arms and try to stand up.
	2. Encourage the children in their efforts. Comment on their attempts to cooperate.

Suggestions Increase the difficulty by having more than two children interlock arms. Another option is to have children sit facing each other with their legs slightly bent and their feet touching. They can clasp hands and try to pull each other up.

---

84 Basket Catch-It (four years +)

Purpose To help children learn how to cooperate. Key concept is *cooperation*.

Setting Partner arrangement preferably in a safe outdoor location

Materials One small basket for each child
One ball (or bean bag) per pair

Activity **1.** Tell the children you would like to give them an opportunity to work together. Ask them to choose partners and give two baskets and ball to each pair. Ask them to use their baskets to try to catch the ball thrown by their partners. When they are throwing they can set their basket on the ground.
2. When finished, talk briefly with the children about their reactions to the activity. How did they feel about cooperating? How successful were they?

Suggestion The difficulty of the game can be affected by increasing or decreasing the size of the basket and the distance between partners. Try to establish conditions which maximize children's opportunity for success and let them decide when they want a greater challenge.

---

85 Group Soup (three years +)

Purpose To help children learn how to cooperate. Key concept is *cooperation*.

Setting Community group and learning center arrangement

Materials Kitchen utensils and a pot for the preparation and cooking of soup
Food brought by children and teachers (see activity instructions)
Soup bowls and spoons
Crock pot Hot plate, if no stove is available

Activity **1.** A couple of days before actually cooking the soup, gather the children together and decide who is responsible for bringing soup ingredients to class. Basic soup items might be carrots, potatoes, celery, tomatoes, onions, and cabbage. Just about any vegetable can be added. The teacher can bring beef or chicken bouillon. Send notes home with the children requesting the specific food items. Ask that all food be fresh rather than canned or frozen.

2. When the children arrive on the cooking day (you might bring a potato or a few carrots for the children who forgot to bring food) ask them to gather in a circle with the food they brought. Take a piece of each type of food and circulate it around the group. Do not allow children to eat the food, but encourage them to get a feeling for the texture, visual aspects, and odors of each vegetable. Following this meeting the children should wash their hands and reconvene at the tables to prepare the food.

3. Supervise all food preparation. Peeling and cutting utensils can hurt. As food is prepared it can be immediately put into the pot or into plastic bags for later use. Rinse all food after it is prepared. Add bouillon and water to the soup pot.

4. While the soup is cooking under close supervision children can continue with other classroom activities. When the soup is finally cooked and served, discuss the children's cooperative efforts to complete the task.

---

86   Balloon Bounce (three years +)

Purpose	To help children learn how to cooperate. Key concept is *cooperation*.
Setting	Community or small group arrangement
Materials	One balloon
Activity	**1.** Tell the children that you have an activity for them to do which requires them to cooperate. Explain that you will toss a balloon into the air and that you will count how many times they can hit the balloon without letting it touch the ground. The important rule they must follow is that *no child may hit the balloon more than two times.* Following their second hit, children must move to the edge of the group.
	2. Then toss the balloon and encourage the children's efforts. Watch carefully to make certain all follow the primary rule. After the balloon touches the ground begin again and encourage them to increase the previous score.
Suggestion	Children around the outside of the group (who have already hit the balloon twice) may be allowed to hit the balloon back into the center if it will help to keep the balloon bouncing. Feel free to relax this rule if children find it confusing or too difficult.

---

87   Balloon Pick-Up (three years +)

Purpose	To help children learn to cooperate. Key concept is *cooperation*.
Setting	Small groups of three children
Materials	About twenty-five balloons

1. Blow up all the balloons and put them where they will not drift all around the room (e.g., in a corner behind some chairs).

2. Tell the children that you would like to see how well they can cooperate by seeing how many balloons each group can get off the ground. One child can be the "balloon getter" while the other two hold the balloons between their heads, hands, tummies, legs, etc. The third child can help hold the balloons up after the other two are holding as many as they can.

3. When the first group is finished, another group can have a turn.

---

88   Tug of Peace (three years +)

Purpose   To help children learn how to cooperate. Key concept is *cooperation*.

Setting   Community group arrangement in a safe outdoor location

Materials   One rope (one-inch), about forty to fifty feet long

Activity   **1.** Tell the children that you have an activity for them to do that involves working together to move something heavy.

2. Select an object that is very heavy and tie the rope around it. The object should be heavy enough that the children really have to work to move it. Also, both ends of the rope must be equally long after it is tied. Divide the children into two equal groups and assign each group to one end of the rope. On command, both groups can begin to pull the rope and try to move the object (e.g., a large wooden box, a large rock, a log, etc.) to a reasonable point designated by the teacher. Supervise closely for safety.

3. If the object is heavy enough, do not hesitate to become involved. Shout words of encouragement and praise as the children pull, and when finished discuss the merits of cooperation to accomplish a difficult task. Point out (and let anyone try if they wish) that no single individual could move the object alone. Only a group could do it.

---

89   Cooperative Musical Chairs (four years +)

Purpose   To help children learn how to cooperate. Key concept is *cooperation*.

Setting   Community group arrangement

Materials   Record player   Record

Activity   **1.** Tell children that they are going to play musical chairs, but that the rules for this game will be quite different. In this game they will have to cooperate to stay seated in the chairs. The game is played exactly like traditional musical chairs except that when the music stops everyone must be seated on a chair *or in someone's lap.*

2. Start the music and take away a chair after each round so that the children are forced to share a diminishing number of chairs.

Suggestion   Younger children might experience less frustration if the class is divided into groups of six.

---

90   **Dividing My Pie** (four years +)

Purpose   To help children understand fairness. Key concepts are *fair* and *unfair*.

Setting   Community, small group or learning center arrangement

Materials   Two "pies" cut out of construction paper, one divided and cut evenly, the other unevenly. For example, for eight children the "pies" could be divided as shown below.

Activity   **1.** Ask the children if they know what *fairness* is and briefly discuss it. Tell the children that you would like them to participate in a pretend activity with you.
2. Take out the unevenly divided pie and ask the children to pretend that it is real. Distribute a piece to each person and discuss whether or not the distribution is fair. What is the problem?
3. Distribute pieces of the evenly divided pie and ask the children to compare these pieces with the ones they received first. Discuss the idea of fairness in terms of equal division. Relate this situation to other experiences the children may have had.

---

91   **Got What?** (five years +)

Purpose   To help children negotiate conflict and learn to cooperate. Key concepts are *cooperation* and *problem*.

Setting   Small groups of four children at a learning center

Materials	(for each group)

Materials   (for each group)
One sheet of paper   One pair of scissors
A bottle of paste   One piece of construction paper
Two crayons

Activity   **1.** Give each child in the foursome either a pair of scissors, a piece of construction paper, a bottle of paste, or the crayons. Then give each group one sheet of paper and ask the children to make something with all the materials they have. They can share their materials or each child can perform a separate task.

2. When the project is finished set the results out for all children to see.

Suggestion   This activity can be simplified by dividing the children into pairs instead of groups of four.

---

92   **Not Enough** (four years +)

Purpose   To help children learn to negotiate in response to conflict. Key concepts are *problem, disagreement,* and *agreement.*

Setting   Community group arrangement

Materials   About three or four objects to give to the children (e.g., balloons)

Activity   **1.** In this activity something is provided for the group which cannot be easily divided among all members. This situation is intended to produce a conflict which can then be resolved by the group.

2. Tell the children that before you can give them something there is a *problem* that they must solve. Set out the objects and say something like, "I would like to give you these things, but I think we might have a problem. What do you think it is?" After the children identify the problem (not enough to go around), ask for their help to find a solution.

3. Engage the children in a discussion about how the objects are to be given out. Do not impose your solutions, but try to have the children discover some mutually agreeable solution of their own. Try to see that everyone's ideas are discussed, and encourage the children to make their own decisions. Point out and discuss the inevitable *disagreements* that will occur. If the group cannot find a solution, the teacher can offer suggestions for discussion.

Suggestions   One group of fifteen four-year-olds solved the problem of being given four balloons by first suggesting such solutions as going to the store to buy more, not handing them out at all (most disagreed), cutting them in half (a humorous nonsolution), etc. Finally, someone suggested that those who did not get one immediately could obtain one tomorrow if the teacher found more that evening. The group agreed that this would be a good idea, and through a gradual process of elimination four children were identified as the immediate recipients. The teacher never had to ask or suggest that certain children would have to drop out.

93   Won or Two (four years +)

Purpose   To help children learn to negotiate in response to conflict. Key concepts are *problem, disagreement,* and *agreement.*

Setting   Small group or learning center arrangement

Materials   One bowl
One nutritious cookie (or other consumable) for each child

Activity   **1.** Tell the children that you have some cookies to give them. Mention, though, that first they will have to solve a problem. Ask for two volunteers to sit facing each other in the center of the circle.
2. Place the bowl between the two children, put one cookie in the bowl, and say, "Here is the problem. I have only one cookie. The rule is that for you to get the cookie your partner must give it to you. *You cannot take it for yourself.''* Remind the children of this guideline if they should forget.
3. Continue the cycle until only one child remains. The teacher becomes that child's partner. If the child does not give the cookie to you, then you can give it to him or her. If the child gives the cookie to you, break it in half and return a portion to your partner.

Suggestions   Children may respond to this activity in several ways: (1) the cookie may be promptly consumed by the recipient, (2) the cookie may be accepted but then divided and a portion returned to the giver, and (3) the cookie may be given only after considerable verbal or nonverbal negotiation. Many possibilities may occur in a second round. Children who divide the first cookie usually repeat this strategy. Most of the children who "give without getting" in the first round wait to be given the cookie in the second round (and are successful). In a few cases the child who gives the first time will repeat the offer the second time.

References on conflict and cooperation

Eronson, E. *The Jigsaw Classroom.* Beverly Hills: Sage Publications, 1978.

Fluegelman, A., ed. *The New Games Book.* Garden City: Doubleday and Company, 1976.

Johnson, D. W., and Johnson, R. T. *Learning Together and Alone: Cooperation, Competition, and Individualization.* Englewood Cliffs: Prentice-Hall, 1975.

Orlick, T. *The Cooperative Sports and Games Book*. New York: Pantheon Books, 1978.

Orlick, T. *Winning through Cooperation*. Washington, D.C.: Acropolis Books, 1978.

Palomares, U., and Logan, A. *A Curriculum on Conflict Management*. La Mesa, California: Human Development Training Institute, 1975.

Pearson, C. *Resolving Classroom Conflict*. Palo Alto, Ca.: Learning Handbooks, 1974.

Prutzman, P., Burger, M. L., Bodenhamer, G., and Stern, L. *The Friendly Classroom for a Small Planet*. Wayne, N.J.: Avery Publishing Group, 1978.

Redl, F., *When We Deal with Children*. New York: The Free Press, 1966.

Stanford, B., ed. *Peacemaking: A Guide to Conflict Resolution for Individuals, Groups, and Nations*. New York: Bantam Books, 1976.

Chapter seven
Kindness: The child's expression
of care and affection

If I can stop one Heart from breaking
  I shall not live in vain
If I can ease one Life the Aching
  Or cool one Pain

Or help one fainting Robin
  Into his Nest again
I shall not live in Vain

No. 919
Emily Dickinson

Two-year-old Martin hears his mother crying in an adjacent room. He is alarmed because she and his daddy just had a heated argument over an issue he couldn't understand. Now his father has stormed out of the house, and his mother is sad and alone. After watching her for a few moments he runs to his room and returns with Tickles, the teddy bear, in his arms. He timidly approaches his mother and hands her his trusted friend. His mother takes the bear and gives Martin an affectionate hug.

June (five years old) is having a frustrating time tying her shoes after arriving at her kindergarten class. Sharon, another five-year-old, notices June's problem and offers her help. June accepts the offer, and after her shoes are tied, she invites Sharon to play a table game with her until class begins.

In these situations both Martin and Sharon demonstrated their willingness to lend another a helping hand. Within the limits of his own perspective Martin tried to respond to his mother's distress. Sharon took the time to help a friend.

Our educational programs can deal with kindness by helping children better understand kindness and learn how to demonstrate it. Body and emotional awareness, affiliation, and influence contribute to a sense of significance and competence in children. These skills are completed by the growth of kindness. Without caring other social skills will wither. If caring for others is missing in our educational programs than what hope can our children have? Knowledge unaffected by kindness can easily be used in service to cruelty.

What is kindness?

Two characteristics we might consider in our definition of kindness are voluntariness and internal reward. If we view kindness from the perspective of one who makes the offer, *voluntary behavior* is an important guideline which we must emphasize. If Sharon had been forced to help her friend we probably would not consider what she did as being kind. Do we often overlook this issue when we try to show children how to care? An adult who demands that a child apologize to a playmate may be doing both children a disservice. The child who makes the statement may learn to hide behind a mask of deceit, and the child who hears it may learn to expect such ritualistic insincerity.

On the other hand, the person who offers a kind act *emphasizes benefit to the recipient* rather than gain for one's self. Kindness is not completely self-serving. If someone does something for us because they were paid to do so or because they expect to be rewarded we are not likely to consider their help an act of kindness. Martin probably shared his beloved teddy bear to relieve his mother's distress rather than to get a piece of candy or pat on the head. Sharon seems to have helped because she felt responsible for easing her friend's frustration rather than because she expected some form of payment.

Even so, kindness can have favorable consequences for those who offer it. The Chinese proverb, "a bit of fragrance always clings to the hand that gives you roses," describes the indirect benefit that may accompany kindness. When his mother stopped crying Martin may have felt relieved of some of his own distress and pleased with what he had done. Sharon may have also felt proud of her ability to successfully offer help. Such personal consequences may or may not have been the primary reason these children decided to offer their assistance, but when we encourage kindness in children we can emphasize the pride that can result from kindness and the satisfaction of sharing in the other's success. We can define kindness, then, as ". . . *voluntary behavior that is carried out to benefit another without anticipation of external rewards . . .*"[1]

The source of kindness

According to Schutz, affection and intimacy are possible only if inclusion (feeling accepted) and control (feeling respected) are evident in our relationships with others.[2]

SELF STUDY 20

The people who nurtured you

Find a quiet spot where you can think without being distracted. Relax and let your mind wander back to your childhood. Try to remember someone who was significant to you, someone who took care of you and provided you with love and attention. Try to imagine this person caring for you. How do you feel?

Now try to remember others who nurtured you as you grew older. Maybe they were teachers, relatives, neighbors or youth group leaders. Try to recall how each one looked and what they contributed to your life.

On one side of a sheet of paper list the names of these individuals in chronological order. To the right of each name describe the effect this person had on you. For example:

| Mr. Scheullman, High School History Teacher | His love for history and his interest in students increased my own hunger for knowledge. He became the model of an educated professional that I wanted to become. |

Look over this list of effects. Is there any continuity or flow from one to the other? Are there gaps in your life when no one emerged as a special person? Did others appear just at the right moment for you? If all these people were together in the same room, what might you say to them?

Kindness is made possible by belief in our own *significance*. If children feel important and are recognized as individuals, they are more likely to reach out to people with support and assistance. If they feel insignificant and worthless, they may either attempt to manipulate or withdraw from others. Children who feel rejected may believe they have nothing to offer. Acceptance nurtures kindness.

Kindness also depends on confidence in our own *competence*. If children believe they can influence others and have a positive effect on social events, they are more likely to offer kindness. Powerlessness creates apathy because children who believe they are incompetent and cannot influence events will not take action to benefit another. Respect provides a foundation for kindness.

We cannot help children to feel affection and to care for each other unless we first nurture a sense of significance and competence. When children have the opportunity to know and accept each other, when they have the responsibility to make decisions, and when they feel respected by others, affection and kindness will begin to emerge in their relationships

Kindness as problem solving

Although feelings of significance and competence provide a foundation for kindness, children are faced with a sequence of perceptions and decisions they must make before kindness can result. The following story illustrates this point.

Stephen, a four-year-old, was a gentle, quiet little boy who had an aura of melancholy that seemed to cling to him everywhere he went. Whatever somber burdens Stephen may have had in the back of his mind, however, did not prevent him from showing concern for others. Stephen cared. One afternoon his teacher was feeling sick and withdrew from the activity of the classroom to sit at the far end of the room near the children's lockers. Stephen walked over and sat quietly next to the teacher as he rested. After a few moments the teacher turned to him and said, "Oh, Stephen, I don't feel so well. I'm sick." Stephen thought for a moment, smiled, and then hugged his teacher. Finally, he suggested, "Now, Mr. Carver, you go home to bed. Your mommy will take care of you." At that moment the teacher felt very touched by this child's sincere concern for his welfare.

Stephen's thoughtful suggestion was the final result of a sequence of decisions we all make when we offer kindness.[3] First, Stephen *noticed that something was happening*. He saw the teacher sitting alone, but he had been preoccupied with something else he might never have noticed. (This step depends on sensing or intuitive ability we examined in Chapter Two.)

Second, Stephen *interpreted what he saw and heard*. The initial idea, that something was wrong with his teacher, was confirmed when the teacher said he was sick. That word triggered images in his mind about how his teacher felt.

Third, Stephen *assumed responsibility for helping*. He could have decided that someone else was responsible for providing aid, but Stephen wanted to do something.

Fourth, after assuming some responsibility Stephen had to *decide what to do*. Initially, he sat quietly and close. After he had more information about the problem he decided to offer physical reassurance and suggest home care. Stephen based his suggestion on his own experience with illness. Even though he was technically incorrect, his suggestion was intended to be kind.

Fifth, Stephen had to actually *offer kindness*. He could have gone through the first four steps and then decided not to take action. He might have kept quiet if he thought his teacher would laugh or criticize his ideas. However, he felt secure enough to offer the hug and make the verbal suggestion.

We can help children in this problem-solving process. We can urge them to become more aware of problems. We can help them interpret signs of distress and explore their values about taking responsibility for kindness. We can examine with them the causes and consequences of distress as well as alternatives for helping others. Finally, we can try to create conditions which encourage kind behavior.

The kind skills matrix

The problem-solving process involves two basic issues. First, a person who *receives* a kindness could be anywhere from totally dependent to being very active and involved in the act. For example, a child's mother could be very ill and confined to bed or she might only have a simple problem like cleaning up the kitchen. Second, the person who *offers* the kindness may extend physical resources, psychological resources, or both depending on how they evaluated the other's need. Thus a child might offer a physical resource like a teddy bear or a psychological resource like a hug. By combining the type of need with the resource offered, a matrix of kindness skills can be determined (see Table 7.1).

Generosity and *caretaking* result when children offer a physical resource to a distressed person who is relatively inactive or dependent. When showing generosity children *give up* ownership of a resource to someone who is in need. For example, a child might give a cookie to a friend who has none or give some of his or her allowance to charity. Caretaking occurs when children devote time caring for someone who cannot take care of him or herself because of sickness, injury, or disability. A child finding a washcloth for a sick father or a child feeding a hungry kitten are demonstrating caretaking behavior.

Table 7.1
The kind skills matrix

		Recipient's condition	
		Inactive/Dependent	*Active/Involved*
Resources offered	Physical action	Generosity Caretaking	Sharing Helping
	Psychological action	Compassion	Affirmation Affection

Sharing and *helping* are physical resources like donating and caretaking but this type of kindness is extended to a person who is more actively involved in what is happening. Because of this, the demands on children are not as great when they share or help. Unlike giving up something, sharing involves only a *temporary* loss of a resource. Sharing a toy with another child is a common example of this form of kindness.

Sometimes we confuse sharing and generosity. For example, when we tell a child to share her cookie and later tell her to share her truck, we are giving the same label to two different outcomes. Children also can confuse these two issues. A toddler who gives a bite of his cookie to an adult may scream when he cannot get it back. Another child may panic because she fears total loss of ownership when a peer plays with her toys. Thus, children allow someone else to benefit from using their resources when they share, but they actually give up ownership of a resource to benefit someone else when they are generous.

Helping occurs when children assist someone in resolving a problem. Children help when they open a door for a parent whose arms are full, find a crayon for a friend, or get a toy from a high shelf for a shorter peer. In each of these instances children are actively helping another reach his or her own goal. (Helping should not be confused with cooperating which is aimed at reaching *mutual* goals.)

Comforting or *compassion* is a psychological resource offered to someone in distress. Stephen's gentle hug was an act of compassion. Anything a child might say in an effort to give someone hope or reassurance would be considered an expression of comforting.

Affirmation and *affection* are psychological resources which children might extend to someone to promote the other's sense of well-being in the absence of any "emergency." A child who gives his teacher a hug and then says, "Teacher, I like you. You are really nice." is affirming her worth. Likewise, a child who says to a friend, "Gee Marsha, you are really smart. You have lots of good ideas," is sending a message that the other person is really worthwhile. The primary difference between affirming and caretaking is that caretaking occurs under emotionally stressful conditions.

These definitions can help us better understand how the kindness skills relate to each other. Sharing, for example, can become generosity if a child decides to give something to another permanently. By defining these terms we also have a clearer picture of what to look for in children's behavior.

Sharing and helping may be the easiest behaviors for children to learn. Because these skills involve physical resources, they are easier for a child to understand and are more easily associated with positive outcomes. Also, they are not likely to occur under intense or stressful conditions. Comforting may be the most difficult kindness for children to learn because its impact is more difficult to detect and it is most often expressed during apprehensive moments.

Children's ideas about kindness

The way children express or fail to express concern for others is influenced by their ideas about kindness. For example, a child may see a friend fall off her bike but not try to help her because he thinks his teacher is responsible for this type of aid. Also, he might be confused by her crying and not understand the problem. It is possible that he wants to help but has no immediate solution to the problem. Each of these ideas could stop the child from taking action.

Kindness begins in the mind and we need to understand what ideas our children have about kind behavior. Can they think of ways to solve another person's distress? Can they describe what *gentle* means? Do they believe kindness is a sign of weakness or strength? How do television, movies, and children's books portray kindness? Every child begins to form his or her own view about the meaning of another's distress, the relevance of help, and the role of compassion.

SELF STUDY 21

Messages about kindness

When you were a child, what messages did you hear about kindness? What statements did your parents or caretakers make about the following issues?

> Generosity and sharing
> Caretaking
> Helping
> Showing compassion
> Showing affection

Did their actions correspond to what they said? How did their words and actions about kindness affect you? Do you find yourself saying and doing these things now? Are you pleased or dissatisfied with your current attitude about kindness? Can you devise a plan for change?

It's a happy kind of feeling:
Children's reflections on kindness

Most of the research on children's thinking about kindness deals with how they justify their behavior, discriminate between various forms of kindness, and take another's perspective. Little research has been done to reveal how children actually describe kindness and how would they go about offering kindness to others. The words of Jenny and Jason provide us with two examples of children's ideas about these issues.

INTERVIEWS   *JASON (five years)*

Jason, can you tell me what kindness is? *That's when you help people in trouble.* Tell me something that is kind. *Well, if an old lady has trouble of getting across the* **203** *street we could help her.* How would you help her? *I would just take her hand and help her across the street.* Why would you do that? *'Cause if she tripped 'cause she was old she would hurt herself, and a car might run over her.* Why are people kind to other people? *'Cause they love each other.* You were talking about helping, Jason. What does that mean? *That means helping people do other things.* How do you know if someone is helping? *If they help people God will bless them.* Tell me about a time when you helped someone else. *Yea . . .when Christine hurt herself on her bike, I went to get a bandage for her.*

How about generosity, Jason? What does *generosity* mean? *I don't know.* Let's pretend there's a child you don't know, and this child has no cookies. If someone gave you three cookies and this child wanted some, what would you do? *I would just let her have one. And if her friend came she could have the other one, and I could have the other one.* So each of you had one. What if her friend did not come? *Well, we could both split the other cookie in half.* So you would have one and she would have one and each of you would have half a one.

How about sharing? What does *sharing* mean? *That's when you share food like when we were just talking.* Can you think of another time when you shared something with someone? *Oh, yea, when the babysitter came over and I had chips and I let Jeremy have a few and I had a few too.* What if Jeremy came over to your house and you had only one truck to play with. If that's the only toy you both have to play with, what would you do? *We would share it. He could push the other side and I could push the other side. The two doors will have two men in it and maybe get one of his trucks, or we could get my puppets like my elephant puppet and my monkey puppet.* Why would you share those with Jeremy? *'Cause he's a nice friend.*

What would you do if someone you knew was very sick? Can you think of a way to be kind? *Yea, I would pick some flowers, and I would give him some flowers.* What else could you do? *I don't know.* How about if I was very sick and there were only you and I—no one else. How could you help me? *I could give you some medicine when it's time, and when it's time for lunch I could get one of those tables and give you some lunch. And when you wanted a book I could get one for you.*

What would you do, Jason, if you were outside and saw a child who was crying but you did not know who he was? *Why?* I don't know. What could you do that was kind? *I could ask him what's wrong.* What would you do if he wouldn't tell you? *Well, I could go tell his mother or father. Or I could tell you.* What would you do if there were no grownups around? *Well, I would just help him up and take him to my house and ask what's wrong. And if he had a bloody knee I could just get a Band-Aid.*

What could you do, Jason, to be kind to someone if they don't have a problem and you just want to give them a happy feeling? What do you and other people do to give each other a happy feeling? *Play together. That gives us happy feelings, like when we were playing over there [points] and we were happy. And I was happy when I was a baby, a little baby.* Can you think of something you could say to someone your age to give them a happy feeling? *I could say, "What's a clown, it's a town!" [laughs]* Make up a joke, huh? Can you think of anything else you want to say about being kind? *I don't think of anything else. I think I used up all my things.*

Kindness: The child's expression of care and affection

204

Jenny, what is *kindness? It's a happy kind of feeling! It's when somebody helps each other.* Tell me about a time when you were kind to someone. *Yesterday at school I helped our teacher clean off the chalkboard.* Why did you do that? *'Cause I like to help people.* Why are people kind? *To make friendships.* Can you think of any other reasons? *Just for the fun of it, like, I just like to be kind.* What happens when you're kind? *Most people get blessed . . . if you die you would surely go to heaven.* That's one reason why you're kind? *Jesus was kind to others when he died he had his halo and he went up.*

Jenny, what does *helping* mean? *Means be kind to others.* Give me another example of helping. *If there was somebody who couldn't skate very well . . . like Christin. When she came down with her new beginner roller skates and she fell down, Bill saw her and said, "Christin's hurt!" And me and Michelle skated up and helped her down the hill.*

Can you tell me what *generosity* is? *Another word for kindness. . .sharing.* What is sharing? *That's kind of in the Bible. There was a little boy and he had two loaves of bread and three "mackramels." And Jesus, he broke everything up so it could feed a hundred people.* And that's sharing? *Yes.* Give me an example of being generous. *Hmm. Well, generous, I think, would mean if you had a piece of bread and there was some other kids playing with you then it would be real kind and nice to share with them. That's generosity.* What would I do with the bread? *Split it up, and if you gave it to them that would be generosity.*

What could you do if someone was very sick? How could you be kind to someone who was sick? *I'd buy a little present for them and a get well card and maybe bring them some soup. That's a good cure for a cold nose.* What would you do, Jenny, if you saw a child who was crying, but you did not know who this child was? *I would go over and try to comfort him anyway.* What would you do to comfort him? *Oh, talk to him, make funny faces, joke.* Can you think of something you might say to him? *I can ask him if he wanted to come over to the house. If it was a boy, I could ask him if he would like to come over and play with my brother. Maybe he'd like to do that.*

What do you do, Jenny, if someone doesn't need your help but you just want to be kind to them, to give them a happy feeling? What are some things you could do? *Just leave them alone. That's what Mom likes me to do.* Let's say you want to give a child on the playground a happy feeling. What might you do? *Ask her, he, if he wanted to play with me, he or she.* What else might you do? *Go dig holes and make little bowls out of them. That's what me and Sandy did. We took some dirt out of the little holes . . .and then we made plates and for forks we found sticks.* If you want to say something kind to someone what might you say? *Hi! That would be my first word. . .or howdy!*

Jenny's and Jason's comments provide us with a glimpse of what children might think of kindness even though their ideas do not represent all children their ages. Their concepts and convictions are similar in that both children indicated that they understood the concept of kindness and its various forms. They could identify a variety of **205** options for showing kindness to others, and both children used the term *sharing* to refer to the temporary loan of a resource and to outright generosity. Even though Jason was not familiar with the term *generosity* he could describe generous behavior. Both children referred to religious convictions to explain their motives for kindness and emphasized mutual play as an everyday way of showing kindness. Finally, both emphasized physical, rather than the verbal, forms of kindness and had difficulty describing how words could be used to convey kindness.

Jenny and Jason were different in some of their ideas about kindness, but we do not know whether these differences are due to age or personality. Jason's immediate view of kindness emphasized aiding "people in trouble." In contrast, Jenny referred to the everyday give-and-take between friends. Possibly because of her age, Jenny was more aware of the psychological benefits of kindness in friendships. As she intially stated, "It's a happy kind of feeling!"

Even though there may be many other ways to analyze their responses, Jason's and Jenny's ideas can serve as a contrast to the opinions of other children we might talk to. As we begin to focus on kindness with children, our first objective might be to find out what they think about being gentle, taking care of someone, sharing, helping, comforting, and affirming others.

James Youniss asked children to tell him a story about a child their age who did something for another child their age.[4] The majority of stories created by six- to eight-year-old children emphasized themes of sharing, generosity, or cooperative play. This youngest age group believed strongly in the self-evident rule of equality: If one has or is doing something then the other should also possess or do the same thing. Unlike older children in this study, this age group showed no concern for the physical or social well-being of their peers as unique individuals. These young children portrayed kindness toward adults as consisting of obedience or being pleasant and polite.

Young children can demonstrate a concern for another's welfare even though they do not fully comprehend the other's perspective. Both Jason and Jenny revealed a concern for another's unique problem. Jason was quite worried about the safety of an elderly lady, and Jenny was concerned about the struggles of a beginning skater. Whether differences are due to age changes or to personality and socialization is difficult to determine.

Gary Ladd and Sheri Oden asked third and fifth grade children how they might help someone who was being victimized by other children. The children agreed that if they arrived while others were teasing or yelling at the other child, they would order them to stop. If the child was alone they would console or comfort the victim, instruct him or her how to avoid the taunts of others, or suggest an alternative activity.[5]

How did Jenny and Jason respond when asked what they might do if they found another child crying and alone? Jason was concerned about knowing the specific cause of the distress before he could do anything for the child. He was eager to help, but he would depend on an adult if he couldn't determine what the problem was. Jenny, similar to the children in the Ladd and Oden study, suggested both comforting and an alternative activity. Such responses may be more likely from older children who are more aware of the psychological solutions to the problems.

Children's reasons for kindness:
From self-interest to commitment

Beliefs which explain why a person should do something or describe a standard of behavior are called *norms*. Children have two very different norms which they use to explain their reasons for being kind.

The *reciprocity norm* holds that people have an obligation to be kind to those who are kind to them and, conversely, have no obligation if there is no debt of kindness. David Rosenhan describes the behavior which results from the reciprocity norm as "normative altruism."[6] The central feature of this form of kindness is concern for one's self. Children who have this norm may say they help someone because he or she is their friend, because they want that person to play with them, or because they want their parents or God to approve of them.

In contrast to this norm of self-interest is the norm of *responsibility* which states that people have an obligation to relieve the distress of others and to promote their development without the expectation of reward. Rosenhan describes the kindness that results from this belief as "autonomous altruism."[7] The central feature of this form of kindness is self-sacrifice and less regard for personal benefit. Children who have the norm of responsibility might explain their kindness by saying they wanted the other person to be happy or become well. Their focus is on benefitting someone other than themselves.

Rosenhan believes that normative altruism emerges first in young children and is followed in later childhood and adolescence by autonomous altruism. "In all of our experiments," he states, "we have been able to elicit considerably more normative altruism (i.e., generosity in the presence of the model) than autonomous altruism (i.e., generosity in his absence) at whatever age."[8] Initially, children may be very conscious of gaining adult approval for their kindness, or, they may act in other ways for their own self-interest.

Support for this position is provided by Robert Leahy who interviewed six-year-olds, seven-year-olds, and adults about how they would reward someone who was kind.[9] He described an act of kindness and then asked each group to allocate rewards to the person who performed the act. Six-year-old children used an *additive* principle and allocated more rewards to someone whose kindness led to positive consequences for himself or avoided negative consequences. Older children and adults preferred a *discounting* principle which gave greater reward if the helping or generosity produced no benefit or occurred under threat of harm.

Both younger and older children believed in *facilitory obligation*, allocating more reward to one who was kind because of an obligation to return a previous kindness. Adults, however, believed in *inhibitory obligation*, giving more reward if the person who accepted the kindness had previously denied a favour to the person who offered it. Apparently, the younger children were more concerned about personal benefits for being kind than were the adults.

A different picture of children's reasoning is provided by the research of Dreman and Greenbaum.[10] These researchers gave kindergarten children a bag of seven candies and asked them to give some, if they would, to a child in their class who did not receive any. After children gave, investigators asked them to describe their reasons for sharing. About 47 percent of the children gave altruistic (e.g., "I gave so he will be happy.") or socially responsible reasons (e.g., "If I don't give, he won't have.") while only 19 percent emphasized self-interest (e.g., "He's a friend of mine," or "I gave so he will play with me."). About 33 percent gave no answer or their responses could not be classified.

How many candies did each of these three groups donate? The children who held responsibility norms donated an average of about 3.57 candies (about one-half of what they had). Those who held a reciprocity norm donated an average of about 2.68 candies. Those who designated no answer or were unclassified donated about 3.42 candies. Although no causal relationship can be determined, reciprocity norms may serve to inhibit generosity.

Clara and Alfred Baldwin have demonstrated how judgments of kindness can change from kindergarten through adulthood.[11] They offered paired responses to children and adults and asked them to identify which were more kind. Several of the alternatives discriminated between the responsibility and reciprocity norms. For example, "Is giving another child a block you need more kind than giving one you don't need?" About 47 percent of the kindergarteners, 68 percent of the second graders, and 81 percent of the fourth graders thought so. "Is giving a toy without receiving anything in return more kind than giving one and receiving a toy in return?" About 66 percent of the kindergarteners, 92 percent of the second graders, and 90 percent of the fourth graders thought so. "Is allowing a child to use your wagon more kind than doing so after he has offered to take you to see some puppies?" About 40 percent of the kindergarteners, 72 percent of the second graders and 87 percent of the fourth graders agreed. In each of these circumstances we see children becoming more aware as they grow older that acting in self-interest contradicts the meaning of kindness. Even at kindergarten age, however, some children demonstrate this socially responsible point of view.

In a related study, Ervin Staub demonstrated that, when temporarily left alone, kindergarten and second grade children who were told to help "if anything happens" were more likely to investigate distress sounds in another room than children who were not given the responsibility.[12] Children who were not told to help may not have investigated because they feared adult disapproval. Those who were told that they could help did not have to worry about breaking an adult rule and may have anticipated adult approval. These results indicate that children might interpret some rules as constraints on kindness. They might say to themselves, "Don't get involved, or you might get into trouble."

Children's causal explanations regarding helping may be influenced by the way adults respond to their efforts. When given praise and penny rewards for donating or a rebuke and fines for not donating, second and third graders were likely to attribute their help giving to external sources (reciprocity norm). When given only praise or rebuke, however, children attributed their actions to a desire to help or a concern for the other person (responsibility norm).[13] We must ask ourselves, therefore, if younger chidren are concerned about self-interest because adults tend to emphasize material rewards in their relationships with them.

Children's sensitivity to others:
From sympathetic to empathetic distress

Children's ability to take the perspectives of other people influences their responses to people in need. Children who are affected by another's distress and who can relate to another's pain are more likely to respond with assistance than those who remain preoccupied with themselves.

Martin Hoffman has suggested three stages of responding to distress which parallel the first three levels of perspective taking identified in Chapter 4.[14] In the first stage, infants and toddlers react emotionally to another's distress by experiencing what the other person seems to feel. Hoffman gives the example of this sympathetic distress in an eleven-month-old girl who saw another child fall and cry. She first watched and stared at the child who was hurt, then appeared about to cry, and finally put her thumb in her mouth and buried her head in her mother's lap. The child was emotionally affected by the incident and responded as though she had been the one to get hurt. Because children are not aware that another child is uniquely different from them, at this stage they will do or offer what they themselves find comforting. Thus, a toddler might offer his teddy bear to his mother who is feeling sad since he assumes his mother will respond in the same way he does.

At the second stage, preschool and kindergarten children typically begin to make adjustments in their care, because they have become more aware that the other person is different from them. They may try to find the true source of distress in another person. In Jason's comments (pp. 203-204) about helping a crying stranger, he was first concerned about the real cause of the child's problem. He wanted to adjust his actions to meet the other child's needs. At this stage a child might get her brother's toy for him when he is unhappy or get a newspaper for her mother to read when she talks about being tired. Children at this age are beginning to look at the world through the other person's eyes and adjust what they do to be more effective.

During the early grade school years, children move into the third stage. They begin to take the other's personality into account and to show concern for the other's general condition. They are more capable of understanding a person's distress while not being overcome or distracted by their own feelings. Their help becomes more effective because they know the other person better and can begin to demonstrate a concern for the welfare of others in general.

Nancy Eisenberg-Berg and her colleagues demonstrated that four- and five-year-old children who focused on another person's needs rather than self-gain are more likely to share or be generous.[15] The same relationship did not occur with helping or comforting behavior. Research by Kenneth Rubin, though, demonstrated a positive relationship between the ability to take another's perspective and helping among seven-year-olds.[16]

Children's attitudes toward people in distress may also influence their responses. Young children may believe in "imminent justice," the conviction that someone who is hurt must have done something wrong to deserve it. They will rate this person as more "bad" than someone who is not hurt. A belief in imminent justice can provide a reason for not helping, but this negative attitude toward victims fades during the middle years of childhood.[17]

Confusion of terminology, differences in research procedures, and differences in instruments designed to measure various aspects of kindness are stumbling blocks in making firm conclusions about the relationship between what children think about kindness and their kind behavior. Despite these limitations, we can make a few tentative conclusions. Research leads us to believe that although some children may show a special concern for others at a very young age, they will be limited in what they can do because of their narrow perspective. Also, young children may act in self-interest because they are not aware of another person's need, and some children may be unwilling to offer kindness under some conditions because they hold convictions which emphasize self-gain.

The genesis of social responsibility

Generosity, caretaking, helping, sharing, compassion, and affirmation change with age and can be influenced by different conditions.

CHILD STUDY 16

Generosity

On three separate days give three children of different ages a bag containing five very small and nutritious cookies or inexpensive party favors. Tell the children that whatever is in the bag is a gift from you and now belongs to them to use in any way they would like. Unobtrusively observe these children and record what they choose to do with their gifts. Do they give anything away? If so, how much do they distribute and who is chosen? Do they give away more than half of the items? Are there any differences between children? If so, why do these differences exist? Does age or personality influence generosity?

How did other children respond to their peer's generosity or selfishness? Is there any relationship between generosity and popularity?

Generosity: to give from the heart

Most of the research on children's kindness has focused on generosity. This emphasis may be due to the simplicity of prompting and measuring generous behavior. In the typical laboratory study a child wins or is given something and is then allowed to donate any portion of that resource to another child. Generosity can then be measured by counting the number of items donated.

Studies of generosity typically reveal an increase in giving with an increase in age.[18] S. B. Dreman gave seven candies to Israeli children from six to thirteen years old as a prize for drawing. They were then given the opportunity to donate a portion of their reward to a child who was not there but was participating in the same activity. The youngest children donated an average of 2.93 candies, and the oldest donated an average of 3.98 candies.[19]

Kindness: The child's expression of care and affection

Green and Schneider investigated generosity and helping in boys from kindergarten to high school age. They found an increase with age in the number of candy bars children were willing to give to other students. Out of the five they were given, kindergarteners donated an average of 1.36 candy bars. This amount gradually increased to 4.24 candy bars donated by thirteen- and fourteen-year-olds.[20] Handlon and Gross investigated how many pennies preschool through sixth grade children would give to their partners who participated in the game played to win the pennies. Nursery and kindergarten children gave an average of 28 percent of their winnings, whereas sixth graders gave 60 percent.[21]

Ugurel-Semin asked children between four and sixteen years old to divide an uneven number of nuts between themselves and a peer. Children were classified as generous if they gave away more than what they kept. About 33 percent of the four- to six-year-olds, 63 percent of the seven- to eight-year-olds, 77 percent of the nine-year-olds, and 10 percent of the twelve-year-olds were generous.[22] These studies demonstrate not only that generous behavior may increase with age but also that even some young children are capable of making sacrifices for the benefit of others.

SELF STUDY 22

Generosity

Think of someone who is special to you. What is this person like? What does he or she enjoy doing? Make a list of objects that you own that this person might like to have. Pretend you are this person and rank order the list from most to least wanted. Now select something from the list to give to your special friend.

What procedure did you use to select the gift? Did you decide which of the things you were or were not willing to part with? How important is your selection for the person who will receive it? How important is it to you? How do you feel about giving away this object?

Give the gift to your friend. How did he or she react, and how do you feel? Does the appreciation your friend demonstrates make your loss worthwhile?

Not all studies have demonstrated age changes in generosity. Marian Yarrow and Carolyn Waxler provided children three to seven years old with opportunities to give, share, help, and comfort.[23] To measure generosity, children were given more snacks than an adult. The adult comments about the inequality and expresses disappointment in the amount. A prosocial response occurred if a child gave some of his or her snack to the adult. Children's performance scores on this task were combined with their scores in another task. In the second situation, a child has the only available pole in a fishing game. An adult who wants to participate in this game expresses an interest in trying but does not actually ask to use the pole. Children are then observed to see if they share the fishing pole with the adult. About 33 percent of all children responded prosocially to at least one of the above two tasks, and, in free play situations, acts of generosity or sharing occurred about 2.1 times in a forty-minute block of time. Comforting occurred about as frequently as sharing, and helping was the most frequent. No behavioral differences due to age were observed. It might have been interesting to observe the characteristics of the two-thirds who failed to give or to share in the structured tasks.

Children's generosity may be influenced by the length of ownership of the resource. In one study five- and six-year-old children who gained either gum, candy, or pennies in a guessing game were more likely to donate more of the rewards if they had them for one hour than if they were asked to donate them immediately.[24] Under these conditions, familiarity made the resource easier to give up. Either the novelty wore off or more satisfaction was gained by giving things they felt they owned. Of course, more meaningful items may not be given away so easily. Some children, for example, may experience a great deal of distress parting with an old toy even though it has outlived its usefulness.

Age changes in generosity may be due to factors other than an increase in altruism. Children may be changing in the value they attribute to the resource. Older children may be more willing to part with candy, pennies, or nuts because they no longer consider these items so important. Such changes with age may also be due to an increase in awareness of social desirability. Older children may be more aware that they are supposed to be generous. Thus, their giving may be an attempt to live up to this expectation. Younger children may not be as generous because they are not as concerned about adult approval.

Caretaking and compassion:
To respond to distress

Responding to someone in distress is not an easy task for children. They first must overcome anxiety in an emotionally intense situation and then actually respond. Their effort can involve caretaking, an active physical attempt to resolve the problem, or compassion, a psychological effort to provide support. Getting a bandage, cleaning a wound, and serving soup to a sick person are examples of caretaking. Hugging, holding soneone's hand, and giving verbal reassurance are examples of compassion.

Children's responses to distress have been examined in a series of intriguing studies carried out by Ervin Staub. The results of one of these studies are shown in Table 7.2.[25] In this study, kindergarten, first, second, fourth, and sixth grade children were left either alone or in pairs in a room. They then heard a tape of severe distress (the sound of a child falling off a chair followed by crying) and were observed to see if they would leave the room to investigate. Several important conclusions can be made from the results. First, distress helping increased then decreased with age. Second, distress helping was most likely to occur when a child was with someone. Third, some children offered help at all ages, alone or in pairs. Additional research by Staub demonstrated that the frequency of helping by children increased when adults gave them permission to leave the room.[26] As previously mentioned, older children may not offer aid because they are more conscious of adult disapproval.

Table 7.2
Children's responses to distress[25]

Percentage offering help

	When in pairs	When alone
Kindergarteners	50%	20%
First graders	85%	25%
Second graders	95%	50%
Fourth graders	40%	50%
Sixth graders	30%	15%

CHILD STUDY 17

Compassion

Separately approach three children of different ages and comment about not feeling well. You might say something like, "Oh Annie, I feel so yucky! I've got a pain in my tummy and my head aches. I feel like a sick bear." Make this comment when your target child is not preoccupied with a friend or a classroom task.

How do these children respond to your comments? What do they say and what do they do? Do they simply offer psychological support (e.g., "You feel better tomorrow!") or do they make specific suggestions to resolve the problem (e.g., "If you go home and go to bed, you will be better!)? Do they do nothing?

How did the children differ in the way they responded to your disclosure? What factors contributed to these differences? How did age seem to influence the children's compassionate behavior?

In their study of children's prosocial behavior Marion Yarrow and Carolyn Waxler investigated whether children of ages three to seven and one-half would offer comfort to an adult who either hurts her finger or cries over a sad story.[27] About 37 percent of all children responded with some form of caretaking in at least one of the two distress situations. Consistent with the findings of Staub, there was a decline in comforting with age, as older children failed to respond when the adult pinched her finger. When children were alone with a crying adult, they demonstrated a wide range of differences in their responses to distress. Some were very pleased with themselves whereas others sought approval for what they had done. Some of the children became upset. Others tentatively approached the adult but hurried back to what they were previously doing when they heard another adult returning. Some refrained from helping because they thought their intrusion might be embarrassing to the person who was upset. Those who did not respond had a reason for not doing so, even though they may have been sympathetic to the other's distress.

Both young and older children have an age-related barrier to caretaking and showing compassion. Young children may want to respond to someone in distress, but they also may be confused by the situation and not know what to do. Older children are more likely to understand the other's problem and know what to do, but they are more likely to be afraid of breaking a rule and getting into trouble. These differences suggest a twofold task for teachers: (1) To help children understand and evaluate the alternatives for responding to another's distress and (2) to affirm the norm of social responsibility.

Helping: To extend a hand

Children are helping when they contribute their time and effort to another's success. A child who opens a door for a person whose arms are full, runs to get something for the teacher, or finds a crayon for a friend demonstrates his or her interest in helping.

Knowing when and how much help to offer are two problems children may have as they learn this skill. They must learn that sometimes a person wants to try to accomplish a task without help. A child who rushes over to show her friend how to put a puzzle together may be interfering rather than helping. If the child becomes frustrated

---

CHILD STUDY 18

Helping

With at least two different age groups "accidentally" spill a handful of about twenty-five pennies. Choose a time when children are free to move about the room on their own initiative. Immediately after dropping the money make a complaint that is loud enough for all the children to hear. You might say something like, "Oh no! I dropped all my pennies. I'll never find them all now!" Then get down on the floor and *slowly* begin picking up the money. If no one helps make another unhappy comment. Do not ask the children for help but do observe their behavior.

How do the children react to your accident? Do they take no notice, notice but do nothing, or do they try to help? How many become involved? What do they say? How many pennies does each age group pick up? (You might ask a friend to make notes for you because you will not be able to write until everything is picked up.)

What differences in helping do you notice between children in the same group or between groups? Why do you think these differences occurred? How does age seem to influence children's helping behavior? What other factors might be important?

Kindness: The child's expression of care and affection

and needs help, a friend might show her where one piece goes, giving just enough help so that she can complete the puzzle on her own. Young children are not as sensitive to these subtle cues that indicate when and how much assistance is needed. Consequently, they may become "bossy" and frequently either fail to offer any help at all or try to do more than is needed.

SELF STUDY 23

Researching helping

Try one of the following experiments and keep a record of what happens. Afterwards, think about the tentative conclusions you can make about people's attitudes toward helping.

1. *Directions*: Stop five people in a fairly busy part of town and ask directions to a local store. How do people react to your request?

2. *The Drop*: Accidentally drop twenty-five pennies in five different, but fairly busy, department stores. How many people, if any, stop to help you each time? How many of the pennies do you get back?

3. Make up your own experiment to explore how willing people are to help. You might vary your appearance or the age of the audience to see what effects these differences make. Do not do anything to embarrass or anger others by revealing the nature of your investigation.

Research has demonstrated that helping is one of the most frequent prosocial acts. In the Yarrow and Waxler study, children of ages three to seven and one-half were given the opportunity to aid an adult who accidently spilled a box of tennis balls. In another situation the adult spilled a box of eating utensils. The adult became immediately occupied with another task after the accident, thus giving the children time to gather **215** the fallen objects. About 52 percent of the children helped in at least one of the two situations. This percentage is considerably higher than the number of children who shared, donated, or offered comfort. In a free play context these children were also observed to offer help about 6.2 times in a forty-minute period. Helping occurred about three times more often than other forms of kindness.[28]

Green and Schneider found that helping behavior increased with age.[29] When an adult researcher accidentally knocked pencils off a table, 48 percent of the five- and six-year-olds volunteered to help pick them up. This percentage increased, however, to 76 percent at seven and eight years and 100 percent at nine and ten years. When asked if they would help put books together for poor children, however, 96 percent of the five- to six-year-olds offered to volunteer at least one time period. Apparently some forms of help are more attractive to children than others. Children may, for example, volunteer to help clean up because they enjoy that activity, but they may shy away from another task because they dislike it or are busy doing something else.

Other research, though, has suggested that there are either low levels of helping in older children or that there is a decline in helping with increased age. Joan Grusec and her colleagues discovered that even after being urged to help or observing another donating marbles, less than one-third of their eight- to ten-year olds picked up objects which an adult spilled off a table.[30] In a study involving observation and analysis of teacher ratings, three- to five-year-old children were rated more helpful to peers than eight- to ten-year-old children.[31] The researchers suggested that older children may have been socialized into achievement and independence norms which inhibited helping.

These contradictory results may be the result of a combination of factors. First, the nature of the helping task may have different appeal at different ages. Second, the concern for adult approval for one's actions may vary as well as the norms which underlie kindness. If the task is simple and familiar even young children can help, but research does not clearly explain why some children help while others do not.

Sharing: To make resources available

Sharing happens when one child offers a resource which can be enjoyed or used by another person. Because it involves the allocation of a resource, sharing is similar to generosity. The important difference is that sharing is temporary but generosity is permanent. These definitions do conflict with the informal as well as general research usage of the words. In the vast majority of instances the word *sharing* has been used to refer to generous acts.[32]

The differentiation of these two terms is helpful for clarity because the outcomes of sharing and generosity are different. A toddler may, with some caution, be willing to share her teddy bear with a friend, but she may be completely opposed to actually giving the toy away. Misunderstandings may arise when children confuse these concepts. A young child may put a friend's toy in her pocket because she believes that use or desire implies ownership. Another child may jealously guard his toys because he thinks that allowing someone to use something is the same as actually giving it away. When we use the word *sharing* to refer to both outcomes, we unwittingly contribute to this misunderstanding.

There is very little research on children's sharing behavior. Harriet Rheingold and her associates found that children as young as fifteen months will share without prompting by showing objects to other persons, by giving them objects to view and manipulate, and by engaging in partner play with the objects.[33] More research is needed, though, to investigate how older children share what they own with others.

Compassion and affirmation: To touch the heart

Compassion and affirmation are both psychological forms of kindness. The emphasis of these behaviors is on influencing another's emotions or state of mind. Compassion is a response to another's distress and affirmation can occur as a part of everyday relationships. The other forms of kindness mentioned earlier in this section are task oriented because their goal is to resolve a specific problem.

Several research studies have examined psychological forms of kindness. Lawrence Severy and Keith Davis differentiated between helping with tasks and helping with emotional distress. They noted that three- to five-year-old children were more likely than eight- to ten-year-old children to show concern and engage in psychological helping.[34] Valerie Perdue and Jane Connor investigated patterns of touching between preschool children and male and female teachers.[35] They found that teachers offered friendly, helping, attentional, and incidental contact more to children of their own sex than to those of the opposite sex. Male teachers offered considerably more friendly touching to boys than to girls, and children offered more friendly than helping or attentional physical contacts. On the average, boys displayed about 12.5 friendly forms of contact per hour in contrast to 8.4 for girls. Boys offered more friendly physical contacts than girls, especially in their relationships with male teachers. This form of touching is an example of affirmation, a gentle response which conveys support and interest to another person. Finally, observation of two- to five-year-old children has revealed that they offered affectionate, supportive contacts more frequently than aggressive overtures in both initiating and maintaining relationships.[36]

SELF STUDY 24

Ten things you like about yourself

Make a list of ten or more things that you like about yourself. Tape the list somewhere (like on a bathroom mirror) where seeing them might lift your spirits. After each key word or phrase identify some real or fictional person that shares the same quality. For example:

> I really care for my spouse   Like the hero in Richard Matheson's book, "What Dreams May Come."

When you think of your quality, think of the other person or character. This may serve to reduce your sense of isolation and build a sense of connection between yourself and others.

Education and kindness

The first step in nurturing kindness skills in children is to have a clear picture of the types of skills we can encourage. In Table 7.3 nine kindness skills are identified. These skills undergo transformation as children grow older, and this fact must be taken into account when planning an educational program. Thus, a three-year-old would talk about kindness much differently than a seven-year-old. The information presented earlier in this chapter may help us understand the kinds of

Table 7.3
Summary of kindness skills for children.

Skill	Definition	Social/cognitive processes
1. Identifying and discussing kindness issues.	1. The ability to identify and describe kind behavior and to become more aware of and identify values regarding kindness. *Examples*: Child sees mother struggling to open a door with her arms full of bags and says, "Wait mommy, I *help* you!" A three-year-old pats his baby brother's head and says, "Gentow!" (gentle) A seven-year-old defines "selfish" as "being mean, not being kind to others, not giving anything you have to others. You know, it's the same thing as being greedy."	Defining *Generosity* *Caring* *Sharing/selfishness* *Affection* *Gentleness* *Kindness/cruelty*
2. Demonstrating a sensitivity to distress.	2. The ability to recognize a situation in which a person needs help, compassion, affection, sharing, generosity, or care. *Examples*: A three-year-old sees an older brother crying and runs to him and says, "Oh, oh, Danny sad!" A five-year-old hears another child cry out in a nearby room and leaves to investigate.	Defining Sensing
3. Describing alternatives and their consequences for resolving misfortunes.	3. The ability to list the various responses which could be initiated to resolve social concerns (strategies should increase in appropriateness as age increases). *Example*: A three-year-old reports he would get a bandage for a friend who scraped his knee. A five-year-old says she would bring her friend to the washroom, clean the scrape, and put a bandage on the cut if her friend was hurt.	Deciding
4. Offering, accepting, and requesting generosity.	4. The ability to give up a resource to benefit another; the ability to accept such offerings when they are wanted and request them when they are needed. *Examples*: A three-year-old gives a friend a bite of his cookie. A five-year-old donates twenty-five cents to charity.	Defining Sensing Deciding Acting

Skill	Definition	Social/cognitive processes
5. Offering, accepting, and re-questing caretaking.	5. The ability to take some direct form of action to alleviate the distress of another living creature; the ability to accept this care when offered and request it when needed. *Examples*: A child works with parents to set his dog's broken leg. A preschooler brings food to the bed of her sick father. A three-year-old feeds a cat.	Defining Sensing Deciding Acting
6. Offering, accepting, and re-questing help when such assis-tance is needed.	6. The ability to respond to another to resolve a task-oriented problem, accept it from another when it is need-ed, refuse it when it is not wanted, and ask for it when it is not readily available. *Examples*: A five-year-old asks her teacher to help her with a puzzle. A three-year-old gets a book from an adjacent room for his older sister.	Defining Sensing Deciding Acting
7. Offering, accepting, and re-questing compas-sion.	7. To ability to show concern and support both nonverbally and verbally; the ability to accept and request well-inten-tioned offerings of psychological support. *Examples*: A toddler hugs her crying mother. A four-year-old holds the hand of a frightened younger sibling when in a strange environment.	Defining Sensing Deciding Acting
8. Offering, accepting, and re-questing sharing.	8. The ability to relinquish control of a resource by allowing another to use it for a temporary period of time; the ability to accept such offerings when they are wanted and re-quest them when they are needed. *Examples*: A three-year-old lets a friend ride her tricycle. A three-year-old lets a friend play with his truck.	Defining Sensing Deciding Acting
9. Offering, accepting, and re-questing af-fectionate and gentle affirmation.	9. The ability to demonstrate one's positive feelings for an-other both verbally and nonverbally; the ability to accept and request other's expressions of affection when needed; the ability to handle or touch something softly and tender-ly; the ability to respond verbally in a calming and caring manner; the ability to enjoy such expressions of kindness and to request it when it is needed. *Examples*: A preschooler approaches his teacher and says, "I love you." A preschooler is hugged and returns the show of affection from her teacher. A child approaches father and asks for a hug. A three-year-old is handed an uncooked egg and deli-cately turns it over and hands it back A two-year-old boy softly pats his napping mother on the face. A preschooler approaches an infant and, with her face close to the child, speaks in a very soft voice.	Defining Sensing Deciding Acting

ideas young children may express. In addition to age, individual personality influences how these skills are acquired. Two kindergarten children may show very different personal styles in the way they offer help to others. One child may proceed very quietly and another may be more outgoing, but both are demonstrating an ability to help.

Kindness is more than offering something to another. It also means accepting and even asking for some form of aid. From this perspective kindness is a mutual activity involving both a giver and a receiver who need each other. The giver needs the receiver to provide the opportunity for demonstrating kindness, and the receiver can benefit from what the other has to offer. Some children can offer kindness but cannot bring themselves to ask for it even when it is needed. Others may have difficulty accepting another's personal generosity, help, or care. When working with children, we might keep these three forms of kindness in mind.

Our relationships with children

How can we best use our everyday relationships to nurture kindness in children? Helping children acquire both a healthy self-interest and a concern for others is not always a simple task. We may want our children to be properly assertive, to decide on what is important to them, and to protect themselves, but this concern for individualism may need to be tempered by a consideration for others. Without social concern, individualism may degenerate into self-indulgence, and our capacity for caring is what makes us distinctly human.

The suggestions for developing kindness may not, by themselves, have significant impact on children's behavior, but when combined with others they may have a greater effect. Each issue can challenge us to reconsider how we relate to children and how we organize our classrooms.

First, we can talk with children about their ideas regarding kindness. We can ask children to describe forms of kindness like sharing, helping, or being generous. We can encourage them to reflect on the consequences of acting (or failing to act) to benefit another and to evaluate the merits of various solutions to distress. These conversations can take place while driving to visit a hospital, across the lunch table, or under a tree during outside play.

When a child is unfamiliar with a concept or cannot describe causes, consequences, or solutions to problems, we can introduce an issue as simply as possible (see Chapter 2). We can talk about kindness, for example, about being gentle or taking care of someone. Such descriptions can be personal messages which reveal our understanding of kindness.

A teacher once returned to visit a preschool class where he had been a student teacher. When he entered the classroom one of his former pupils enthusiastically ran up to him and punched him in the stomach. The child was neither angry nor seeking revenge. He was apparently very happy to see an old friend, but he did not know how to express his joy and affection effectively. After recovering, the teacher hugged the boy and said, "Keith, I'm really happy to see you again, and I'm glad you're so happy too. But you know what? I would much rather have a *gentle* hug from you than a punch. That hurt." At that point the child responded with a warm embrace. He either

Kindness: The
child's expres-
sion of care
220   **and affection**

did not know how to express affection in a positive way or was too preoccupied. Helping children understand a situation and how they might effectively respond is likely to be more effective than simply saying something like, "Hey, don't you know you're not supposed to hit?"

When children reveal an idea about kindness which appears to be a misconception or an irrational point of view, we can gently encourage them to consider other possibilities (see Table 7.4). Instead of telling children they are wrong, we might use a problem-solving dialogue (see pp. 21–25) to help them explore their idea and discover its limitations and contradictions. If children are encouraged to do their own thinking and draw their own conclusions, they are more likely to modify their ideas (unless they are too young to comprehend an issue).

Table 7.4
Contrasting examples of irrational and rational beliefs about kindness

Irrational beliefs		Rational beliefs
• I can't be kind.	vs.	• I can use my skills to be kind to others.
• I am a sissy or failure if I ask for kindness.	vs.	• No matter how smart I am, I will sometimes need help.
• If I'm kind there has got to be something in it for me.	vs.	• I can find pleasure in being kind even if I don't get anything for it.
• No one needs me.	vs.	• Other people need me.

Secondly, we can encourage children to become more aware of distress when it appears in others. Noticing and then being affected by another's need for aid are important stages in offering kindness. In one research study seven- to twelve-year-old children who recalled sad experiences of someone they knew were more generous than children who thought of other experiences.[37] In another study children who participated in role playing of kind behavior and emotional sensitivity actually increased their nonverbal helping behavior.[38] We can invite children to acquire this awareness by discussing the meaning of such cues as crying, frustration, or withdrawal and how they might respond to the person who displays them. For example, a teacher could ask a child what he might be able to do for a peer who is upset after being rejected by another group of children. Also, while reading a story a teacher might ask a small group of children how they would feel if, like one of the characters in the book, one of their pets died. The point here is to encourage children to sense the impact that distress can have on others.

Third, we can emphasize sincerity in kindness. Kindness is an act of the heart that may quickly fade under pressure from adults. If we try to force children to be kind we may actually be teaching them to view kindness as an impersonal ritual, something that people should do because others expect it. A forced kindness is a counterfeit gift.

Being forced to say, "I'm sorry" is a common example of phony kindness. One four-year-old was an "I'm sorry" expert. Whenever he hurt someone (which happened to be quite often) he would immediately say, "I'm sorry!" If an adult confronted him about his misbehavior he would complain with righteous indignation, "But teacher, I *said* I was *sorry!*" Used in this manner, the statement assumes a mantle of ritualistic vindication. As soon as it is uttered wrongdoers may believe that it absolves them of any blame for their acts.

Fourth, we can create an environment which promotes kindness. Three aspects of our classrooms are important for nuturing kindness—children's affect, reinforcement of kindness, and the teacher's example. Happy children are likely to be more generous than those who experience unpleasant emotions.[39] Children who are sad, frightened, or angry are more likely to be distracted by their own needs, but a happy child feels more like sincerely reaching out to others. Anything we can do to enhance children's sense of well-being can have a positive effect on their concern for others.

Research has also shown that social reinforcement in the form of praise can have a positive effect on the generosity of children from kindergarten through second grade.[40] Comments like, "Wow, Jason, you sure did a good job taking care of Karen's cut knee!" and "Janice, you give such nice and gentle hugs!" emphasize the importance of being kind and give recognition to kind acts. If such reinforcement is overdone, though, children may act in order to obtain adult approval. To offset this risk we can emphasize the consequences a child's act may have on another rather than simply give approval to what the child has done.

We can also look to ourselves and consider the example we set for children. Research has demonstrated that children from preschool through grade school are influenced by the actions of nurturant models who demonstrate kind behavior.[41] Marian Yarrow and her colleagues concluded that, ". . . the parent who is an altruist in the world but is cold with his child reaps a small harvest in developing altruism in his child. Further, the parent who conveys his values to the child didactically as tidy principles, and no more, accomplishes only that learning in his child. Generalized altruism would appear to be best learned from parents who not only try to inculcate the principles of altruism, but who also manifest altruism in everyday interactions."[42] Children look to us as examples of how to act. How frequently do we demonstrate what we hope to see in them?

Finally, *we can create opportunities for children to be kind.* We can influence a situation so that it provides children with a chance to practice some aspect of kindness. Instead of assuming control in most situations we might look for ways to involve children. For example, if one child needs help we may be able to encourage another child to respond instead of us. If some treat is to be distributed, we can allow a child to distribute it. Instead of getting something down from a shelf ourselves, we can lift a child up to get it for one of his or her peers. If a child has a minor cut, we can supervise another child in performing first aid. The possibilities are endless. Instead of the teacher being the center or source of kindness, we can give children opportunities to assume some of these nurturant responsibilities and help them learn the actual mechanics of being generous, helping, caring, and sharing. By doing so we may enhance their feelings of self-competence and confidence as they begin to look to each other as sources of kindness.

Activities to promote kindness

The following activities may be helpful to you as you design a program to nurture kindness in children. Please review Tables 3.3 and 3.4 (pp. 53-54) before beginning. For additional activities on kindness see the following:

29 Lotion Motion
32 Still Water
38 Know Hear
39 Know Talk
40 Know See

94

Wishing Well (four years +)

Purpose To help children offer and accept gentle affection and affirmation. Key concept is *wishing*.

Setting Community group arrangement

Materials None

Activity **1.** Teach children to chant the following poem.

Mind Gifts

If my mind was a wishing well
I'd wish a wish
To wish you well
I'd reach back in my mind
For a wish of smiles and fun
A thought for me to find
To warm you like the sun.

2. When one full verse is finished, describe a wish you would like to make for one of the children in your group. For example, you might say, "Sarah, my wish for you is that every morning ten beautiful teddy bears wake you up with gentle hugs and songs of sunshine." Then have the group sing the chant once more and ask a volunteer to offer a wish to anyone they would like. Repeat the process and continue as long as children want. Be sure to stop before they become tired, and give children who did not have a turn an opportunity to do so at another time.

Suggestion Your wishes may be pure fantasy or they may be something you know a child really wants to have or do. At any one time, though, make your wishes at the same level and type for all children in your group.

---

95 Yay Say . . . A Strength Bombardment Exercise (four years +)

Purpose To help children offer and accept gentle affection and affirmation and to help them become more aware of personal strengths in themselves and others. Key concepts are *like*, *kind*, and *appreciate*.

Setting Community group arrangement

Materials None

Activity 1. The teacher can begin the activity by saying something like, "I think sometimes many people have a difficult time telling other people what they like about them. I would like to give us a chance to tell other people in the group what they do that we like and appreciate. Would anyone like to hear what other people like about them?"

2. When a child volunteers you might say something like, "Chris would like to hear what we like about her [or him]. Chris, I like the way your bright smile cheers me up in the morning." The strength which is identified should be clear and specific, for example, "I like the way you try to help the other children when they can't do something. You don't boss the other person, but you give them just enough help so they can do it." When you are finished, invite other children to describe those traits or behaviors they are attracted to in the child that volunteered. Ask the child who hears the positive comments to listen to what others are saying without feeling obligated to say anything in return.

3. If someone voices a complaint you might respond with, "Yes, that is something you want to tell Chris, but this is a time for talking about those things we like about other people. Dan, what does Chris do that you like?" If a child cannot think of anything, you might introduce a few of your own observations, for example, "Dan, you really seem to enjoy Brad's company when you ride together. I think you like to be with Brad when you get the trikes out. Is that true?"

Suggestions You may choose to focus on only one child each day. This can avoid the problems of children comparing their comments to those of others. If no one volunteers you might begin by hearing their positive comments about you.

Even children for whom you may feel some antagonism have qualities or have done something you have appreciated. This activity challenges us to emphasize the positive aspects of our relationships with them.

---

96 It's OK to Brag Because I'm Well Worth It (four years +)

Purpose   To help children express self-affection and acknowledge their own personal strengths. Key concepts are *like, kind,* and *pride.*

Setting   Community group arrangement

Materials   None

Activity   **1.** The teacher can begin the activity by saying something like, "I think everyone can think of something they really like about themselves. One of the things I like about myself is _____ ." Be clear and specific (e.g., . . . the way I like to play dress-up with children or . . . the way I tell a story).
2. After your comments, encourage other children to identify those characteristics they like in themselves. Do not force anyone to mention something. Those who choose to remain quiet are listening and watching. They will feel more comfortable talking if they don't feel pushed.
3. Following all comments, talk about the importance of feeling proud of ourselves.

---

97 Gentle People (three years +)

Purpose   To help children understand kindness and offer gentle affection and affirmation. Key concept is *gentleness.*

Setting   Community group arrangement

Materials   A small, tame pet (e.g., mouse or hamster)

Activity   **1.** Ask the children if they understand what *gentleness* means. Discuss various ways people can be gentle to each other. Tell the group that you would like to give them the opportunity to be gentle.
2. Bring the pet into the circle, and mention that you would like to see how gentle all of the children can be. Giving assistance where needed, pass the animal around the circle. Bypass children who do not want to handle the animal, and gently take the animal away from those who are too rough. Clearly identify any inappropriate behavior and suggest more suitable responses. Comment on any gentle behavior you may see.

Suggestions   Be particularly cautious with children who have a background of being   **225** rough. Even the most interpersonally aggressive child can be very gentle when it comes to handling animals. (One four-year-old with a history of seriously aggressive behavior was capable of being very gentle with animals.) Be aware that rough treatment of an animal is usually preceded by silly behavior.

The same activity can be done with an egg if you are hesitant to have an animal passed around.

98 Kind and Gentle Hands (three years +)

Purpose   To help children understand kindness and offer and accept gentle affection and affirmation. Key concepts are *like, kind,* and *gentle.*

Setting   Small groups of about six children, each with an adult leader.

Materials   None

Activity   **1.** Talk briefly with the children about the importance of touching in building friendships and becoming close to people. Try to elicit as many examples of pleasant contact as possible (e.g., hugs, kisses, shaking hands, back rubs, etc.). Talk also about some of the negative types of contact. Tell the children that you would like to give them the opportunity to show kindness by being gentle with their hands.

2. One of the adults should then move to the center of the circle and lie on his or her stomach. The other adult then say something like, "Oh, Nancy is tired. She would like to see if your hands can help wake her up. I will gently and softly slap her back so she will feel all awake and tingly!" After a few moments the teacher returns to his or her spot so a child can volunteer.

3. At some point change from a full-hand slapping and tapping to a finger-tip tapping. As the finger tapping subsides the group can slowly massage the recipient's back and legs. When finished, remain by the recipient's side while he or she describes the experience. Allow any children who are interested to have a turn as the recipient.

Suggestion   The primary purpose of this activity is to help children understand that physical contact, and even gentle slapping, does not have to be unpleasant. Show children who are too rough how to slap more gently.

99 Arm Lifting (four years +)

Purpose   To help children understand kindness and offer and accept affectionate and gentle behavior; to help children learn how to cooperate. Key concepts are *like, kind,* and *gentle.*

Setting   Community group and partner arrangement

Materials   **None**

Activity   **1.** Briefly discuss the concept of *gentleness*. Tell the children that you have a simple activity for them to do in which they will have the opportunity to be gentle and kind to other children in the class.

2. Demonstrate the activity by lifting first the arms and then the legs of a reclining volunteer. Ask the children to form partnerships. Have one child in each pair become the "lifter" and the other the "rag doll." The rag doll lies down on his or her back and relaxes while the lifter kneels at his or her right side. When everyone is ready, ask the lifters to gently and slowly lift their partner's right arm. The rag dolls do nothing other than let their partners lift their arms. After a brief moment, have them gently and slowly lower their partners' arms. Ask them to remain quiet while doing this.

3. Repeat the same process with the other arm and the legs. Then have the children switch roles.

Suggestions   The teacher can help the children understand the activity even better by becoming the first rag doll and allowing several children lift his or her arms and legs. Watch for silly or rough behavior, and show children how to lift gently and slowly.

This activity gives children the opportunity to experience the gentle care of another child. Under close supervision by an adult, a child can also gently lift and lower the partner's head.

---

100   Body Lifting (four years +)

Purpose   To help children understand kindness and accept affectionate and gentle behavior; to help children learn how cooperate. Key concepts are *like, kind, gentle,* and *cooperate.*

Setting   Small groups of about eight children, each with an adult leader

Materials   **None**

Activity   **1.** Engage the children in a discussion similar to that suggested at the beginning of *Kind and Gentle Hands* (Activity 98). Introduce the idea of lifting as a form of gentleness. Tell the children that you would like to see if they can work together to gently lift someone in their group. After briefly describing the activity, ask if any of the children would like to be picked up by the others.

2. Ask the volunteer to lie on his or her back with arms at the sides and legs together. All the children who elect to help should kneel on both sides of the **227**

child who is about to be lifted (the recipient). The recipient is then asked to close his or her eyes. The rest of the children should then slide their hands, palms up, underneath the back and legs. For security, the teacher should be at the recipient's head with one hand underneath the head and the other under the spine. On the teacher's signal everyone lifts and comes to a standing position. Try to keep as quiet as possible. If the child being lifted is securely held and the children seem comfortable, they might try rocking him or her and singing part of a song.

3. After a few moments, slowly lower the recipient back to earth. Once he or she is down, ask the children to slowly take their hands from underneath the body and wait for him or her to get up. Ask the recipient to talk about how he or she felt. Take a few moments to discuss what happened and begin again with another volunteer.

Suggestions Children are typically quite serious when they participate in this activity. Remind the children how important it is to be quiet if they do start acting silly.

The child who is being lifted can choose about five children to do the lifting or volunteers can be requested.

101

Kind Find Crayons (three years +)

Purpose To help children understand kind behavior and offer, accept, and ask for task-oriented help. Key concepts are *help* and *kindness*.

Setting Community group and learning center arrangement

Materials One sheet of paper for each child
Bowl of crayons
Scissors
Paste
Collage materials, in individual cups

Activity **1.** Ask the children if they know what *help* means. Discuss various ways people can help each other, for example, if someone drops a bag of groceries then people nearby can *help* pick them up or if a parent has a big job to do at home their children can *help* them complete the task. Tell the children that you have an activity for them to do which will give them an opportunity to help each other.

2. Distribute one sheet of paper to each child and adult in the group. (Don't forget yourself.) Discuss the various tasks the children can do with the paper (e.g., drawing on it, cutting it, pasting materials on it, etc.). Ask them to think of something they would like to do with the paper. After a moment of thought tell them that you would like to see if they can help each

Kindness: The child's expression of care
228 **and affection**

other get the things they need. Begin the activity by saying something like, "I would like some *help*, [*name child*], can you *help* me? Can you please get me two crayons?" When the helper returns, thank him or her. The child should then return to his or her previous place.

3. Then ask, "Who else would like to have some help?" Go around the circle and ask each child to make a specific request to a potential helper. If any child refuses to help, ask the child making the request to choose some-one else. If any children decline to ask for assistance, first ask the rest of the children to indicate their willingness to help (to let them know of the others' interest). If they still refuse to request a helper, they may get the materials on their own.

4. When everyone has what they need, summarize the activity by saying something like, "Sometimes we really like to get help from other people, and sometimes we like to be helpful." Name the children who helped and asked for help. Then say, "Sometimes we don't want help, like [name those who refused to ask for help], and sometimes we don't feel like helping, like [name those who refused to help], but everyone at some time or the other needs help. Sometimes it is important that we help them." Following the summary discussion have the children go to their tables and complete their tasks.

---

102   Nature Tribute (four years +)

Purpose   To help children understand kindness and offer affection, especially as they apply to nature. Key concepts are *kindness*, *caring*, and *nature*.

Setting   Community group in a safe outdoor location

Materials   Arts and crafts materials as appropriate (see below)

Activity   **1.** Discuss the idea that people can be kind to nature as well as to other people. Try to identify as many examples as you can, for example, keeping a picnic area clean or leaving wild flowers for all to see rather than picking them. Tell the children that you have an activity for them to do which will give them an opportunity to be kind to nature.

2. Choose to pay tribute to some nearby object of nature, such as a tree, rock, or plant. Each group member finds something outside that he or she finds interesting to decorate the object. Have the children sit around or near the object and encourage them to talk about it, emphasizing those aspects that are liked and appreciated. Following this, the children can approach the object and attach or place their decorations nearby. When all are finished, sing a song or play a game around the object.

103

Flower Power (three years +)

Purpose   To help children understand kindness and offer and accept generous behavior; to help children become aware of feelings associated with interpersonal attraction. Key concepts are *happiness, giving,* and *friends.*

Setting   Community group and learning center arrangement

Materials   Precut pieces of paper flowers (stems, leaves, buds, etc.)
Small cups of paste
Paste appliers
Crayons

Activity   **1.** Tell the children that you have a flower-making activity for them to do. Pass out the materials and demonstrate how the various pieces can be put together to make a flower. Mention that the children can draw happy faces on them if they would like, and ask them to make at least two flowers. Dismiss the children to desks or tables to complete their work.

2. When the children return to the circle, discuss the types of feelings people can have when they give and receive something worthwhile. Mention that it might be interesting if they would give one or more of their flowers away to other people in their class. Ask something like, "Would anyone like to give one or both of their flowers to someone else in the group?" The teacher can begin by giving his or her flowers to others. Children interested in giving their flowers can take turns doing so.

3. When finished, ask the children to discuss what happened and acknowledge any feelings they might want to share. Reemphasize the important aspects of kindness and generosity.

Suggestions   The group leader should be very alert to what is happening in the group. Which children give flowers but do not receive any from the others? Who refuses to participate? Do any negative feelings need to be acknowledged and dealt with in the group? How can learning be reinforced outside of the group?

Do not pressure children to give away their flowers. Their generosity should be sincere.

104

Sad Person (four years +)

Purpose   To help children understand kindness, affection, and those feelings associated with loss, deprivation, or separation; to practice offering and accepting compassionate and generous behavior. Key concepts are *friendly, kind,* and *sad.*

Setting	Community group arrangement
Materials	Bowl of handouts or consumables (cookies, trinkets, sugarless gum, etc.)
Activity	**1.** Discuss the question, "What are some friendly things people can do for you when you feel sad?"
	2. Tell the children that you are going to do an activity with them in which they will have a chance to be friendly to someone who is pretending to be sad. Set the bowl in front of you. Ask if anyone would like to be a pretend-sad person, and have the volunteer go to the center of the circle. The children forming the circle chant, "Sad person, sad person, it's okay to feel sad and blue. Can one of us be friendly to you?"
	3. The center child then names someone in the group who goes to the bowl and gets a gift to give to the sad person. Another child then goes to the center to be the sad person, and the game continues as before.
Suggestions	Be alert to children who are not asked to be "friendly." Go to the center yourself and ask a child who needs the experience to be a giver. Without being too obvious, talk about the sadness that might result from not being chosen to be friendly.
	Let the children "ham it up" in their pretending. You might even suggest that they mention pretend reasons for feeling sad.

---

105   **Caring Sharing** (three years +)

Purpose	To help children understand the meaning of kindness and to develop the ability to offer and accept generosity. Key concepts are *friendly behavior, kindness, affection, like,* and *friends*.
Setting	Community group arrangement
Materials	Bowl of handouts or consumables (e.g., cookies, trinkets, sugarless gum, etc.)
Activity	**1.** Set the bowl in the center of the circle (or in your lap) and ask the children if they know what *giving* and *friendly* mean. Briefly discuss how you felt when someone gave something to you. Comment that since everyone in the class is learning to become friends, you would like to give them an opportunity to give something to each other.
	2. Take something out of the bowl and say, "I would like to be friendly to Cheryl." After giving the gift, ask the others if they would like to be friendly to someone. Allow volunteers to individually select a "gift" for someone of their choice, and let the children give them, one at a time, until everyone has received something. You may have to take a second turn to give a "gift" to someone who is likely to be overlooked by the others. This should be done

with great tact to avoid embarassing the child. Remind children that giving something to someone is one way of showing affection, showing that you like them. *No one should leave the group without having received at least one share.*

Suggestion   This is an excellent activity at all times. It is especially effective when children are getting to know each other better.

---

106 Being Generous (four years +)

Purpose   To help children understand kindness and to offer, ask for, and accept generosity; to help learners develop the ability to make a negotiating response to conflict. Key concept is *generous.*

Setting   Community group arrangement

Materials   One small cookie (or other nutritious consumable) for each child
One paper bag

Activity   **1.** Tell the children that you have a sharing activity for them to do. Take out the bag and say something like, "Here is a bag of _____ that I am going to give to someone in the group. When this person gets the sack he or she may decide to keep them all, give them all away, or give some away and keep some. When he or she is finished, we will talk about what happened."
2. Give the bag to one of the children, choosing a typically generous child the first time around, and describe the options. When finished, ask the children who received something to raise their hands. Talk about how they feel. Ask those who did not receive anything to raise their hands, and encourage them to talk about how they feel.
3. Try to help children understand that sometimes others will not want to give things to them. Explain that they might feel sad since it is not fun to be left out. Also, tell them that if they are patient and if they ask, they may find someone who will be generous.

---

107 Won or None (four years +)

Purpose   To help children understand generosity and to offer, ask for, and accept generous behavior; to help learners understand and express feelings of rejection. Key concepts are *generous, sadness,* and *anger.*

Setting   Community group arrangement

Materials   One nutritious cookie for every two children

Activity   **1.** Pass out a cookie to every other child sitting in the circle. Tell them they cannot eat the cookie until you tell them it is time. Ask the children who have cookies to raise their hands. Then ask all those who did not receive cookies to do likewise. Explain that you will give an opportunity to those who received cookies to be generous to others. Then ask those who would like to do so to give some of their cookie to others in the group. (They still should not eat their cookies.)

2. Ask those who still do not have any cookie to raise their hands. Then say "Some children do not have cookies. Would anyone like to give some to them?" Following this round of generosity, encourage children to talk about their experiences. Try to ensure that children who received cookies understand the feelings of those who failed to get any. Then give the group another opportunity to be generous. Following this, the children can eat their cookies.

Suggestion   Avoid making a big fuss over those who did not receive cookies. Some children may take this mild rejection in stride. If you act *as though* they *should* feel angry or sad, they may become upset. Those who are upset will have their feelings resolved if they are confident that others are aware of those feelings.

108

The Blind Child and the Children (four years +)

Purpose   To help learners understand kindness and to offer and accept helping and sharing behavior; to promote children's sensitivity to touch. Key concepts are *kindness, sharing, help,* and *gentle.*

Setting   Community group arrangement

Materials   One blindfold
Interesting objects

Activity   **1.** Tell the children that you are going to play a game in which one of the children will pretend to be blind and the rest of the children will get things for him or her to touch. Discuss some of the ways people can be kind to those who have a physical disability.

2. Blindfold a volunteer who remains seated on the floor or ground throughout the game. Have the rest of the children bring interesting objects for the "blind" child to touch. As each child gives something to the recipient, mention their name, for example, "Here is something Jim would like to give you."

3. After two or three minutes have the blindfolded child exchange places with another.

Suggestion   Show the children how to gently hand something to someone who is blind. Some may want to drop objects into their hands, and this can be frightening to the recipient.

Emphasize the idea that sometimes people *do not* want help. For example, sometimes blind people want to find things for themselves.

---

109   Are You Sick? (three years +)

Purpose   To help children understand physical discomfort, kind behavior, and feelings associated with being ill; will practice offering and accepting kindness. Key concepts are *sick/ill, doctors, nurses, yucky feelings,* and *taking care of.*

Setting   Community small group arrangement

Materials   Blanket
Various medical aids (e.g., thermometer, filled hot water bottle, washcloth, toy syringe, pretend medicine

Activity   **1.** Show the materials and ask the children if they know what they are used for. Generate a brief discussion about illness, the feelings of people who are sick, and the importance of good care.
2. Tell the children that you have a pretend game about being sick. Have a volunteer lay down on the blanket in the center of the circle. Fold the blanket over so it covers the child. Pretend you are a doctor and, in a gentle manner, complete the ritual of attending to someone ill.
3. Let another child pretend to be sick, let another be the doctor, and encourage him or her to care for the sick individual. After several rounds, discuss the importance of good care during illness. Set up a play hospital or room with the medical aids so that young children can role play the sick/caretaker situation.

Suggestion   Discuss the sex-role stereotypes related to the medical profession and emphasize the fact that many girls now become doctors and many boys decide to be nurses when they grow up.

This is also a good opportunity to discuss the dangers of medicines and precautions for their proper use.

---

110   Where Are You Hurt? (four years +)

Purpose   To help children understand physical discomfort and to learn awareness of the behavior and feelings associated with physical harm; to practice offering and accepting kindness. Key concepts are *hurt, blood, helping, taking care of fear,* and *sadness.*

Setting	Community group and partner arrangement
Materials	Thick red paint and small brush
	Small wet sponges or paper towels (one for each child and teacher)
	Adhesive bandages (one for each child and a few extras)
Activity	**1.** Tell the children that they are going to do an activity in which they will have the chance to help each other with a pretend problem. Ask the children if they understand what *hurt* means. Elicit a variety of responses. Guide the discussion into a conversation about bleeding, first aid, and feelings about being hurt. Talk about the various responses people can make to help someone who is hurt.
	2. Take out the paint and brush and tell the children that you need someone to put a bandage on a pretend cut. Dot your finger (or hand, arm, etc.) with paint and have a volunteer wash, dry, and bandage the "wound." Mention that you would like them to have a chance to help each other with a pretend hurt.
	3. Go around to each pair and ask the children to tell you who is pretending to be hurt and who is the helper. The hurt child indicates where he or she wants the wound to be and the helper is given the cleaning cloth and bandage. A teacher's aide might help in handing out materials. Repeat the process by suggesting that the children switch roles.
	4. When all pairs are finished, discuss their responses to the activity. Describe your own observations of their behavior.
Suggestions	Do not be concerned with the proper application of bandages. Young children often find them somewhat difficult to apply. If application seems too frustrating, offer assistance. This is not a technical lesson on first aid.

 Hospital Gifts (three years +)

Purpose	To help children understand physical discomfort, kind behavior, and feelings associated with separation; to practice offering kindness. Key concepts are *sick/ill, hospitals, sadness, loneliness, fear,* **and** *kindness.*
Setting	Learning center arrangement
Materials	Paper
	Crayons
Activity	**1.** Ask the children to describe what *being sick* means. Direct the conversation to a discussion of hospitals and hospital experiences. Ask the children to consider how hospitalized sick people feel. Discuss how it feels to be separated from family and familiar things.

2. Tell the children that you are going to give them an opportunity to do something kind for some sick children (or grandparents). Pass out the paper and crayons and ask the children to draw a special picture for someone who is in the hospital (or nursing home).

3. When finished emphasize the positive feelings that the pictures might produce in the people who get them. Place all pictures in an envelope and mail it to the pediatric or geriatric ward of a local hospital.

Suggestions Drawing can include comments written by the children. Those children who are unable to write might dictate their thoughts to an adult.

The pediatric or geriatric ward of a hospital or nursing home should be notified before the drawings are sent. Instead of mailing, the gifts can be dropped off as part of a field visit to a hospital or nursing home. If you receive any responses from patients or hospital staff members, be sure to read them to the children.

References on kindness

Clarke, J. I. *Self-Esteem: A Family Affair.* Minneapolis: Winston Press, 1978.

Elkins, D. P. *Glad to Be Me.* Englewood Cliffs: Prentice-Hall, 1976.

Gaylin, W. *Caring.* New York: Avon Books, 1976.

Mayeroff, M. *On Caring.* New York: Harper and Row, 1971.

Montagu, A. *Touching: The Human Significance of the Skin.* New York: Columbia University Press, 1971.

Mussen, P., and Eisenberg-Berg, N. *Roots of Caring, Sharing, and Helping.* San Francisco: W. H. Freeman, 1977.

Staub, E. *Positive Social Behavior and Morality, Vol. 2: Socialization and Development.* New York: Academic Press, 1979.

Appendix
The Personal/Social Skills Rating Scale

The Personal/Social Skills Rating Scale (Individual Form) is a simple, informal instrument teachers can use to keep records of a specific child's progress over three periods of time. To define more clearly and find examples for any of the forty-three skills listed on the form consult the text chapters that examine the skills in more detail. You may wish to use the form as it is or reduce the number of skills to include only those you would like to emphasize in your program. Keep in mind that no total score is given, and the child's performance is compared to a standard of behavior rather than to the performance of others. You may also elect to use these skills as general guidelines to derive more specific objectives appropriate to the developmental levels of the children you work with. As they are currently stated, the skills may be too abstract to be measured accurately. On the other hand, this scale may serve its purpose if it is used as an informal record of a child's progress and consulted when introducing classroom experiences to meet individual needs.

Personal/Social Skills Rating Scale
Individual Form

Name: _____ Sex (M/F) _____

Birthdate: _____ Today's Date _____

Instructions: To the right of each skill note the child's performance by using one of the following symbols:

> **?** = Unknown, insufficient observation
> **0** = Observed no evidence of skill
> **+** = Some evidence but needs opportunities to learn more
> **++** = Proficiency in skill, considering age

Three columns have been provided for assessment at different times.

This chart can be useful as a guide for determining strengths and weaknesses of children and making decisions regarding the types of learning experiences children need, and as a record for use with parents or administrators.

Themes	Skills	Assessment		
		First	Second	Third
Body awareness	1. Identifies human characteristics			
	2. Identifies body parts and functions			
	3. Describes and accepts learning limits			
	4. Describes developmental changes			
	5. Attends to body processes			
	6. Uses senses to make contact			
	7. Uses sensory vocabulary			
	8. Uses sensory media			
	9. Engages in uninhibited movement			

Themes	Skills	Assessment		
		First	Second	Third
	10. Applies problem solving to body distress			
Emotional development	11. Recognizes, describes, and accepts emotions			
	12. Applies problem solving to emotions			
	13. Communicates emotions			
	14. Expresses emotions nonverbally			
	15. Shows sensitivity to the emotions of others			
Affiliation	16. Makes approval and disapproval statements			
	17. Applies problem solving to social isolation			
	18. Differentiates between and describes functions of family.			
	19. Identifies friends			
	20. Applies problem solving to friendship			
	21. Attracts and holds attention of others			
	22. Achieves social contact			
	23. Initiates and maintains friendships			

Themes	Skills	Assessment		
		First	Second	Third
Conflict and cooperation	24. Identifies restraints on behavior			
	25. Applies problem solving to conflict			
	26. Applies problem solving to cooperation			
	27. Makes requests and shows pride			
	28. Makes reasonable assertions			
	29. Offers protection and assistance			
	30. Leads and follows peers			
	31. Demonstrates cooperation			
	32. Can engage in cooperative competition			
	33. Makes a negotiating response to conflict			
	34. Protects self from harm			
Kindness	35. Describes concepts of kindness			
	36. Demonstrates sensitivity to distress			
	37. Applies problem solving to distress			
	38. Offers, accepts, and requests generosity			
	39. Offers, accepts, and requests caretaking			

Themes	Skills	Assessment		
		First	Second	Third
Kindness	40. Offers, accepts, and requests help			
	41. Offers, accepts, and requests compassion			
	42. Offers, accepts, and requests sharing			
	43. Offers, accepts, and requests affirmation			

Date

Recorder

Reference notes

Chapter one

1. Rollo May, "Contributions of Existential Psychotherapy," in *Existence: A New Dimension in Psychiatry and Psychology*, Rollo May, Ernest Angel, and Henri Ellenberger, eds. (New York: Simon and Schuster, 1958), pp. 37-91.

2. William Damon, *The Social World of the Child* (San Francisco: Jossey-Bass, 1977).

3. Stella Chess, Alexander Thomas, and Herbert Birch, *Your Child Is a Person* (New York: Viking Press, 1965).

4. William Schutz, *Profound Simplicity* (New York: Bantam Books, 1979); *see also* William Schutz, *The Interpersonal Underworld* (Palo Alto, Ca.: Science and Behavior Books, 1966), pp. 17-33.

5. Benjamin Bloom, J. Thomas Hastings, and George F. Madaus, *Handbook on Formative and Summative Evaluation of Student Learning* (New York: McGraw-Hill, 1971), pp. 19-41.

Chapter two

1. William Damon, ed., *Social Cognition* (San Francisco: Jossey-Bass, 1978).

2. Erving Goffman, *Interaction Ritual* (Garden City: Doubleday, 1967).

3. Peter Berger and Thomas Luckman, *The Social Construction of Reality* (Garden City: Doubleday, 1966).

4. Malcolm W. Watson and Kurt W. Fischer, "Development of Social Roles in Elicited and Spontaneous Behavior During the Preschool Years," *Developmental Psychology*, 16 (1980), 483-494.

5. Jerome Kagan, *Understanding Children: Behavior, Motives, and Thought* (New York: Harcourt Brace Jovanovich, 1971), p. 85.

6. Jerome Bruner, Jacqueline J. Goodnow, and George A. Austin, *A Study of Thinking* (New York: Wiley, 1956), pp. 243-245.

7. Paul H. Mussen, John J. Conger, Jerome Kagan, *Child Development and Personality* (New York: Harper and Row, 1974), pp. 272-277.

8. John H. Flavell, "Concept Development," in *Handbook of Child Psychology,* Paul H. Mussen, ed. (New York: Wiley, 1970), pp. 983-1060.

9. Jean Piaget, *The Moral Judgment of the Child* (New York: Harcourt, 1932).

10. Jean Piaget, *The Origins of Intelligence in Children* (New York: International Universities Press, 1952).

11. Kagan, 1971, pp. 92-101.

12. Victor Daniels and Laurence Horowitz, *Being and Caring* (San Francisco: San Francisco Book Co., 1976), pp. 238-239.

13. Albert Ellis, *Humanistic Psychotherapy: The Rational-Emotive Approach* (New York: The Julian Press, 1973).

14. Charles A. Smith and Duane Davis, "Teaching Children Non-Sense," *Young Children,* (September 1976), pp. 438-447.

15. Jean Piaget, *The Language and Thought of the Child* (New York: Harcourt Brace Jovanovich, 1926).

16. Frances E. Vaughan, *Awakening Intuition* (Garden City: Anchor Press, 1979).

17. Robert Summer, *The Mind's Eye: Imagery in Everyday Life* (New York: Dell, 1978).

18. Robert E. Ornstein, *The Psychology of Consciousness* (New York: Penguin, 1972), pp. 65-89.

19. Louis M. Savary and Margaret Ehlen-Miller, *Mindways: A Guide for Exploring Your Mind* (New York: Harper and Row, 1979).

20. Richard de Mille, *Put Your Mother on the Ceiling: Children's Imagination Games* (New York: Penguin, 1976).

21. Jerome Singer, *The Inner World of Daydreaming* (New York: Harper and Row, 1975), pp. 123-148; *see also* Dorothy G. Singer and Jerome L. Singer, *Partners in Play: A Step-by-Step Guide to Imaginative Play in Children* (New York: Harper and Row, 1977), pp. 1-15.

22. George I. Brown, *Human Teaching for Human Learning* (New York: Viking Press, 1971).

23. Robert Plutchik, "A Language for the Emotions," *Psychology Today* (February 1980), pp. 68-78.

24. George Spivak, Jerome Platt, and Myrna Shure, *The Problem-Solving Approach to Adjustment* (San Francisco: Jossey-Bass, 1976), pp. 18-55.

25. Myrna B. Shure and George Spivak, *Problem-Solving Techniques in Child Rearing* (San Francisco: Jossey-Bass, 1978), pp. 36-37.

26. Charles A. Smith, "Puppetry and Problem-Solving Skills," *Young Children* (March 1979), pp. 4-11.

27. Spivak, *et al.,* 1976, pp. 18-55.

Chapter three

1. Bennet Berthanthal and Kurt W. Fischer, "Development of Self-Recognition in the Infant," *Developmental Psychology,* 14(1978), pp. 44-50.

2. L. Joseph Stone and Joseph Church, *Childhood and Adolescence* (New York: Random House, 1975).

3. Stone and Church, 1975, p. 287.

4. Jean Brooks-Gunn and Wendy S. Mathews, *He and She: How Children Develop Their Sex-Role Identity* (Englewood Cliffs, N.J.: Prentice-Hall, 1979); Janet Chafetz, *Masculine/Feminine or Human? An Overview of the Sociology of Sex Roles* (Itasca, Il.: F. E. Peacock, 1974).

5. Spencer K. Thompson, "Gender Labels and Early Sex-Role Development," *Child Development*, 46(1975), pp. 339-347.

6. Walter Emmerich, Karla S. Goldman, Barbara Kirsh, and Ruth Sharabany, "Evidence for a Transitional Phase in the Development of Gender Constancy," *Child Development*, 48 (1977), pp. 930-936; Ronald Slaby and Karen Frey, "Development of Gender Constancy and Selective Attention to Same-Sex Models," *Child Development*, 46(1975), pp. 849-856.

7. Spencer K. Thompson and Peter M. Bentler, "The Priority of Cues in Sex Discrimination by Children and Adults," *Developmental Psychology*, 5(1971), pp. 181-185.

8. Dorothy C. Ullian, "The Development of Conceptions of Masculinity and Femininity," in *Exploring Sex Differences*, Barbara Lloyd and John Ascher, eds. (London: Academic Press, 1976), pp. 25-47.

9. Lawrence Kohlberg, "A Cognitive-Developmental Analysis of Children's Sex-Role Concepts and Attitudes," in *The Development of Sex Differences*, Eleanor Maccoby, ed. (Stanford, Ca.: Stanford University Press, 1966), pp. 82-173; Eleanor Maccoby and Carol Jacklin, *The Psychology of Sex Differences* (Stanford, Ca.: Stanford University Press, 1974), pp. 1-2; 364-365.

10. T. Parsons and R. F. Bales, *Family, Socialization, and Interaction Process* (Glencoe, Il.: Free Press, 1953).

11. Maccoby and Jacklin, 1974, pp. 349-360.

12. Maccoby and Jacklin, 1974, p. 362.

13. Laura Sidorowicz and G. Sparks Lunney, "Baby X Revisited," *Sex Roles*, 6(1980), pp. 67-73.

14. John Condry and Sandra Condry, "Sex Differences: A Study of the Eye of the Beholder," *Child Development*, 47(1976), pp. 812-819.

15. Carol Seavy, Phyllis Katz, and Sue Zalk, "Baby X: The Effect of Gender Labels on Adult Responses to Infants," *Sex Roles*, 1(1975), pp. 103-110.

16. Hannah L. Frisch, "Sex Stereotypes in Adult-Infant Play," *Child Development*, 48(1977), pp. 1671-1675.

17. Beverly Fagot and G. Patterson, "An *In Vivo* Analysis of Reinforcing Contingencies for Sex-Role Behaviors in the Preschool Child," *Developmental Psychology*, 1(1969), pp. 563-568.

18. Kohlberg, 1966; Michael Lewis and Marsha Weinraub, "Origins of Early Sex-Role Development," *Sex Roles*, 5(1979), pp. 135-153; Maccoby and Jacklin, 1974.

19. John C. Masters, Martin E. Ford, Richard Arend, Harold D. Grotevant, and Lawrence V. Clark, "Modeling and Labeling as Integrated Determinants of Children's Sex-Typed Behaviors," *Child Development*, 50(1979), pp. 364-371.

20. Fagot and Patterson, 1969; Michael Lamb and Jaipaul Roopnarine, "Peer Influences on Sex-Role Development in Preschoolers," *Child Development*, 50(1979), pp. 1219-1222.

21. Chafetz, 1974.

22. Deanna Kuhn, Charon Nash, and Laura Brucken, "Sex-Role Concepts of Two- and Three-Year-Olds," *Child Development*, 49(1978), pp. 445-451.

23. David G. White, "Effects of Sex-Typed Labels and Their Source on the Imitative Performance of Young Children," *Child Development*, 49(1978), pp. 1266-1269.

24. Ullian, 1976.

25. Bette W. Tyron, "Beliefs about Male and Female Competence Held by Kindergarteners and Second Graders," *Sex Roles*, 6(1980), pp. 85-97.

26. Sally G. Koblinsky, Donna F. Cruse, and Alan I. Sugawara, "Sex-Role Stereotypes and Children's Memory for Story Content," *Child Development*, 49(1978), pp. 452-458.

27. Mary E. Goodman, *Race Awareness in Young Children* (New York: Collier Books, 1964), p. 252.

28. E. S. Brand, R. A. Ruiz, and A. M. Padilla, "Ethnic Identification and Preference: A Review," *Psychological Bulletin*, 81(1974), pp. 860-890.

29. A. S. Rice, R. A. Ruiz, and A. M. Padilla, "Person Perception, Self-Identity, and Ethnic Group Preference in Anglo, Black, and Chicano Preschool and Third-Grade Children," *Journal of Cross-Cultural Psychology*, 5(1974), pp. 100-108.

30. B. Hunsberger, "Racial Awareness and Preference of White and Indian Canadian Children," *Canadian Journal of Behavioral Science*, 10(1978), pp. 176-180; B. G. Rosenthal, "Development of Self-Identification in Relation to Attitudes Toward the Self in the Chippewa Indians," *Genetic Psychology Monographs*, 90(1974), pp. 43-141.

31. J. E. Williams and C. A. Rousseau, "Evaluation and Identification Responses of Negro Preschoolers to the Colors Black and White," *Perceptual and Motor Skills*, 33(1971), pp. 587-599; K. B. Clark and M. P. Clark, "Racial Identification and Preference in Negro Children," in *Readings in Social Psychology*, G. E. Swanson, T. M. Newcomb, and E. L. Hartley, eds. (New York: Henry Holt and Co., 1952); *see also* Hunsberger, 1978, pp. 176-180, and Rice, Ruiz, and Padilla, 1974, pp. 100-108.

32. Goodman, 1964, pp. 256-261.

33. Shirley C. Samuels, *Enhancing Self-Concept in Early Childhood* (New York: Human Sciences Press, 1977), pp. 153-159.

34. J. D. Porter, *Black Child, White Child. The Development of Racial Attitudes* (Cambridge, Mass.: Harvard University Press, 1971); H. W. Stevenson and E. C. Stewart, "A Developmental Study of Racial Awareness in Young Children," *Child Development*, 29(1958), pp. 399-409; *see also* Hunsberger, 1978, pp. 176-180.

35. Robert Coles, *Children of Crisis: A Study of Courage and Fear* (Boston: Atlantic Monthly Press, 1967).

36. J. A. Green and H. B. Gerard, "School Desegregation and Ethnic Attitudes," in *Integrating the Organization*, H. Fromkin and J. Sherwood, eds. (Glencoe: Il: The Free Press, 1975).

37. Karen K. Dion, "Young Children's Stereotyping of Facial Attractiveness," *Developmental Psychology*, 9(1973), pp. 183-188.

38. Judith H. Langlois and Cookie Stephen, "The Effects of Physical Attractiveness and Ethnicity on Children's Behavior Attributions and Peer Preferences," *Child Development*, 48(1977), pp. 1694-1698.

39. Karen K. Dion and Ellen Berscheid, "Physical Attractiveness and Peer Perception," *Sociometry*, 37(1974), pp. 1-12.

40. Lyn E. Styczynski and Judith Langlois, "The Effects of Familiarity on Behavioral Stereo-

types Associated with Physical Attractiveness in Young Children," *Child Development*, 48(1977), pp. 1137-1141.

41. Langlois and Stephen, 1977, pp. 1694-1698.

42. Karen K. Dion, "The Incentive Value of Physical Attractiveness for Young Children," *Personality and Social Psychology Bulletin*, 3(1977), pp. 67-70.

43. Dion, "Young Children's Stereotyping," 1973, pp. 183-188.

44. Langlois and Stephen, 1977, pp. 1694-1698.

45. Judith H. Langlois and Chris A. Downs, "Peer Relations as a Function of Physical Attractiveness: The Eye of the Beholder or Behavioral Reality," *Child Development*, 50(1979), pp. 409-418.

46. Richard M. Lerner and Jacqueline V. Lerner, "The Effects of Age, Sex, and Physical Attractiveness on Child-Peer Relations, Academic Performance and Elementary School Adjustment," *Developmental Psychology*, 13(1977), pp. 585-590; Margaret M. Clifford and Elaine Walster, "The Effects of Physical Attractiveness on Teacher Expectations," *Sociology of Education*, 46(1973), pp. 248-258.

47. John Salvia, Robert Algozzine, and Joseph Sheare, "Attractiveness and School Achievement," *Journal of School Psychology*, 15(1977), pp. 60-67.

48. Karen K. Dion, "Physical Attractiveness and Evaluation of Children's Transgressions," *Journal of Personality and Social Psychology*, 24(1972), pp. 207-213.

49. Anne Bernstein and Philip Cowan, "Children's Concepts of How People Get Babies," *Child Development*, 46(1975), pp. 77-91; Anne C. Bernstein, "How Children Learn about Sex and Birth," *Psychology Today* (January, 1976), pp. 31-35.

50. H. Kreitler and S. Kreitler, "Children's Concepts of Sexuality and Birth," *Child Development*, 37(1966), pp. 363-378.

51. Carolyn P. Edwards and Michael Lewis, "Young Children's Concepts of Social Relations: Social Functions and Social Objects," in *The Child and Its Family*, Michael Lewis and Leanord A. Rosenblum, eds. (New York: Plenum Press, 1979), pp. 245-266.

52. Edwards and Lewis, 1979, pp. 251-265.

53. I. Alexander and A. M. Alderstein, "Affective Responses to the Concept of Death in a Population of Children and Early Adolescents," *Journal of Genetics and Psychology*, 93(1959), pp. 166-167.

54. Jean Piaget, *The Child's Concept of the World* (New York: Harcourt Brace, 1929); G. A. Safier, "A Study in Relationships Between the Life and Death Concepts," *Journal of Genetic Psychology*, 105(1964), p. 283; P. M. Smeets, "The Influence of MA and CA on the Attribution of Life and Life Traits to Animate and Inanimate Objects," *Journal of Genetic Psychology*, 124(1974), pp. 17-27.

55. J. D. Melear, "Children's Conceptions of Death," *Journal of Genetic Psychology*, 123(1973), pp. 359-360.

56. P. Childers and M. Wimmer, "The Concept of Death in Early Childhood," *Child Development*, 42(1971), pp. 1299-1301; R. Kastenbaum, "The Child's Understanding of Death: How Does It Develop?" in *Explaining Death to Children*, Earl A. Grollman, ed. (Boston: Beacon Press, 1967), pp. 89-110.

57. Maria H. Nagy, "The Child's View of Death," *Journal of Genetics and Psychology*, 73(1948), pp. 3-27.

58. Alexander Lowen, *Pleasure: A Creative Approach to Life* (New York: Penguin Books, 1970), pp. 207-226.

59. Stone and Church, 1975, pp. 236-237.

60. Abraham Maslow, *The Farther Reaches of Human Nature* (New York: The Viking Press, 1971), pp. 251-266.

61. Gay Hendricks and Russel Wills, *The Centering Book: Awareness Activities for Children, Parents, and Teachers* (Englewood Cliffs, N.J.: Prentice-Hall, 1975), pp. 29-34; Ron Kurtz and Hector Prestera, *The Body Reveals* (New York: Bantam Books, 1976), pp. 18-44.

62. Ida Rolf, *Rolfing: The Integration of Human Structures* (Santa Monica, Ca: Dennis-Landman, 1977).

63. Don Johnson, *The Protean Body: A Rolfer's View of Human Flexibility* (New York: Harper-Colophon Books, 1977); Will Schutz and Evelyn Turner, *Body Fantasy* (New York: Harper and Row, 1976).

64. Stone and Church, 1975, pp. 240-243.

65. Cathy Neuhauser, Beulah Amsterdam, Patricia Hines, and Margaret Steward, "Children's Concepts of Healing: Cognitive Development and Locus of Control Factors," *American Journal of Orthopsychiatry*, 48(1978), pp. 335-341.

66. John D. Campbell, "Illness as a Point of View: The Development of Children's Concepts of Illness," *Child Development*, 46(1975), pp. 92-100.

67. Campbell, 1975, pp. 92-100.

68. Chuck Smith, "The First Year Journal," Unpublished Manuscript, Bowling Green State University, 1972, p. 18.

69. Chuck Smith, "Will They Call Me Teacher? Part II," Unpublished Manuscript, Texas Tech University, 1973, p. 7.

70. Sandra Bem, Wendy Martyna, and Carol Watson; "Sex Typing and Androgeny: Further Explorations of the Expressive Domain," *Journal of Personality and Social Psychology*, 34(1976), pp. 1016-1023; June Singer, *Androgeny: Toward a New Theory of Sexuality* (Garden City: Anchor Press, 1976).

71. Ashley Montagu, *Touching: The Human Significance of the Skin* (New York: Columbia University Press, 1971).

Chapter four

1. Robert Plutchik, "A Language for the Emotions," *Psychology Today* (February 1980), pp. 68-78.

2. J. C. Coleman and C. L. Hammen, *Contemporary Psychology and Effective Behavior* (Glenview, Il.: Scott Foresman, 1974), pp. 462-463.

3. P. T. Young, *Understanding Your Feelings and Emotions* (Englewood Cliffs, N.J.: Prentice-Hall, 1975), p. 12.

4. Robert Plutchik, *Emotion: A Psychoevolutionary Synthesis* (New York: Harper and Row, 1980), pp. 152-172.

5. Plutchik, 1980, pp. 160-165.

6. Helen Borke, "Interpersonal Perception of Young Children: Egocentrism or Empathy?" *Developmental Psychology*, 5(1971), pp. 263-269; Helen Borke, The Development of Empathy in Chinese and American Children between Three and Six Years of Age: A Cross-Cultural Study," *Developmental Psychology*, 9(1973), pp. 102-108.

7. W. A. Bousfield and W. D. Orbison, "Ontogenesis of Emotional Behavior," *Psychology Review*, 59(1952), pp. 1-7.

8. David H. Bauer, "An Exploratory Study of Developmental Changes in Children's Fears," *Journal of Child Psychology and Psychiatry*, 17(1976), 69-74.

9. Plutchik, 1980, pp. 96-99.

10. Sidney M. Jourard, *The Transparent Self* (New York: D. Van Nostrand, 1964), pp. 19-30.

11. Chuck Smith, "The First Year Journal," Unpublished Manuscript, Bowling Green State University, 1972, p. 67.

12. T. R. Sarbin, "Role Theory," in *Handbook of Social Psychology*, G. Lindzey, ed. (Cambridge, Mass.: Addison-Wesley, 1954), pp. 223-258.

13. John H. Flavell, Patricia Botkin, Charles Fry, John Wright, and Paul Jarvis, *The Development of Role-Taking and Communication Skills in Children*, (Huntington, N.Y.: Robert E. Krieger Publishing Co., 1975), pp. 4-8.

14. Robert L. Selman and Diane F. Byrne, "A Structural-Developmental Analysis of Levels of Role Taking in Middle Childhood," *Child Development*, 45(1974), pp. 803-806.

15. Jean Piaget, *The Language of Thought of the Child* (New York: Harcourt, Brace, 1926); K. H. Rubin, "Egocentrism in Childhood: A Unitary Contruct?" *Child Development*, 44(1973), pp. 102-110; S. Weinheimer, "Egocentrism and Social Influence in Children," *Child Development*, 43(1972), pp. 567-578.

16. Jean Piaget and B. Inhelder, *The Child's Conception of Space* (London: Routledge & Kegan Paul, 1956).

17. N. Burns and L. Cavey, "Age Differences in Empathic Ability among Children," *Canadian Journal of Psychology*, 11(1957), pp. 227-230.

18. Michael C. Smith, "Cognizing the Behavioral Stream: The Recognition of Intentional Action," *Child Development*, 49(1978), pp. 736-743.

19. D. G. Mossler, R. S. Marvin and M. T. Greenberg, "Conceptual Perspective Taking in 2- to 6-Year-Old Children," *Developmental Psychology*, 12(1976), pp. 85-86.

20. Henry M. Wellman and Jacques D. Lempers, "The Naturalistic Communicative Abilities of Two-Year-Olds," *Child Development*, 48(1977), pp. 1052-1057.

21. Helen Borke, "Piaget's Mountains Revisited: Changes in the Egocentric Landscape," *Developmental Psychology*, 11(1975), pp. 240-243.

22. Francine Deutsch, "Female Preschoolers' Perception of Affective Responses and Interpersonal Behavior in Videotaped Episodes," *Developmental Psychology*, 10(1974), pp. 733-740.

23. Rona Abramovitch, "Children's Recognition of Situational Aspects of Facial Expression," *Child Development*, 48(1977), pp. 459-463; Rona Abramovitch and Eleanor Daly, "Inferring Attributes of a Situation from the Facial Expression of Peers," *Child Development*, 50(1979), pp. 586-589.

24. Micahel P. Maratsos, "Nonegocentric Communication Abilities in Preschool Children," *Child Development*, 44(1973), pp. 697-700.

25. Susan K. Green, "Causal Attribution of Emotion in Kindergarten Children," *Developmental Psychology*, 13(1977), pp. 533-534.

26. Smith, 1978, pp. 736-743.

27. Lawrence A. Kurdek, "Structural Components and Intellectual Correlates of Cognitive Perspective Taking in First- through Fourth-Grade Children," *Child Development*, 48(1977), pp. 1503-1511.

28. Smith, 1972, pp. 22-24.

29. Dorothy C. Briggs, *Your Child's Self-Esteem* (Garden City: Doubleday, 1970), pp. 104-111.

30. Smith, 1972, p. 19.

31. Smith, 1972, p. 31.

Chapter five

1. James Youniss, *Parents and Peers in Social Development* (Chicago: University of Chicago Press, 1980), pp. 1-42.

2. Zick Rubin, *Children's Friendships* (Cambridge, Mass.: Harvard University Press, 1980), p. 1-11.

3. Albert Bandura, J. E. Grusec, and F. L. Menlove, "Vicarious Extinction of Avoidance Behavior," *Journal of Personality and Social Psychology*, 5(1967), pp. 16-23; Albert Bandura and F. L. Menlove, "Factors Determining Vicarious Extinction of Avoidance Behavior through Symbolic Modeling," *Journal of Personality and Social Psychology*, 8(1968), pp. 99-108.

4. W. W. Hartup and B. Coates, "Imitation of a Peer as a Function of Reinforcement from the Peer Group and Rewardingness of the Model," *Child Development*, 38(1967), pp. 1003-1016.

5. H. F. Harlow and M. K. Harlow, "Social Deprivation in Monkeys," *Scientific American*, 207(1962), pp.136-146.

6. Emory L. Cowen, Andreas Pederson, Haroutun Babigian, Louis D. Izzo, and Mary Ann Trost, "Long-term Follow-up of Early Detected Vulnerable Children," *Journal of Consulting and Clinical Psychology*, 41(1973), pp. 438-446.

7. Eric Fromm, *Man for Himself* (New York: Holt, Rinehart, and Winston, 1947), p. 23.

8. Bobby R. Patton and Kim Giffin, *Interpersonal Communication* (New York: Harper and Row, 1974), pp. 172-173.

9. Lee C. Lee, "A Cognitive Theory of Interpersonal Development," in *Friendship and Peer Relations*, Michael Lewis and Leonard Rosenblum, eds. (New York: Wiley, 1975), pp. 213-215.

10. Lee, 1975, p. 215.

11. William Damon, *The Social World of the Child* (San Francisco: Jossey-Bass, 1977), pp. 154-157; Robert L. Selman and Anne Selman, "Children's Ideas about Friendship: A New Theory," *Psychology Today* (October 1979), 71-114; James Youniss and Jacqueline Volpe, "A Relational Analysis of Children's Friendship," in *Social Cognition*, William Damon, ed. (San Francisco: Jossey-Bass, 1978), pp. 1-22.

12. Selman and Selman, 1979, pp. 71-114.

13. Rubin, 1980, pp. 38-40.

14. Erving Goffman, *Relations in Public* (New York: Harper and Row, 1971), p. 79; Erving Goffman, *Interaction Ritual* (Garden City: Doubleday, 1967), p. 71.

15. William A. Corsaro, "'We're Friends, Right?': Children's Use of Access Rituals in a Nursery School," *Language in Society*, 8(1979), pp. 315-336.

16. K. Garvey, "Some Properties of Social Play," *Merrill-Palmer Quarterly*, 20(1974), pp. 163-180.

17. Michael Lewis and Jeanne Brooks, "Infants' Social Perception: A Constructivist View," in *Infant Perception: From Sensation to Cognition, Vol. II*, Leslie B. Cohen and Philip

Salapatek, eds. (New York: Academic Press, 1975), pp. 102-148.

18. Katherine M. Bridges, "A Study of Social Development in Early Infacy," *Child Development*, 4(1933), pp. 36-49.

19. Michael E. Lamb, "A Reexamination of the Infant's Social World," *Human Development*, 20(1977), pp. 65-85.

20. Margaret C. Holmberg, "The Development of Social Interchange Patterns from 12 to 42 months," *Child Development*, 51(1980), pp. 448-456.

21. Edward Mueller and Thomas Lucas, "A Developmental Analysis of Peer Interaction among Toddlers," in *Friendship and Peer Relations*, Michael Lewis and Leonard Rosenblum, eds. (New York: Wiley, 1975), pp. 228-237.

22. Mueller and Lucas, 1975, pp. 237-246.

23. Mueller and Lucas, 1975, p. 241.

24. Mueller and Lucas, 1975, pp. 247-252.

25. Mueller and Lucas, 1975, pp. 247-252.

26. Barbara D. Goldman and Hildy S. Ross, "Social Skills in Action: An Analysis of Early Peer Games," in *The Development of Social Understanding*, Joseph Glick and K. Alison Clarke-Stewart, eds. (New York: Gardiner Press, 1978), pp. 177-209.

27. Edward Mueller and Adrienne Rich, "Clustering and Socially-Directed Behaviors in a Playgroup of One-Year-Old Boys," *Journal of Child Psychology and Psychiatry*, 17(1976), pp. 315-322.

28. Michael D. Lougee, Royal Grueneich, and Willard Hartup, "Social Interaction in Same- and Mixed-Age Dyads of Preschool Children," *Child Development*, 48(1977), pp. 1353-1361.

29. Holmberg, 1980, pp. 448-456.

30. Edward Mueller, Mark Bleier, Joanne Krakow, Katherine Hegedus, and Paulette Cournoyer, "Development of Peer Verbal Interaction among Two-Year-Old Boys," *Child Development*, 48(1977), pp. 284-287.

31. Peter K. Smith, "A Longitudinal Study of Social Participation in Preschool Children: Solitary and Parallel Play Reexamined," *Developmental Psychology*, 14(1978), pp. 517-523.

32. N. V. Moore, C. M. Everton, and J. E. Brophy, "Solitary Play: Some Functional Considerations," *Developmental Psychology*, 10(1974), pp. 830-834; Kenneth H. Rubin, "Relation between Social Participation and Role-Taking Skill in Preschool Children," *Psychological Reports*, 39(1976), pp. 823-826.

33. J. Craig Peery, "Popular, Amiable, Isolated, Rejected: A Reconceptualization of Sociometric Status in Preschool Children," *Child Development*, 50(1979), pp. 1231-1234.

34. Bridges, 1933, pp. 36-49; Lamb, 1977, pp. 65-85.

35. See the description of Lee's observations of infants in Willard Hartup, "The Origins of Friendships," in *Friendship and Peer Relations*, Michael Lewis and Leonard A. Rosenblum, eds. (New York: Wiley, 1975), p. 13.

36. Hartup, 1975, pp. 12-13.

37. Michael Lewis, Gerald Young, Jeanne Brooks, and Linda Michalson, "The Beginning of Friendship," in *Friendship and Peer Relations*, Michael Lewis and Leonard A. Rosenblum, eds. (New York: Wiley, 1975) pp. 27-66.

38. Anna-Beth Doyle, Jennifer Connolly, and Louis-Paul Rivest, "The Effects of Playmate

Familiarity on the Social Interactions of Young Children," *Child Development*, 51(1980), pp. 217-223.

39. J. C. Schwartz, "Effects of Peer Familiarity on the Behavior of Preschoolers in Novel Situations," *Journal of Personality and Social Psychology*, 24(1972), pp. 276-284.

40. Willard W. Hartup, Jane A. Glazer, and Rosalind Charlesworth, "Peer Reinforcement and Sociometric Status," *Child Development*, 38(1967), pp. 1017-1024.

41. Hugh C. Foot, Antony Chapman, and Jean Smith, "Friendship and Social Responsiveness in Boys and Girls," *Journal of Personality and Social Psychology*, 35(1977), pp. 401-411.

42. Craig L. Feldbaum, Terri Christenson, and Edgar O'Neal, "An Observational Study of the Assimilation of the Newcomer to the Preschool," *Child Development*, 51(1980), pp. 497-507.

43. Wyndol Furman, Donald F. Rahe, and Willard Hartup, "Rehabilitation of Socially Withdrawn Preschool Children through Mixed-Aged and Same-Aged Socialization," *Child Development*, 50(1979), pp. 915-922.

Chapter six

1. Will Schutz, *Profound Simplicity* (New York: Bantam Books, 1979), pp. 111-137.

2. Schutz, 1979, p. 117.

3. John H. Flavell, *The Developmental Psychology of Jean Piaget* (New York: D. Van Nostrand, 1963), p. 279; Jean Piaget, *The Language and Thought of the Child* (New York: Harcourt, Brace, 1926).

4. George R. Bach and Herb Goldberg, *Creative Aggression* (New York: Avon Books, 1974), pp. 25-38.

5. Rollo May, *Power and Innocence: A Search for the Sources of Violence* (New York: W. W. Norton, 1972).

6. Rene A. Spitz, *The First Year of Life* (New York: International Universities Press, 1965), pp. 268-271.

7. May, 1972, pp. 137-138.

8. Herbert Fensterheim and J. Baer, *Don't Say Yes When You Want to Say No* (New York: David McKay Company, 1975).

9. May, 1972, p. 148.

10. Terry Orlick, *Winning through Cooperation* (Washington, D.C.: Acropolis Books, 1978).

11. Kenneth A. Dodge, "Social Cognition and Children's Aggressive Behavior," *Child Development*, 51(1980), pp. 162-170.

12. May, 1972, p. 151.

13. Ron Adler and Neil Towne, *Looking Out/Looking In: Interpersonal Communication* (San Francisco: Rinehart Press, 1975), pp. 298-299.

14. May, 1972, p. 23.

15. Orlick, 1978, pp. 136-137.

16. Robert L. Selman, *The Growth of Interpersonal Understanding* (New York: Academic Press, 1980).

17. Selman, 1980, p. 107.

18. Selman, 1980, p. 111.

19. James Youniss, *Parents and Peers in Social Development* (Chicago: University of Chicago Press, 1980), pp. 104-148.

20. Roger E. Jensen and Shirley G. Moore, "The Effect of Attribute Statements on Cooperativeness and Competitiveness in School-Age Boys," *Child Development*, 48(1977), pp. 305-307.

21. George Spivak, Jerome Platt, and Myrna Shure, *The Problem-Solving Approach to Adjustment* (San Francisco: Jossey-Bass, 1976).

22. Spivak, Platt, and Shure, 1976, p. 26.

23. Spivak, Platt, and Shure, 1976, p. 68.

24. L. S. Hewitt, "The Effects of Provocation, Intention, and Consequences on Children's Moral Judgments," *Child Development*, 46(1975), pp. 540-544.

25. Thomas J. Berndt, "The Effect of Reciprocity Norms on Moral Judgment and Causal Attribution," *Child Development*, 48(1977), pp. 1322-1330.

26. B. G. Rule, A. R. Nesdale, and M. J. McAra, "Children's Reactions to Information about the Intentions Underlying an Aggressive Act," *Child Development*, 45(1974), pp. 794-798.

27. E. Staub, "The Learning and Unlearning of Aggression," in *The Control of Aggression and Violence*, Jerome L. Singer, ed. (New York: Academic Press, 1971), pp. 93-124.

28. Nancy C. Much and Richard A. Shweder, "Speaking of Rules: The Analysis of Culture in Breach," in *Moral Development*, William Damon, ed. (San Francisco: Jossey-Bass, 1978), pp. 19-39.

29. Much and Shweder, 1978, p. 30.

30. William Damon, *The Social World of the Child* (San Francisco: Jossey-Bass, 1977), pp. 227-281; L. Nucci and Elliot Turiel, "Social Interactions and the Development of Social Concepts in Preschool Children," *Child Development*, 49(1978), pp. 400-408; Elliot Turiel, "Social Regulations and Domains of Social Concepts," in *Social Cognition*, William Damon, ed. (San Francisco, Jossey-Bass, 1978), pp. 45-74.

31. Nucci and Turiel, 1978, pp. 400-408.

32. Elliot Turiel, "The Development of Concepts of Social Structure," in *The Development of Social Understanding*, Joseph Glick and K. Alison Clarke-Stewart, eds. (New York: Gardiner Press, 1978), pp. 25-107.

33. Turiel, "The Development of Concepts of Social Structure," 1978, p. 80.

34. Wanda C. Bronson, "Developments in Behavior with Age Mates During the Second Year of Life," in *Friendship and Peer Relations*, Michael Lewis and Leonard Rosenblum, eds. (New York: Wiley, 1975), pp. 131-152.

35. Katherine M. Bridges, "A Study of Social Development in Early Infancy," *Child Development*, 4(1933), pp. 36-49.

36. Michael Lewis, Gerald Young, Jeanne Brooks, and Linda Michalson, "The Beginning of Friendship," in *Friendship and Peer Relations*, Michael Lewis and Leonard Rosenblum, eds. (New York: Wiley, 1975), pp. 27-66.

37. Robert F. Marcus, Sharon Telleen, and Edward J. Roke, "Relation between Cooperation and Empathy in Young Children," *Developmental Psychology*, 15(1979), pp. 346-347.

38. Willard W. Hartup, "Aggression in Childhood: Developmental Perspectives," *American Psychologist*, 29(1974), pp. 336-341.

39. G. R. Patterson, R. A. Littman, and W. Bricker, "Assertive Behavior in Children: A Step To-

ward a Theory of Aggression." *Monographs of the Society for Research in Child Development*, 32(1967), pp. 1-42.

40. Hartup, 1974, pp. 336-341.

41. Charles G. McClintock, Joel M. Moskowitz, and Evie McClintock, "Variations in Preferences for Individualistic, Competitive, and Cooperative Outcomes as a Function of Age, Game Class, and Task in Nursery School Children," *Child Development*, 48(1977), pp. 1080-1085.

42. A. T. Jersild and F. V. Markey, "Conflicts between Preschool Children," *Child Development Monographs*, 1935, p. 21.

43. S. Feshbach, "Aggression," in *Carmichael's Manual of Child Psychology, Vol. 2*, P. H. Mussen, ed. (New York: Wiley, 1970).

44. Hartup, 1974, pp. 336-341.

45. Linden Nelson and Spencer Kagan, "Competition: The Star-Spangled Scramble," *Psychology Today* (September 1972), pp. 53-56, 90-91; *see also* Masanao Tado, Hiromi Shinotsuka, Charles G. McClintock, and Frank J. Stech, "Development of Competitive Behavior as a Function of Culture, Age, and Social Comparison," *Journal of Personality and Social Psychology*, 36(1978), pp. 825-839.

46. Nelson and Kagan, 1972, p. 56.

47. Nelson and Kagan, 1972, p. 91.

48. Mark A. Barnett, Karen A. Matthews, and Jeffery Howard, "Relationship between Competitiveness and Empathy in 6- and 7-Year Olds," *Developmental Psychology*, 15(1979), pp. 221-222; Mark A. Barnett and James H. Bryan, "Effects of Competition with Outcome Feedback on Children's Helping Behavior," *Developmental Psychology*, 10(1974), pp. 838-842.

49. George P. Knight and Spencer Kagan, "Development of Prosocial and Competitive Behaviors in Anglo-American and Mexican-American Children," *Child Development*, 48(1977), pp. 1385-1394; Barbara Moely, Kurt Skarin, and Sandra Weil, "Sex Differences in Competition-Cooperation Behavior of Children at Two Age Levels," *Sex Roles*, 5(1979), pp. 329-342.

50. Karen Matthews and Julio Angulo, "Measurement of the Type A Behavior Pattern in Children: Assessment of Children's Competitiveness, Impatience, Anger, and Aggression," *Child Development*, 51(1980), pp. 466-475.

51. David G. Perry and Louise C. Perry, "A Note on the Effects of Prior Anger Arousal and Winning or Losing a Competition on Aggressive Behavior in Boys," *Journal of Child Psychology and Psychiatry*, 17(1976), pp. 145-149.

52. Leonard D. Eron, Leopold O. Walder, and Monroe M. Lefkowitz, *Learning of Aggression in Children* (Boston: Little, Brown, 1971).

53. Owen Aldis, *Play Fighting* (New York: Academic Press, 1975), p. 3.

54. Willard Hartup, "Peer Interaction and the Behavioral Development of the Child," in *Child Development, Deviations and Treatment*, E. Schopler and R. J. Reichler, eds. (New York: Plenum, 1976).

55. David W. Johnson and Roger T. Johnson, *Learning Together and Alone: Cooperation, Competition, and Individualization* (Englewood Cliffs, N.J.: Prentice-Hall, 1975); *see also* Doran French, Celia Brownell, William Graziano, and Willard Hartup, "Effects of a Cooperative, Competitive, and Individualistic Sets on Performance in Children's Groups," *Journal of Experimental Child Psychology*, 24(1977), pp. 1-10.

56. Brenda K. Bryant, "The Effects of Interpersonal Context of Evaluation on Self- and Other-Enhancement Behavior," *Child Development*, 48(1977), pp. 885-892.

57. R. Cornelius, "Cooperative and Noncompetitive Games," Handout available from the Peace Research Laboratory, 6251 San Bonita Avenue, St. Louis, Missouri 63105.

Chapter seven

1. D. Bar-Tal, *Prosocial Behavior: Theory and Research* (New York: Wiley, 1976), p. 4.

2. Will Schutz, *Profound Simplicity* (New York: Bantam Books, 1979), pp. 111-137.

3. Robert A. Baron, Don Byrne, and William Griffitt, *Social Psychology* (Boston: Allyn and Bacon, 1974), pp. 231-232.

4. James Youniss, *Parents and Peers in Social Development* (Chicago: University of Chicago Press, 1980), pp. 63-103.

5. Gary Ladd and Sherri Oden, "The Relationship between Peer Acceptance and Children's Ideas about Helpfulness," *Child Development*, 50(1979), pp. 402-408.

6. David Rosenhan, "The Kindness of Children," *Young Children*, 25(1969), pp. 30-44.

7. Rosenhan, 1969, pp. 36-37.

8. David Rosenhan, "Prosocial Behavior of Children," in *The Young Child: Reviews of Research, Vol.2*, Willard Hartup, ed. (Washington: NAEYC, 1972), pp. 340-359, p. 356.

9. Robert Leahy, "Development of Conceptions of Prosocial Behavior: Information Affecting Rewards Given for Altruism and Kindness," *Developmental Psychology*, 15(1979), pp. 34-37.

10. S. B. Dreman and C. W. Greenbaum, "Altruism or Reciprocity: Sharing Behavior in Israeli Kindergarten Children," *Child Development*, 44(1973), pp. 61-68.

11. Clara P. Baldwin and Alfred L. Baldwin, "Children's Judgments of Kindness," *Child Development*, 41(1970), pp. 29-47.

12. Ervin A. Staub, "A Child in Distress: The Effect of Focusing Responsibility on Children and Their Attempts to Help," *Developmental Psychology*, 2(1970), pp. 152-153.

13. Cathleen L. Smith, Donna M. Gelfand, Donald A. Hartmann, and Marjorie Partlow, "Children's Causal Attributions Regarding Help Giving," *Child Development*, 50(1979), pp. 203-210.

14. Martin L. Hoffman, "Developmental Synthesis of Affect and Cognition and Its Implications for Altruistic Motivation," *Developmental Psychology*, 11(1975), pp. 607-622.

15. Nancy Eisenberg-Berg and Michael Hand, "The Relationships of Preschooler's Reasoning about Prosocial Moral Conflicts to Prosocial Behavior," *Child Development*, 50(1979), pp. 356-363.

16. K. H. Rubin and F. W. Schneider, "The Relationship between Moral Judgment, Egocentrism, and Altruistic Behavior," *Child Development*, 44(1973), pp. 661-665.

17. Jerry Suls and Robert Kalle, "Children's Moral Judgments as a Function of Intention, Damage, and an Actor's Physical Harm," *Developmental Psychology*, 15(1979), pp. 93-94.

18. Ervin Staub, *Positive Social Behavior and Morality, Volume 2: Socialization and Development* (New York: Academic Press, 1979), p. 64.

19. S. B. Dreman, "Sharing Behavior in Israeli School Children," *Child Development*, 47(1976), pp. 186-194.

20. F. P. Green and F. W. Schneider, "Age Differences in the Behavior of Boys on Three Measures of Altruism," *Child Development*, 45(1974), pp. 248-251.

21. B. J. Handlon and P. Gross, "The Development of Sharing Behavior," *Journal of Abnormal and Social Psychology*, 59(1959), pp. 425-428.

22. R. Ugurel-Semin, "Moral Behavior and Moral Judgment of Children," *Journal of Abnormal and Social Psychology*, 47(1952), pp. 463-474.

23. Marion Yarrow and Carolyn Waxler, "Dimensions and Correlates of Prosocial Behavior in Young Children," *Child Development*, 47(1976), pp. 118-125.

24. Joseph R. Canale, "The Effect of Modeling and Length of Ownership on Sharing Behavior of Children," *Social Behavior and Personality*, 5(1977), pp. 187-191.

25. Ervin Staub, "The Influence of Age and Number of Witnesses on Children's Attempts to Help," *Journal of Personality and Social Psychology*, 14(1970), pp. 130-140.

26. Ervin Staub, 1970, pp. 152-153; Ervin Staub, "Helping a Person in Distress: The Influence of Implicit and Explicit 'Rules' of Conduct on Children and Adults," *Journal of Personality and Social Psychology*, 17(1971), pp. 137-144.

27. Yarrow and Waxler, 1976, pp. 118-125.

28. Yarrow and Waxler, 1976, pp. 118-125.

29. Green and Schneider, 1974, pp. 248-251.

30. Joan E. Grusec, Peter Saas-Kortsaak, and Zita M. Simutis, "The Role of Example and Moral Exhortation in the Training of Altruism," *Child Development*, 49(1978), pp. 920-923.

31. Lawrence J. Severy and Keith E. Davis, "Helping Behavior among Normal and Retardate Children," *Child Development*, 42(1971), pp. 1017-1031.

32. Britomar J. Handlon and Patricia Gross, "The Development of Sharing Behavior," *Journal of Abnormal and Social Psychology*, 59(1959), pp. 425-428; Gary Y. Larsen and Jeffrey Kellogg, "A Developmental Study of the Relationship between Conservation and Sharing Behavior," *Child Development*, 45(1974), pp. 849-851.

33. Harriet L. Rheingold, Dale F. Hay, and Meredith J. West, "Sharing in the Second Year of Life," *Child Development*, 47(1976), pp. 1148-1158.

34. Severy and Davis, 1971, pp. 1017-1031.

35. Valerie P. Perdue and Jane M. Connor, "Patterns of Touching between Preschool Children and Male and Female Teachers," *Child Development*, 49(1978), pp. 1258-1262.

36. J. Walters, D. Pearce, and L. Dahms, "Affectional and Aggressive Behavior of Preschool Children," *Child Development*, 28(1957), pp. 15-26.

37. Mark A. Barnett, Laura M. King, and Jeffery Howard, "Inducing Affect about Self or Other: Effects on Generosity in Children," *Developmental Psychology*, 15(1979), pp. 164-167.

38. Lynette K. Friedrich and Aletha H. Stein, "Prosocial Television and Young Children: The Effects of Verbal Labeling and Role Playing on Learning and Behavior," *Child Development*, 46(1975), pp. 27-38.

39. D. L. Rosenhan, B. Underwood, and B. Moore, "Affect Moderates, Self-Gratification and Altruism," *Journal of Personality and Social Psychology*, 30(1974), pp. 546-552.

40. J. H. Bryan, J. Redfield and S. Mader, "Words and Deeds about Altruism and the Subsequent Reinforcement Power of the Model, *Child Development*, 42(1971), pp. 1501-1508; D. M. Gelfand, D. P. Hartmann, C. C. Cromer, C. L. Smith, and B. C. Page,

"The Effects of Instructional Prompts and Praise on Children's Donation Rates," *Child Development*, 46(1975), pp. 980-983.

41. J. H. Bryan and N. Walbek, "The Impact of Words and Deeds Concerning Altruism upon Children," *Child Development*, 41(1970), pp. 747-757; Grusec, Saas-Kortsaak, and Simutis, 1978, pp. 920-923; Ervin A. Staub, "A Child in Distress: The Influence of Nurturance and Modeling on Children's Attempts to Help," *Developmental Psychology*, 5(1971), pp. 124-132.

42. Marian R. Yarrow, Phyllis M. Scott, and Carolyn Z. Waxler, "Learning Concern for Others," *Developmental Psychology*, 8(1973), pp. 240-260, pp. 255-256.

Index